INTO EACH LIFE

BEULAH BROWN

For my parents, Sam and Sarah,
G-d's blessing.

Her selfless devotion and love for her husband Leon, her sons Robert and Michael,
her daughters-in-law Ava and Richelle, and her grandchildren Jessica, Sarah, Danielle,
Samantha, Madeleine, Thomas, Clement and Peter, will long abide in memory
and in their love for others.

ISBN: 1468111299
ISBN-13: 978-1468111293

1

I can hardly believe it! I'm 74! An old cliché dances through my head. How did I move into old age without fighting for the value of each day? Every moment slipped by easily, happily, ruthlessly, inevitably.

Am I really thinking about the advantages of cremation over burial? Why do I turn back to a misted recollection on my fourth birthday of an automobile accident observed from a short distance away? I see a dimly lighted street lamp surrounded by fog. I view the dark scene from my seat in a car that also holds Mama, Papa, and the kind relatives who had invited us for a ride. It was a decided case of noblesse oblige. We could never afford a car. Time generally softens memory, but this early childhood recollection of a frightening scene lingers and flows into old age.

Shortly after this unforgettable incident, my family moved to an apartment in an area of Brooklyn called Williamsburg. I'm sure my parents considered it a step up in their world peopled with immigrants who had come from Poland and Russia. They had firmly settled into the New World, and were in love with America.

Our new four-room apartment was located on the fourth floor of a six-story tenement building in Brooklyn, N. Y. How proud my mother felt when their solid dark mahogany dining room table, six chairs and beautiful serving pieces were established in the most important room. The moving men had great difficulty, half carefully dragging and half carrying these heavy pieces of furniture up four terrible flights of stairs. Their endurance seemed remarkable to us. How we pitied them.

The most respected and loved piece of furniture that my parents owned was their big black upright player piano. It had to be hoisted up four floors in a terrifying display on the outside of the building and into the apartment through the window frame where the windows had been temporarily removed.

The family waited with great apprehension and labored breathing until this huge whale of melody inched back into our lives and settled into a corner of the dining room. Music was the soul of the family and the piano could not be left behind. Our kitchen was delightfully large and homey and would make a great gathering place for all of us. Two bedrooms were available in our new home. My parents shared the larger, and my brother, sister and I shared the smaller, which we barely fit into.

I loved sitting on a cotton mat on the floor of the dining room after dinner, listening to our new stand up radio. While I listened to my favorite program "Buck Rogers," I would pull out, one by one, the varied colored threads from the mat and roll them into a ball. Fortunately, there seemed to be an inexhaustible supply. I felt warm and secure in the enveloping folds of my family.

Nevertheless, I often remembered the day, shortly after we had moved in, when my mother preceded me up the steps to the fourth floor and I trailed slowly behind immersed in my childish dreams and fantasies. I lost sight of her and felt the intense pounding power of fear at not really knowing where our particular apartment #43 was located. Each floor had five apartments, and each landing seemed so far apart.

"Ma," I called. "Ma, Ma, where are you?" Her sweet response was velvety, leading me to love and safety.

"Just hold on to the banister tight and keep walking up the steps," she called down to me softly but clearly, in her accustomed European accent. "It's pretty far up, but I'll wait for you right here. Before you know it," she slowly continued, "you'll be here too. I've got cookies in the house that you like and you'll have a nice glass of milk with it when we go in together, but be careful coming up. Don't fall."

I knew that I would follow that voice anywhere.

As I was the youngest in the family, I had to go to sleep before the others. Sylvia, who was five years older than I, slept with me in our single bed and my brother Jack, sixteen months younger than Sylvia, slept in the other single bed, barely two and one half feet away. When Jack first saw the minute size of the room, he commented in his booming eight-year old voice.

"I can't believe how small this room is, and I hate walking up all those steps to get here."

"Calm down," my big sister answered. "You'll get used to it. We all have to." Jack and I looked up to Sylvia. We listened to her. To us she was a mature realist and easily commanded our respect.

During the cold winter nights I loved to snuggle up to my sister's warm body in that small single bed. Summers presented the other side of the coin.

2

Papa lost his business in the '29 crash and went to work as a salesman for a "somewhat friend" who was able to hold on to his. He worked six days a week and arrived home every night at 7:45 P.M. I can almost taste the Nestles chocolate bars with almonds that he would bring home for the children. He always had a little smile on his face when he came home, and he brought a feeling of joy into our lives when that door opened and he walked in. His greetings were always warm and affectionate, and we all knew that we were well loved. He wore a smiling mask when he saw us that covered any daily discouragement and painful encounters of the workday. Little failures and successes were held in reserve for late evening talks with Mama, his Sarah. She was his confidant, his pillar of support, and they shared all of the burdens of responsibility for the family. I never saw my father kiss my mother, but a special look was reserved for her.

Once in a while, he would playfully ask the children, "Did you ever see such a beautiful little nose like your mother's? And look at those eyes!"

"Sam, please," was my mother's smiling delighted response. We were all happy to be part of the ongoing fun of love that was expressed.

I never went to kindergarten. Mama kept me home with her since I was somewhat frail and always seemed to be in the midst of a cold or catching one. I did not think that I was missing anything of great importance. Of course there was no basis for comparison. I loved being home with my mother and had no desire to experience the realities of separation. She was such good company. However, first grade was fast approaching and I was gradually developing a case of mild anxiety. Everyone in the family was offering positive support and insisting that I was going to love school. I probably thought they did protest too much.

Outfitted with a little briefcase that every self—respecting schoolgirl needed, I rechecked the contents to make sure that I had the pre-requisites: crayons, sharpened pencils, notebooks and a little ruler. The sweet orderliness of my supplies eased my doubts about "loving school." My mother held my hand in hers as we walked along the street towards the old giant of a building that housed P.S. 44. Our palms pressed and blended into each other's affording me much comfort and a sense of security. All was not lost. Mama would pick me up directly after school, and I completely trusted her reliability. She kept up a soft running conversation with her decided accent, like a cool stream of water floating over little stones, occasionally lapsing into small Jewish phrases. It almost made me feel as though I was listening to music.

Melodies were constantly floating through my mind and evolving into sound. I could not always restrain the inner music escaping from my lips. Mama had a glorious voice and had taught me many Yiddish songs from the time that I was two years of age. Everyone in the family could sing well except for Papa, and he was a great listener. Songfests were a common occurrence and we all wanted to outdo one another with what we hoped was the beauty of our song and voices. Our enthusiasm, no doubt, outweighed our talent, but if I sit very quietly, I can still hear within my mind my brother Jack's beautiful tenor voice singing, "With Someone Like You," and feel the fun of the lyrics when Sylvia sang her special song, "Lazy Bones."

Mrs. Busch, my first grade teacher, was a soft-spoken, middle-aged woman. It was love at first sight when she greeted the class with her welcoming words. She promised us the special gift of reading if we gave her our careful attention. "We'll work hard together and have many good times, children. I can tell that you are all very smart." Her psychology worked. She was adored. I actually looked forward to going to school.

One Friday at noon, Mama was preparing for the approaching Sabbath. She was down on her hands and knees washing the large kitchen floor with one of her favorite household weapons, a soapy scrub-brush. I was in my parents' bedroom in their bed, recuperating from a bout with the "Grippe" as it was known at that time. I heard someone knocking at the kitchen door.

"Who is it, Mama? Who is it?" I kept shouting impolitely.

I could hear Mama speaking in her soft, heavily accented English. "Please come in. Come in," she urged, "and please, excuse the floor."

The cultured response silenced my shouts. I felt my fever rise with the pure improbability of it. Could it really be Mrs. Busch walking several blocks to our building and hiking up four flights of stairs during her lunch hour to see how I was feeling? I was overwhelmed with gratitude, and my timid self-esteem rose accordingly. I was pleased and proud that my mother insisted on serving Mrs. Busch a simple, but delicious lunch. My elegant first-grade teacher seemed delighted to share her limited time with us. My love for her grew accordingly.

It was a good year, surprisingly healthy and happy. At promotion time in June, I learned that I had been placed into a second grade rapid-advance class. I had "skipped!" My parents were quietly ecstatic and proud.

3

Sarah was trying to remember some of the advice that her mother had given her. "I know that fourteen is very young to be leaving your family," she said in Yiddish, "but it's a golden opportunity for you to get to America. Papa and I talked about it and thought about it for a long time, and we hope that the rest of the family can join you eventually. Poland, Sarah, is a land of pogroms. Officials here have always encouraged anti-Semitism by passing laws that make it difficult for Jews to earn a living. They restrict our choice of professions and our freedom to live where we choose. These restrictive laws are often accompanied by organized violence.

We do the best we can under these trying circumstances, but it's very hard." She sighed and softly repeated, "It's very hard. We're happy to think that you'll escape these terrible unfair hardships."

"But Mama," Sarah protested. "I really don't want to go. I already feel lonely, even before I leave, and I'm so afraid of going all by myself. I know that the ship that will take me to America is very big and I'll feel afraid and lost in it. There will be nobody to take care of me or give me advice."

"That's absolutely true, Sarah. The ship is tremendous, and you'll be in steerage. Steerage is very common and crowded, and that's why it doesn't cost too much to make the crossing. I know that it will be uncomfortable for you, but you'll get through it. You have to get through it, and you'll get to America."

"I don't want to go, Mama," I moaned. "I want to stay with the family."

"I know, my sweet daughter, but you must be brave. Uncle Panush and Tante Lakie will be there, waiting for you at Ellis Island, and they'll take you to their home. They'll love you and treat you like family. You have to start thinking like a responsible grown-up person. Sarah, listen carefully. I want to warn you that you must be very cautious and concerned about who you speak to and who you spend time with on the ship. I'm sure that there will be some people who will make you feel uncomfortable, but perhaps you can get near a nice motherly type to keep you company. Most of all, Sarale, I want to warn you to stay away from men. You're a beautiful girl and you're very young. Someone may try to take advantage of you and your sweet nature."

"Oh, Mama, don't be silly. You know that I can take good care of myself."

"Of course you can, in our little town, but steerage is a different, dangerous kind of town and you must protect yourself." Sarah listened with great concentration, and attempted to absorb her mother's wise advice. She realized that she did not have a choice in this matter. Decisions had been made for her and she had to follow them. She would do the best she could.

4

The lonely voyage to the "Golden Land" filled Sarah with pounding moments of self-doubt and fear. It was difficult to deal with the nausea that accompanied her on the long seemingly never-ending trip. The crowded conditions, the varied odors and smells arising from the ill-prepared and poor quality of the food and the multitudes of human flesh in close contact contributed to Sarah's depressive feelings and ongoing waves of illness.

On the third day out, the feather pillow that her mother had given her as a loving gift to take with her to the new country disappeared. Sarah's childish despair raged and could hardly be restrained. This seemed the greatest loss of all at the moment. She secretly suspected that the pillow was stolen because of her irresponsibility. Her formerly repressed emotions were unlocked and her tears and self-recriminations flowed freely. They would not be held back any longer.

"Oh, why am I here? I want to be with Mama and Papa. I miss my family. Muttel, I want to hear you play the violin once again." Muttel was only a year younger than Sarah, and closest in spirit. Sarah permitted herself the pleasure and relief of a good cry and then remembered her mother's words about being brave. She strove to internalize that message. She wanted her parents to be proud of her.

After an exhausting and depressing voyage, the big ship was entering the New York harbor. Sarah, having taken her mother's advice, stood next to her middle—aged friend who had taken her under her wing. Together, they could see the Statue of Liberty at

Bedloe's Island standing tall, holding the torch of freedom from oppression, and welcoming the teeming masses to America.

When they disembarked, they were herded like cattle into long lines for a doctor's hasty examination. Those who failed the test, for a myriad of reasons, would be sent back from whence they came. Sarah started to tremble as she approached the doctor's table. She felt feverish. The tension in her mind and body was almost unbearable and could hardly be contained and controlled. Finally, she was next in line. The doctor wearily examined her and completed his cursory inspection covering all necessary details. Sarah had come through the ordeal. The doctor muttered, "O.K. Next!" Sarah heaved a sigh of profound relief and felt that she had been dipped in a pool of ecstasy. She laughed aloud with joy until she glanced at the adjacent line and saw her friend, her protector, crying. She had some seemingly slight infection in her eyes and was not allowed to pass through. She was to be returned to Poland. Meanwhile, she was temporarily quarantined.

Sarah's joy rapidly dissipated, and she sadly proceeded to search for her benefactors who were supposed to be there to greet her. She scrutinized the waiting area with eyes blinded by tears. "My friend is going back. My friend is going back," her mind kept repeating. Acceptance was difficult, but that was the way life was. Suddenly she saw them! There they were, Tante Lakie and Uncle Panush! She saw them! They were holding up a large sign, which said, "Sarah Kubersky."

Sarah recognized them from the sepia photograph that they had long ago mailed to her family in Poland. She ran towards them. Uncle Panush was a small man with dark hair and full mustache. His expression was reserved and severe, but upon seeing Sarah, his eyes gleamed and Sarah could see him attempting to restrain tears. A deep reserve of strength welled up within her and welcomed her to this new land. She felt the renewal and warmth of family love.

Tante Lakie embraced her warmly and started comforting Sarah with hushed ongoing conversational Yiddish. Her voice had a quavery quality like a singer who was not quite sure where the next note would land. "How do you feel, my sweet child? It's so good to see you. I can imagine how terrible the voyage was, but now you're home and safe. You'll be like a daughter to us and our two sons will be like brothers to you." Her softness was like a healing balm for Sarah's battered mind and body "Thank you, Tante. Thank you, Uncle. Thank you, Thank you," she kept repeating, filling up with gratefulness. However, a stark picture of her older and protective friend who had accompanied her on the ship and was now being detained for a return to Poland kept insisting its way into her mind. She could hardly concentrate on what Tante Lakie was saying, but the sounds and sweetness of her voice were gently and firmly caressing her and were more important than her words.

She met her new brothers when they finally arrived home after a long train and bus ride. In the small apartment, a tiny side room had been prepared for her. A cool ray of sun had found its way through the freshly laundered curtains that had been hung with great care on a miniature-sized window. A small desk resting under the window had an old-fashioned lamp on it with a few books placed nearby. Sarah realized that she was blessed with a new family, remarkably generous, who cared about her even though they did not know her. "I'll do everything in my power to earn their caring," she silently promised herself.

Her new brothers were just that. They treated her with disdain, love and compassion. They were wonderful! They were special, reflecting the orthodox Jewish teaching and ethics of their parents. They insisted and subtlety demanded that she take part in dinner and family conversations. They gradually taught her to understand English and to be able to converse imperfectly in her new language. She attended classes for the foreign born and learned to read and write English, in addition to her knowledge of Yiddish, Polish and some Russian.

"Sarah," young Hymie would tease. "It isn't enough to be pretty and have green eyes. In this country, you have to know how to speak like an American, not like a greenhorn." Sarah's good humor prevailed and she once again learned how to laugh. Her new brothers and their loving parents gradually helped to lessen the loneliness and the longing for her family in Europe.

Sarah became a woman under the watchful eyes of her new family.

When she was nineteen, she was married under the "Chupah" in their house to Sam Dlugash, who had fallen deeply in love with this lovely green-eyed young lady, ten years his junior. The year was 1917, more than a decade before the great depression. Sam was a respected and well-liked young businessman and it looked like a successful match. Their love was reciprocal and never failed to follow them and rule them through hardships and joys.

5

We waited impatiently. Mama and Papa were due home with a brand new baby boy. It was a clear cool spring day but the anticipation made me feel feverish. It was time for me to relinquish my place as the youngest in the family. As a matter of fact, I felt quite grown up and ready for the change. After all, I would be nine in two months and had finally graduated into the role of big sister. Sylvia, almost fourteen years old, had moved into the little mother slot and was destined to have me as the "monkey on her back" and intermittent companion for the next few years. She accepted this new role with unbelievable grace. Of course there were frequent reprieves when I played with my friends. My brother, Jack, was my friendly torturer. He could turn my life into Heaven or Hell, which was determined by his irregular moods.

The three of us sat and waited nervously on our white kitchen chairs until suddenly, we could hear the sounds of someone coming up the stairs outside of our apartment. The movement seemed slow and careful and stopped outside our door. We remained transfixed and in a stupor of expectation. The door opened and there before us was our glowing Mama and Papa. Papa was carrying a little blue bundle in his arms. Their obvious happiness and joy made a quick entry into our hearts.

Mama was the first to speak. "This is your new little brother, Murray. Isn't he beautiful?" Papa handed the baby to a smiling patiently waiting Sylvia. A look of pride and pleasure showed on her face as she welcomed him with a gently rocking motion, and as she rocked, it seemed as though she and the tiny infant were one. How serene my sister looked. She was so patient and caring. So lovely. Could I ever aspire to be like her?

She was now a mature fourteen-year old young lady in junior high school, the very same age that our mother was when she came to America, all alone, in the bottom-dwelling steerage of a very big ship. How had my little mother been strong enough to be able to internalize those bitter days and turn her mind and voice toward optimism and joyous song? Her Tante Lakie and Uncle Panush were her initial support system, and my father, who loved her so dearly, was always there for her when she cried for her family still remaining in Poland.

Her darker moods were well hidden from us, but we knew they existed when she would say to me in a voice that was filled with pain, "Beulah, please run down to the drug store and get me a special headache powder." I would quickly descend the four flights of stairs with wings on my shoes. The pharmacist, our trusted druggist, would give me a little packet of blessed relief for my mother. He was a good friend to all of the tenants in the building. He was the one who often removed the tiny something that entered our eye and caused us great discomfort. We put on a brave front and hardly minded the approach of the thin stick with a little piece of cotton on it. He gently but firmly rolled back the lid of our eye, looked deeply into it, and removed the offending bit of dirt with great dexterity and speed. He had a face that smiled with compassion and he happily treated our minor emergencies. We depended upon his kindness and free treatment.

Sylvia held our new little baby and as usual, looked so competent. It seemed to me that she did everything well. I remembered that she had written a prize-winning play on fire prevention when she was in the sixth grade graduating class in elementary school. It was a competition sponsored by the New York City Fire Department and included all the elementary schools in the city. Several teachers and judges decided which six entries deserved to win, and the winners were to be awarded a special medal by Mayor Jimmy Walker. Sylvia, our Sylvia, was one of the six young playwrights to be selected for this tremendous honor. How puffed up and proud we were as we watched her receive her medal. She was a source of perpetual pleasure and we all tried to restrain our bragging. Some of our relatives seemed less pleased. They obviously preferred to hear about their own children's achievements. We outwardly quieted our enthusiasm and pride in Sylvia's accomplishments while we retained its inner pleasure. It was difficult to be quiet.

6

Our tiny brother weighed five and a half pounds, but Mama repeated one of her favorite bits of old world wisdom. "It's a big world," which translated into the meaning that things change day by day and there are always good hopes and expectations for the future. Murray was an adorable little fellow who seemed skinnier and skimpier than my mother's Sabbath chicken. He was promptly moved into my parent's bedroom where he contentedly slept every day in his little crib for several years.

He initially lost a few ounces which we were informed was not at all unusual, and we all waited impatiently for him to gain the necessary weight so that he could be ceremoniously circumcised and enter into the family of Judaism. Ordinarily this occasion takes place on the eighth day after birth, but our religion always paid special attention to the needs and health of the individual, and Murray had to achieve the minimal weight before the event could occur.

Tante Lakie, Uncle Panush and their young handsome sons were at our apartment to help celebrate this important event, and Papa's brothers and sister, who lived within walking distance, arrived with their spouses and children. It was always much fun to be with my cousins. My aunts and uncles treated us lovingly and had taken Mama into their lives. Once again, she had a family outside of her own little nest with whom we could exchange visits on a regular basis and with whom we could share food, fun and warm companionship.

In spite of my mother's condition as a "kimpatur," a brand new mother, and in spite of general weariness and serious lack of sleep, she prepared copious quantities of baked goods, delicious delicacies and treats for all of her guests. Even though my father and Sylvia attempted to help her, the burden was mainly hers, and she was exhausted but irrepressible. Her feelings of pleasure at having fulfilled her responsibilities were great. It was an important celebration and our little Murray handled the situation ably. No doubt the tiny sip of wine that had been given him helped ease the pain of the circumcision. After the ceremony, there was lots of animated and lively conversation, lots of good eating, and a good time was had by all, except perhaps for our little baby brother. However, his ordeal was satisfactorily concluded, and happily, healing was uncomplicated and rapid.

Mama went back to flushing the diaper detritus down the toilet and soaking the cotton diapers in the bathtub, never forgetting to add a little soap and bleach to the water. Her metal washboard was in constant use and was practically a member of the family. She could not function without it. However, I still recall a painful vision of this little woman lifting a huge, heavy white pail filled with water and clean freshly washed diapers up to the stove top, and then proceeding to boil this special stew. Murray had the whitest diapers.

My mother's generation did not have the luxury of disposable diapers or the use of a washing machine.

Outside of the small bedroom window, our clothesline was strung from our apartment to the other side of the building. It traveled across the inner court of the tenement to the opposing window. The little wheels, on which the lines were moved along, were professionally inserted into the brick wall right outside of the children's bedroom window. This feat was accomplished by a person who knew the process for traversing the yard with heavy line rope, and who earned part, or his entire livelihood, doing this job. It always made me feel a little anxious when my mother would hang out the wet wash, slightly leaning out the window of our fourth floor apartment to reach the rope. She carefully set the article of clothing or the diaper on the line and then secured it in place with sturdy clothespins. She then pushed hard on the rope to move it along to make room for the next article to be hung. I learned to swallow the deep fear that she might fall out the window.

The courtyard way down below our apartment loomed in shadow. The sun never seemed to reach the bottom. It appeared unkempt and somewhat littered although there was a janitor who was supposed to swab the halls weekly and keep the building and the yard looking respectable. The arrangement for managing this job was that he did not have to pay any rent. Perhaps there was a little extra compensation. It was not common knowledge. However, it was known that he did not take his responsibilities very seriously. Our janitor was very unfriendly and his lips were permanently set in a frown. He never greeted any of the tenants and faced us all with surly looks. It was whispered that he hated Jews.

In the main entrance landing or what mighty be generously called the "lobby," were thirty brass mailboxes set into the wall. Next to the mailboxes was the dark door leading down a stairway to the inner court or "yard" as we called it.

There was an old gray-bearded man who showed up regularly in our back yard with a large sack on his back. He would sing his short refrain, "Alte zachen, alte zachen," over and over again. We understood this Yiddish phrase, "Old things, old things." The words included clothing or any other item no longer in use, and therefore worthless to the owner. This "ragman" would give a few pennies to the housewives for contributions he considered worthwhile. We could clearly hear his call all the way up to the fourth floor. The women of the building would save their used up scraps of old clothing or any other accumulated junk for the "alte zachen" man, and they were delighted to turn their throw-aways into a few coins.

The very same courtyard witnessed a tragedy one very early morning. My brother, sister and I were sound asleep in our tiny bedroom when we were awakened by a loud noise that sounded as though a sack of cement had been thrown from the roof, passing each floor before it landed with a tremendous thud in our enclosed inner yard. It was the body of a young woman. She had come into our building while the darkness still prevailed, walked up to the sixth floor, opened the heavy door which led to the roof of the tenement and thrust herself to her death. We later learned that this young mother of two children could not handle the traumas, the crushing deprivations, and the debt-inducing depression. Her feelings were echoed by many in the building, but they were pushed along by a tentative hope and a prayerful faith in the future. Her devastated husband appeared later to claim her body. He did not bring his children with him.

7

My best friend, whom I did not like, was Goldie Engel. She did not live at the 477 Marcy Avenue tenement, but in a real one family house near the corner of the street. It was set back from the sidewalk as though it deserved its privacy. An untended garden with a few hardy perennials displayed its tenacity. I jealously believed that these living quarters were the height of luxury. Goldie actually had her own room! She was one of the very few children that lived nearby who was my age, and she chose me to be her friend. It therefore appeared as though we were destined to be a team. Little skinny Goldie was a bully and I was an even skinnier wimp. We were both nine years old. I allowed her to boss me around and threaten me on occasion, and this behavior on my part earned me her full loyalty.

Goldie came from a more open and liberal family than mine.

Her older brother, Aaron, had casually informed Goldie how babies were conceived, and she, just as casually and haphazardly, let me in on the hidden secret world of sex. I initially did not believe her filthy lies and mentioned all the horrifying and degrading information to my sister. I waited for her absolute and complete denial, but in spite of my emphatic disbelief, Sylvia verified this abomination. However, she eased my way out of babyhood with her cool and comforting logic, scientific knowledge and general reassurances. She turned chaos into normality.

"As you get older, you'll understand how things work out," she offered. "After all, having adorable babies and having sex really has to do with love and hugging. I'm sure it's pretty wonderful. You'll see. Try to think of it that way, and remember the most important thing. It has to do with love."

Each summer evening, after Goldie and I had slowly ingested our nightly quota of ice cream, which we purchased at the candy store for a nickel, we had to return to our respective homes because it was almost time to go to bed. We would stroll down the street with arms intertwined and sing in unison, "Good Night Sweetheart," which was a well known song sung by Alice Faye, a popular movie star at the time. Singing that song together became somewhat of a ritual. It turned into our theme song. My conscience bothered me a bit since I never felt sincere.

At the base of our six-story tenement, was a series of business spaces, which accommodated the drug store, the large candy store, the tailor shop and the barber's premises where the revolving red and white barber pole outside his large window proclaimed his exclusive talent. Much to everyone's surprise, Goldie's parents, at this time, bought the large dilapidated candy store and proceeded to renovate it. It was slowly turned into a minor showplace with new counters and sparkling large clean shiny glass covered containers that held thrifty penny candy. There were additional and accompanying higher priced delights also for the local spendthrifts who had a few more cents in their pockets. Goldie helped out a little bit in the store and respect for her soared in spite of her unpleasant personality, which strongly resembled her mother's. It was very quickly recognized that Goldie was "Power"! She was able to get as much candy as she wished.

Goldie's mother ran that business with an iron fist. The change was impressive. The store looked clean and successful and the brand new Hamilton Beach malted machines glowed with a silvery sheen. The stainless steel refrigerated ice cream compartments were filled with many different luscious flavors, and were an added incentive towards self-gratification. It was a delightful pastime to window shop in Goldie's candy store. It was even more delightful to spend a penny or two on a well thought out delectable selection.

My sister Sylvia got a job offer she couldn't refuse. She was invited to spend her summer vacation time from school working in Mrs. Engel's candy store dispensing candy, ice cream, and delicious malteds. She was delighted with this opportunity to earn a little money. She would prepare malteds with milk that contained ice crystals, malt, a scoop of ice cream and specific flavoring, which would be decided upon by the discriminating consumer. She learned quickly, and became an all around helper and a malted "maven" or specialist. She would also mix the popular "egg cream" of the time. She raised it to the level of perfection. It consisted of chocolate syrup, seltzer, [club soda] and a good dash of ice-cold milk. This was a favorite drink of the Jewish "bourgeois" especially during the hot summer months. My mind still fills with the nostalgia of its delicious, sweet, icy taste.

Sylvia's summer job was a great advantage for me. She often treated her skinny little sister to free malteds, which I thrived on and loved. Inevitably it was an extra thick drink, no doubt because of the double dose of ice cream beaten into it. Mrs. Engel, Goldie's mother, had no knowledge of Sylvia's sweet generosity. Sylvia liked the job and enjoyed the companionship and conversation of the people who frequented "Engel's Candy Store" and who sat on the tall stools waiting for their orders to be served. The days passed very quickly. Mrs. Engel was very pleased with my hard working sister and so were the customers.

There was a short plump woman with red hair and a pretty middle-aged face who came in every day and spent an hour or two sitting on a tall stool at the counter slowly sipping Coca-Cola and making it last as long as she possibly could. Her loneliness was palpable. As she finished one bottle, she ordered another. She never left Engel's Candy Store until she had finished at least three bottles of Coca-Cola. She was good company for Sylvia, who believed that Mrs. Ames was absolutely addicted to this particular drink. This mature woman began to confide in my very young, inexperienced sister and gave her lots of free, unasked for advice and information. Sylvia learned a lot about what Mrs. Ames considered the real world.

"Men are not to be trusted, Sylvia. You can never believe everything they tell you. As a matter of fact, about ten percent would be about the limit. My husband hardly ever told the truth."

Sylvia listened politely. She did not want to openly disagree with Mrs. Ames, but she could barely hold back her beliefs and attitudes regarding the world of men. Her father was the epitome of ethical behavior and trustworthiness. Her mother trusted him implicitly. Fortunately, her very limited knowledge in the realm of relationships with the opposite sex had always been positive. Mrs. Ames did not have much effect on my sister.

About this time I was lucky enough to meet a new girl who had just moved into our building with her father. They occupied the apartment directly over ours on the fifth floor. She told me that her mother had died two years before. It was very difficult for me to imagine anyone of that age being deprived of a mother's company and love, but when I met her father, I realized that he doubled the devotion and attention that he directed towards his daughter. His rules and loving discipline were an accepted part of her life and no doubt, she became stronger and centered because of it. She retained the lasting influence of her mother, and the appreciation of her father's continual support. They had a close relationship and I enjoyed observing their camaraderie. They were Filipinos and it was the first time in my life that I had an opportunity to experience a new culture, which surprisingly turned out to be not very different from my own.

Ramona invited me to visit her, and after I quickly got my mother's permission, I raced up the flight of stairs to her fifth floor apartment. I knocked at her door and after a few moments, Ramona opened it. She greeted me with a pleasant smile. "I'm so glad you could come."

My eyes were dazzled by the display of the many flowering plants on her windowsills. The sun sent its sharp rays of light through the shiny windows reflecting the flowerpots filled with flowering plants. I was impressed by their living beauty in that scarcely furnished, sad looking apartment. My new nine-year old friend explained that the flowers and plants gave her a feeling of peace and happiness and reminded her of her beautiful mother who had always loved flowers so much. Her eyes filled with unspilled tears as she spoke of her great loss, but I could think of no words to comfort her. "My poor little friend," I thought. "How can you bear it?"

I had always loved having a plant or two to take care of at home and I remember Ramona encouraging me and cultivating this pleasure. Her father had taught her much about the joys of gardening even in such a limited area and she was happy to share her knowledge and pleasure. I would no longer pull flowering weeds that grew in the park and plant them in a little pot at home. I had been promoted in the field of horticulture.

Ramona and I spent many happy hours together after school during the long winter months. We sat on the cold landing between our floors that had been paved with small octagon shaped tiles and played "Jacks," the prevailing popular game. The landing floor was a perfect playing field for this pastime. We loved every moment when we carefully and thoughtfully threw out all of the small seven pointed metal objects at one time, and carefully attempted to pick them up in a regulated order with one hand without dropping any, according to the rules and format of the game. What fun it was to share time with a smiling face that possessed a warm hearted, non-critical attitude, unlike my best friend Goldie!

Ramona told me about the long difficult voyage with her father from the Philippine Islands to the United States. They had hoped to escape the devastating poverty of the islands, but upon their arrival in the United States they quickly learned that they still had to contend with the pervasive harsh depression and the extremely low income that barely covered their restrained, inhibited living expenses. However, even residing in a small deteriorating apartment on the fifth floor of a tenement was better than the conditions generally existing for them in the Philippines. Here they had a private toilet in their own apartment. It was a great improvement over an outhouse that they shared with an occasional rat. Unfortunately, Ramona's mother had sickened and died when Ramona was only seven years old and never knew that her little family would travel to a "New World," and a new life.

I was sadly moved when Ramona told me that her father ironed all of her school dresses. That was a mother's job! A picture of my mother standing at the ironing board meticulously putting the finishing touches on a cotton dress flashed into my mind. She often picked up another item to be ironed and handed it to me. She taught me how to iron simple articles and would often joke upon observing my technique, "Don't tickle it. It will start to laugh". I loved the sound of her voice and the repetition of that little bit of fun. It always made me chuckle and I thought about how much I loved her and needed her. Ramona no longer had that comfort that every child deserved.

8

My brother, Jack, was a great influence in my life. Every Saturday morning he would take me to Tompkin's Park, which housed a public library with a wonderful section and selection of children's books. I loved reading every fairy tale book I could find and the selection was vast. Every Friday night, I was filled with great anticipation and would rush to finish the last acquisition, usually before bedtime.

Unfortunately, the library was about twenty blocks from where we lived and we had to take a trolley car as our mode of transportation, or walk. The trolley moved along rather slowly on tracks, and had an overhead line as a source of electrical power. It stopped at each corner, usually with a great jerk, to allow passengers to step up or out. The fare was five cents. As far as I was concerned, the great disadvantage besides the cost, was that I invariably suffered severe trolley car sickness with symptoms of intense nausea as soon as I stepped up and took my seat. The pervasive and distinctive odor of the trolley car would immediately enfold me and feed me its bad breath. Its jerking movement would complete my misery. My brother would force me to stay on the trolley for as long as I could manage to control the effects of the nausea, and at the last telling moment, he would hastily pull the cord that rang the bell. He did not want the manifestations of my nausea to be evidenced on the trolley. The conductor would stop at the next corner and we would dash down the steps into the sweet smelling fresh air that would quickly dispel my symptoms.

Jack did not take kindly to these unhappy experiences, and he harassed and teased me unmercifully. However, in spite of these little glitches, he kindly continued to take me with him weekly to the library. To him, it was imperative that I read, read, read! We did a lot of walking and he complained a good deal. It was a sacrifice for him to allow me to accompany him, but he did it.

He was an intellectual stimulus for me even at a very early age and always encouraged, urged and bullied me to read more and more. He was already playing chess at an adult level and giving Papa, who had taught him initially how the pieces moved, good competition. They played chess practically every evening and I could always hear my father softly humming to himself while he deliberated and decided on his next move. The camaraderie and bond between them was very strong and they enjoyed their competition and time together. Jack, meanwhile, was regularly taking out books on chess from the library and studying some complex and sophisticated moves of the masters, which he practiced on Papa. Jack kept improving his game, studying and learning, while his worthy opponent stayed thoughtfully at the same level. The first time Jack beat him, Papa was very proud. "You'll be a chess-master some day," he promised. Jack was very pleased with himself, and doubly pleased with our father.

One afternoon, Jack was outside with his friends. They were going to play stickball in the street, which served as a substitute ball field. There weren't many cars driving through our area at that time. The age of automobiles had arrived, but relatively few people could afford them. The streets belonged mostly to the local residents and to the few horses pulling wagons. The boys were having a good time getting ready to compete, and they teased each other unmercifully and good-naturedly. Finally, they were ready to proceed with their game. Everyone was in his proper place. Jack was up first. He carried a large stick masquerading as a bat. Suddenly, a highly polished black car relentlessly turned the quiet corner and unswervingly pursued its terrifying course to where the youthful players were gathered. Too late the driver jammed on the brakes but he could not stop the car quickly enough to avoid hitting my brother. Everyone heard the loud and seemingly hollow thump. Jack's body was lifted and thrown several feet by the impact. He lay on the ground, very still. The well-dressed driver quickly got out of the car, groaned loudly, and shouted to one of the boys. "Hurry. Call an ambulance!" Without delay, the boy dashed into Engel's candy store to use the phone. Several of Jack's friends raced up to the fourth floor barely able to catch their breath or contain their excitement and pounded loudly and continually on our door!

Mama was washing the lunch dishes and I was wallowing in the pleasures of reading the "Grimm's Fairy Tales." I could see the sudden fear erupting in my mother's face at the unprecedented forcefulness of the attack on our door, which she immediately perceived to be a terrible emergency. She swung open the door and when she saw the little group of Jack's friends, she held on to the doorknob for support. She could barely whisper, "What's wrong? What happened?"

They all started shouting, interrupting each other, straining to give Mama their hysterical message. "Jack's been run over and an ambulance is coming. He's lying on the ground, not moving, and the man is with him. Lots of neighbors are outside and the druggist is there, too. We wanted to let you know."

Mama closed her eyes and attempted to overcome her feeling of faintness. She mustered all the strength and courage she was capable of. "Thank you. I'm coming right down."

She turned to me and with slow labored breath said softly, hardly above a whisper, "Beulah, you must stay with the baby. When he gets up, give him a bottle from the icebox. You know how to heat it up. Be careful not to burn yourself. Sylvia will be home soon and Papa and I will be home when we can. Everything will be all right," she promised, as she ran out without a jacket, forgetting to remove her apron. I clung to her promise, "Everything will be alright." I tried not to cry, but my tears seemed to stream down my cheeks of their own accord. I kept picturing my handsome big brother lying hurt and helpless on the ground. Was he going to die? "Please G-d," I prayed. "Please help my brother." I kept repeating my prayer over and over.

The words became meaningless with repetition. I sat at the kitchen table and leaned down. My forehead touched the cold wooden top and my arms embraced my head. The house was silent, but I could feel the comforting presence of our little one-year old baby sleeping quietly and innocently in my parents' bedroom. I had to control my enveloping and resounding fear. I was responsible for the baby's well being and I could not betray my mother's trust in me. I could visualize one of Mama's good neighbors using the public phone in the candy store or drugstore to call Papa where he worked, so that he could meet her at the hospital. They would talk to him softly and would minimize and lighten the sense of Jack's imminent danger in order to make the shock of the accident less fearful and oppressive. He would respond quietly, internalizing and hiding his overwhelming panic and fear.

I later learned that Mrs. Gerber, Mama's closest and respected neighbor on our floor, accompanied her and Jack in the ambulance. Mrs. Gerber was considerably older than Mama and treated her like a younger sister. The relationship was mutually beneficial and Mama trusted and admired Mrs. Gerber. The driver of the car followed the ambulance to the hospital and was overcome with emotion. He could not restrain his tears and attempted to stem their flow with his very white handkerchief.

When they finally reached the emergency entrance, he approached my mother and kept apologizing and telling her over and over again how sorry he was. He was distraught but Mama's thoughts were not of him. They were for her child, and her husband who had not yet arrived. She knew that she had to maintain a calm exterior for her husband's sake. She had strong, protective feelings and instincts for Papa as well as for her children. She was well aware of his great sensitivity as well as his strengths. She knew that he was her very best friend. She knew that he would react quietly to this devastating experience to spare her, but that he would suffer tremendous inner turmoil and pain.

When he finally arrived at the hospital, pale and haggard, he removed his jacket and placed it around her shoulders to shield her from the cold shock of what she had just experienced, and what they might have to deal with together in the immediate future.

He felt the sharp pain and dismay of overwhelming despair. He looked at his harried wife who had always seemed to him so very lovely and young. For the first time, he noticed the fine cobweb lines around her eyes. They were the green eyes that he loved so well, that were now attempting to hide her inner agony from her husband. The subtle wrinkles on her forehead seemed deeper and more pronounced.

"My poor Sarah," he thought. "I was going to provide you with an easy life to make up for the loss of your family in Europe. Many of my promises failed, Sarah, but not my feelings for you. We will do better, I hope, and so will our children."

My mother and father looked at each other and together joined their strengths and determination. They waited patiently for what seemed to be an unbearably long time until the doctor finally emerged from the inner sanctum of the emergency treatment room. He briskly approached my parents and they listened very carefully to what he had to say. "Your son is very lucky," he announced with great authority. "He's got a bad concussion and will have to remain here for a few days, but he'll be all right. He doesn't seem to have any broken bones."

The driver of the car was there standing next to them and upon hearing what the doctor had to say, he kept repeating his muffled and muted phrase, "Thank G-d, thank G-d, thank G-d."

My parents struggled to mute and restrain their reaction to the emotional onslaught of the accident and the ensuing happy prognosis. The relief was overwhelming and Mama started to sob softly. My father attempted to comfort her. "You heard the doctor, Sarah. He'll be fine. He'll be fine," he repeated. "We must go home now and take care of the rest of the family. We'll come again tomorrow to see Jack, and before you know it, he'll be home."

Mrs. Gerber stood stoically nearby, a stolid and comforting figure. She gently and persistently patted my mother's shoulder. "I'll drive you home," insisted the man. "Please allow me to do this. I want to help you and do anything in my power to see that your boy is well taken care of and treated in the best possible way."

My folks listened carefully, and politely thanked him. That was their way. They walked slightly dazed and hesitatingly with Mrs. Gerber to the vehicle that had almost killed their son. They innately knew that the man was sincere and had been punished enough for his reckless and careless driving.

Sylvia had come home from a friend's house in the interim, and when I gave her the fearful news about Jack, we comforted each other. Our little baby Murray had behaved admirably and I felt proud of my motherly role. My sister hugged me and complimented me on doing a good grown-up job. She was my ideal. I looked up to her and her approval always remained important to me.

"Beulah, something inside of me is telling me that Jack will be o.k. We've got to believe that. Look, I'm working tomorrow after school. Come into the candy store and I'll make you the best malted you've ever tasted. You deserve it."

My heart tightened with dread when I thought of Jack's possible injuries, but filled with love and anticipation when I considered my sister's treat for me tomorrow. A double scoop malted could ease the pain a little for a little girl.

The man came up to our apartment with my parents upon their return from the hospital. He took Papa aside, I later learned, and offered him money as compensation, but Papa would only accept payment for medical bills. He absolutely refused the urging of the driver to accept additional money for the pain and grief that he had caused our family. "My son will be fine and that's all the compensation that I want and need," he firmly responded.

My mother was very upset when the man left and Papa subsequently told her about their conversation. She felt that Papa had shown unnecessary pride and had done a foolish thing. "That man could afford the money," she cried, "and we could have done something worthwhile with a little extra. We could have bought new clothes for Jack and the other children. They deserve a little reward for that man's terrible carelessness." But it was too late. The offer had been given and rejected.

Much to our deep satisfaction and relief, the doctor was right. Jack recovered, and was fine after some additional bed rest when he got home from the hospital. He got a great deal of special treatment from the family and he enjoyed the attention and the delicious treats that came his way. We were all so glad to have him home that we happily spoiled him and put up with his constant annoying requests. "This is the best thing that ever happened to me," he secretly confided to me. I assured him with my ten-year old sense of logic that the situation was very temporary and that he had better not accustom himself so readily to the easy life.

9

The summer weather and school vacation were fast approaching and we all looked forward to it. The little household chores and responsibilities seemed light and unimportant especially when we realized that time would be slowing down to a lazy summer rhythm very soon, and we would have the freedom to enjoy it. The happiest thought was of the end of the school year. We would spend so much of our time out of doors and the warmth and sunshine would lead us to new and fun filled activities.

I saw a lot more of Goldie and a new girl Dorothy, who had recently moved into a three-family house directly across the street from where Goldie lived. Her parents had rented the downstairs apartment. She joined our little group regularly when we jumped rope, which was a favorite pastime. We accompanied ourselves with little singsong tunes, which we sang in unison, like "Down the Mississippi where the steam goes push." Two girls would turn the rope and the others would line up to jump in and out at the right time. If one missed the proper moment to jump in or out, she had to take her place as a rope turner. We all became adept at this physical pastime and familiar with the many repetitive ditties that we sang together. Playing with "Jacks" also continued to be a popular pastime and we honed our skills daily. Ramona, my fifth-floor friend, was the champ and I was a close second. Goldie continued to push her almost non-existent weight around, but I was growing up and not taking her too seriously any longer. The two of us continued to sing "Good Night Sweetheart" at the end of each day during the warm summer months, but I didn't really mean it.

Dorothy, the new girl from across the street was easy going and was anxious to please. She wanted to make friends. I was really impressed with Dorothy's mother since she was born in this country, unlike my own, and did not speak with an accent. Her father wore a uniform since he was a train conductor in the subway system. He was tall, slender and very American. How impressive! Dorothy's mother wore her jet-black hair, which I did not realize at the time came from a bottle, severely pulled back and gathered in a fashionable bun at the back of her head. I thought that she looked very sophisticated. I had some guilty moments when I compared her relaxed good looks with my mother's generally harried expression, even though I believed my mother to be much prettier.

Dorothy was an only child and was able to enjoy many of its benefits. I loved visiting her because Mrs. Krasner always treated me as a special guest and spoke so pleasantly and quietly. "Would you like to have lunch with us tomorrow, Beulah? I always make cholent for the Sabbath and I'm sure that you would enjoy it. You can ask your mother if you would like to come, and let me know if she says it's all right. We eat lunch at one o'clock, but you can come earlier and spend some time with Dorothy."

What a heavenly invitation! My mother was a great cook and baker, using all of the limited means at her disposal, but she had never made cholent. It was not part of her particular Polish culture. It seemed as though Jewish women created certain dishes and stressed certain ingredients depending upon what part of the world they and their ancestors had emigrated from.

When I asked Mama if I could have lunch with Dorothy and her parents the following day, she said, "That would be fine, Beulah, and I know that you'll have a wonderful lunch and a good time. They're nice people. Remember to show your good manners when you're there. You know, wherever you go and whoever you're with, you, your brothers and sister represent our family and of course that's very important to me and Papa." She paused for a moment and then continued in a thoughtful manner. "I think it would be very nice to bring something for Mrs. Krasner when you go, maybe a piece of the cake that I baked today."

"That's great. I know she'll love it. She told me she's serving cholent for lunch. Did you ever taste cholent, Mama? Do you know what it is?"

"Well, it's a dish that came from Europe. It's a combination of meat, bones, spices, beans and barley and other good things that are baked together for many, many hours. Back in the old country, the orthodox Jews were not supposed to light the fire and cook on the Sabbath, so on Friday before sundown, the women would take their big pots filled with these special ingredients and bring them to the baker who would put them in his oven that had been adjusted to a very, very low temperature. The pots would remain there until the following day when the ladies would come to pick up their slow, well baked and delicious cholent for the family's Sabbath lunch. The baker was not breaking any religious law because he had adjusted the temperature in the oven just before the Sabbath and did not change it until the sun went down the following day."

That was a long speech for Mama. I enjoyed hearing all that information about cholent, and I loved hearing the sound of her musical voice alternating between her fragmented English, and little Yiddish phrases.

I was quite excited the next day when I put on my best dress that my mother had washed and ironed so carefully. Sylvia put a pretty ribbon in my hair and I was on my way, carrying a large piece of the delicious cake that Mama had baked the day before as an offering of thanks for Mrs. Krasner.

Dorothy was a tall, slender girl whose little nose seemed to tilt to one side. She greeted me warmly and her parents immediately made me feel relaxed and very comfortable.

"I'm so glad you could come," said Mrs. Krasner. Dorothy tells me what fun she has with you and your friends."

"They enjoy her company too and so do I," I politely responded. I wanted to be well thought of. After all, Mrs. Krasner had been kind enough to invite me to eat with her family.

She did serve a most delicious, unusual and perhaps more important, elegant lunch. Their apartment seemed so quietly relaxing and uncrowded, unlike mine.

I happily absorbed the calm atmosphere. However, after a while, the conversation came to a standstill as we all attempted to push it along. I began to think about our busier and bustling household where something was always happening and suddenly, it seemed much more interesting to me. Noisy wasn't so bad! Goldie Engel suddenly came to mind. Dorothy was a nice girl but she could never match the interest or excitement that obnoxious Goldie exuded.

Mrs. Krasner thanked me graciously for the cake I brought and I showed my best manners by acting grateful for being invited for such a lovely meal. The cholent was alien to my taste, but I loved its foreign and exotic flavors. I silently promised myself to ask my mother if she could duplicate this special repast. There was no doubt in my mind that she could and would. She loved to please her children whenever and wherever possible.

10

Our little group was extended when another new girl by the name of Tessie, moved nearby and joined us. Her family had also bought a candy store. I was impressed even though it was a small business compared to Goldie's. She certainly didn't look rich. Neither did Goldie. The small store was located a block and a half away on the other slue of the street.

Tessie was a chubby little girl, our age, with a fun-filled round face framed by curly brown hair. It seemed as though she was constantly eating up the profits of her candy store with her prodigious appetite for sweets. We approved of her without reservation. We particularly approved of her generosity. She often plied us with samples of succulent candies, which she pilfered from her store when her parents weren't looking.

One day she took Dorothy and me into the shoe repair store right next to her candy store. She had to pick up a pair of shoes that her mother had brought in previously to be resoled. A young man took her ticket for the shoes and proceeded to look for them amongst the many that were lined up on the shelves that held all the completed work. The place had a leathery smell.

On the other side of the store was a little balcony fitted with large brown shiny chairs. At the base of each chair was a small stool on which to place your feet if you wanted to have your shoes shined for a nickel.

Dorothy and I scampered up to those chairs while waiting for Tessie. We felt relaxed and important, looking down from that height.

Suddenly, an elderly shoemaker slowly shuffled his way from the back of the store, the area where shoes were carefully restored and repaired and he drew close to where we were sitting. We watched him as he approached, feeling a discomfort that we could not readily identify. He wore a heavily soiled work apron and we noticed that his spotted hands looked lined and dirty. He had a peculiar smile on his face as he glanced up and asked us if we wanted a free shine. He did not wait for a reply but quickly ran his weighty, gnarled and stained hand up Dorothy's leg to her cotton panties. Dorothy's face blanched and was filled with horror and shock. I grabbed her hand and we hastily clambered down, scraping our knees against the metal foot supports to quickly escape the shoemaker's ugly face with its distorted grin. I shouted to Tessie that we would see her later.

We never told anyone about that dreadful, horrifying incident and vowed that we never would. As young as we were, we knew that we had come in contact with a damaged soul and evil personified. We would have great difficulty banishing the memory of that frightening incident from our minds. A strong bond had been established between Dorothy and me. Tessie remained outside of the experience.

11

The "Depression" still weighed heavily upon the minds and hearts of everyone we knew and came in contact with. The women in our building bought their daily ration of groceries from the family run grocery store located almost two blocks away. Early every morning my mom and many other housewives would rush out to pick up fresh bread and hot rolls that had just been delivered. The butter they ordered was scooped out of a large tub with a special little shovel, and cream cheese was cut from a rectangular bar. These items would each be placed on a piece of wax paper and carefully weighed on a scale that sat on Mr. Gelber's counter near a large basket filled with the oversized hot seeded rolls that I loved. Other necessary food items would be picked up at the same time or later in the day by one of the children, meaning me. Meanwhile at home, the coffee had already been prepared by my father for breakfast. Its fragrance captured us and permeated the entire apartment.

Mr. and Mrs. Gelber, who owned and worked in the family grocery store, could always be depended upon to be polite, very friendly and most accommodating. The women did not always have the ready-money to pay for the minimal foodstuff they bought during that difficult depression time, and he would hear the phrase, oft repeated, "Please write it down." Mr. Gelber would take the thick bunch of individual rectangular papers that were held together by a huge safety pin and kept under the counter, and turn each page carefully until he came to the proper name. He would then enter the date and the amount of the sale, giving the customer a pleasant smile.

Each week, after a meager payday, Mama would send me with a small amount to put on the account. Sometimes I was told to say, "My mother said she'll give you next week." Mr. Gelber would always give me a warm smile and a sweet "Thank you." He was a hero.

One reason I did not mind shopping for my mother at the grocery store was because Mr. Gelber had the most delicious individual malomars I had ever tasted. These little cakes were held in cardboard boxes that were kept on the side of the store. They sold for two cents each and I would use my daily allowance for that very special treat. Those malomars, which were covered with delicious dark chocolate, had an unusual creamy filling that I craved, and slowly tasting it and savoring its flavor filled me with temporary ecstasy. Sometimes I could not refrain from buying two. If I concentrate, I can easily travel back in time and can almost taste its rich delicate creaminess now.

Very often I would take Murray along with me to the grocery store. He was now little more than a year old and walking nicely. I would carry him down the four flights of stairs very carefully. I needed to take his carriage since his little legs would not be able to carry him for such a distance. His carriage was hiding behind the stairs of the lobby, near the door that led to the yard. I would gently place this sweet little bundle in it and with great precision strap him in and slowly wheel the carriage through the lobby and into the street. We passed Goldie's house and turned at the corner towards our destination. My mission was to return with a bottle of milk. Cardboard containers to hold milk were not in existence at that time. I felt proud of my role as a little mother and always pleased that Mama trusted me.

Our little baby had gone through a traumatic time when he was only several months old and in turn my mother and father suffered much. For no apparent reason that could be discerned, Murray started having convulsions from time to time. After many examinations and consultations with a number of doctors, there were still no definite diagnostic answers or beneficial results. The convulsions continued with greater frequency and the decision was made to hospitalize our little baby brother so that his condition could be more thoroughly analyzed and studied in depth. He appeared to be the smiling, laughing picture of health, but something had gone wrong and there had to be further investigation. He would be subject to many tests and his discomfort and pain would be deeply implanted in my parents' souls. Their hearts were breaking, but they called upon their joint inner core of strength and hope, and outwardly maintained their equilibrium to try to give a calm and peaceful environment to their children at home.

Little Murray spent two weeks in the hospital undergoing careful scrutiny and unfortunately experienced many different kinds of probings and examinations in the attempt to determine what was creating this horrific problem. We all hoped and prayed he would be given a positive prognosis.

He finally returned home from the hospital, and the family breathed a sigh of relief. After an extended period of time, the convulsions became less frequent and, quite unexpectedly, they completely stopped. They thankfully never reoccurred and, after a while, we all tried to block out the fearful remembrances. A diagnosis had never been made. That brought me to the conclusion, later in life, that the body was possibly a self-healing unit, and that we should allow our minds to accept and welcome this miracle.

Murray sat contentedly in his carriage as we rounded the corner on our way to the grocery store. There were several small houses along that street. They appeared a little run-down, and their small dry gardens seemed sterile and uncared for. I never saw anyone who lived there, even though I had passed that area innumerable times. It almost seemed to me that the houses might have been abandoned.

However, one of the houses had a tiny plot of land in front of it with yellow Irises that bloomed gently and faded quickly during the warm summer months. They looked dry and lifeless most of the time and each time I passed them, I could feel a slight dampening of my spirits. I developed a life-long mild aversive feeling for that beautiful and delicate flower. It was planted in my mind as a negative symbol of closed doors, dry earth, uncaring people and untended places that were meant to display G-d's gift of natural beauty.

We returned to our building with the bottle of cold milk, which was stashed away in a safe spot in the carriage. I wheeled my baby brother into the lobby and under the stairs where his carriage was generally stored. I removed his safety strap, kissed him on that perfect little cheek, and lifted him and the bottle of milk, which rested in a paper sack. I proceeded to walk up the stairs when suddenly Murray turned his little body unexpectedly and loosened my hold on the glass bottle within the paper bag. It dropped with sharp impact and shattered. There were glass shards everywhere resting in a milky marinade. I felt something pointed piercing my ankle and when I looked down, my shoe was covered with blood. I continued to hold tightly to Murray and slowly made my way up to the fourth floor. I attempted to speak soft comforting words to my baby brother. His little face reflected the shock of the accident.

"Don't worry, sweetheart. Everything is fine. I love you and Mama loves you. You'll see her in just a few minutes." I kept babbling along, hoping to sooth him. I don't think he understood my words, but he understood the solace. I gently kissed him once again and refrained from looking down at my bleeding foot.

Mama responded to my anxious knocking at the door and made everything right. She took the baby from my trembling arms, set him safely down in his crib and gave me her full attention and immediate care. "What happened? What happened?" she repeated. "Don't worry. Everything will be fine."

She very carefully removed my shoe and examined my bleeding ankle for any glass splinters that might have remained imbedded. "See, there's no glass left in your foot," she reassured me. "Nothing to worry."

She washed the area very gently and thoroughly and applied a disinfectant, which she had quickly gotten from our medicine chest in the bathroom. It was a deep gash and she was determined to prevent infection. Her bandage was surprisingly professional and I felt secure in the knowledge that I was being well taken care of.

While my mother seemed to be completely concentrating and concerned with me, she nevertheless, loudly and clearly, directed Jack and Sylvia to go downstairs and clean up the mess of glass and milk that remained in the hall. She was fearful that anyone coming up the steps could fall and cut themselves on the hazardous fragments. Many times she repeated her warnings. Her trembling voice betrayed her outward calmness with which she had greeted me at the door. Her inward anxiety and alarm were evident when she started speaking.

"Be careful. Be very, very careful not to hurt yourselves. Please, listen! Take your time and look very thoroughly around so that you notice all the little pieces of glass so you won't cut yourselves. Take a few bags from under the sink to put them in, and in the closet you'll find a lot of rags to wipe up the milk. Be careful! Sylvia, ...after a little while send Jack upstairs so that he can take care of the baby, and then I'll come down to help you. I'll be finished with Beulah in a little while."

Because the gash in my ankle was quite large and deep, I had to rest for a few days and keep my leg elevated. It was wonderful not having to go to school and being treated like a princess at home, even if was temporary. When Papa came home from work that evening, he slipped me an extra piece of Nestles chocolate with almonds to keep my spirits up. As a matter of fact, I was feeling quite content. I was made to feel blameless and brave. I had taken good care of the baby, and that was the bottom line.

12

Across the street from where I lived, near Dorothy's house, were several storefront businesses with rental apartments above them. A glazier occupied one of these stores. Two large windows, which haphazardly displayed different sizes of panes of glass, were separated by a door, which stood shabby and unnoticed. The dirty, hazy exterior of the windows seemed to be shielding its face from the light and warm sunshine. I never saw anyone going in or out of the glazier's door, and for me it remained alien territory, perhaps deserted, perhaps haunted.

One day Goldie and I were enjoying the warmth of the afternoon on the sunny side of the street across from where we lived. We were happily engaged in slowly eating an ice cream and savoring its sweet, creamy taste. It was a delicious Breyer's Mello-Roll, cylindrically shaped and mounted on a sturdy stick. A soft piece of cardboard wrapping had encircled this gustatory delight and had to be peeled off to reach the ice cream. How we loved our summer treats!

Suddenly, much to our surprise, the glazier's door opened wide and a strange looking, rather rotund woman stood on the threshold and beckoned to me. Her dress was vivid in color and constrained by the shape of her somewhat lumpy body. Her very blond tinted hair fired by the sun, had a slightly greenish hue and was tightly fitted to her head like a cap. I hesitated, but courageous Goldie gave me a shove and I slowly approached the figure standing in the doorway.

"I've seen you around," she said, "and I thought you might like to have a little job, that is, if you've got good penmanship."

"As a matter of fact, I do," I quickly and immodestly responded.

The unconsidered idea of working and earning some money at my age, like my sister Sylvia, was immediately appealing to my ten-year-old mentality. How proud my family would be for me to have a "writing" job.

"You would have to address a lot of envelopes and you would get paid a certain amount for every fifty you finish. Do you think you could do it?"

"Absolutely," I replied unhesitatingly, any residue of shyness dissipating at the thought of dollar bills coming my way.

"Well, come in tomorrow after school and I'll set you up."

I left the sunny side of the street with no idea of how much compensation there would be, or how much time would be involved. Goldie was openly annoyed with me for having been selected by this apparition and proceeded to try to frighten me at the thought of my working inside the "ghost" office. I also had second thoughts about my new career when Goldie continued to downgrade the possible benefits of a job that might be terribly boring. However, I decided to discuss this important matter with my parents.

That evening at dinner, I mentioned the possibility of employment by the glazier from across the street and what it would entail. I could see little restrained smiles settling in their faces. They pulled themselves together, however, and very seriously considered the job from many angles. They thought it would be fine for me to try it out for one hour a day to see how I would like it and how it would like me.

After drinking my milk and eating some of my mother's delicious home-baked cookies the next day, I slowly walked down the stairs, contemplating and savoring the idea of the money I would earn. I crossed the street, timidly knocked on the dark door, and heard a voice from within bark loudly, "Come in."

The interior of the store appeared completely insulated against the out-of-doors bright sunshine. The walls looked dark and dusty. The gloomy atmosphere was assailed by sheets of glass of varied shapes and sizes that leaned against the sides of the room. Other pieces, beautifully beveled, lay on top of several very large tables. In the center of this workshop was an old-fashioned huge, grimy looking desk. Indeed, Goldie's imaginative description was apt. I could almost imagine ghosts occupying the store when the owners left for the day. However, I stood bravely and politely waiting for what I hoped would be friendly instruction.

She sat at the desk dressed in the bright colors that she seemed to favor and she wore a heavy perfume that made me feel faint. A small red kerchief covered most of her hair and her heavily made up face looked attractive in the half-light. She proceeded in a succinct, rational manner to give me all the details of the work that I was to do.

"This is an advertising promotion," she said. "You'll address each envelope carefully and put a flyer into each envelope. Then you'll seal it and stamp it."

I nodded my head and attempted to look interested and approving. She seemed satisfied when I explained that I could only give her one hour of my time each day. She set before me a large box of envelopes, a fountain pen and long lists of names and addresses. She turned her back to me and walked over to a nearby cluttered table where she removed a huge box filled with papers that she brought to the desk where I was to sit.

"These are the flyers. They inform our customers about the special sales that are coming up and the prices. Make sure you remember to insert one of them in each envelope after it's addressed. The pay is one cent per envelope."

She looked piercingly into my eyes as she spoke. I felt the pangs of disappointment sear my soul. I had hoped that this would be a get-rich-quick opportunity. Nevertheless, I gave her what I hoped was an enthusiastic nod and smile. Her sharp hawk eyes could read my face and discerned my innermost feelings. She decided not to press charges, and my work began.

I sat at her dirty disheveled desk and started to write very painstakingly in my best penmanship. When I completed my first envelope, I looked up and realized that she was standing over me watching me very carefully. For the first time, I could see a little smile break through her heavily rouged face. She approved! My timid feeling of self worth rose. I decided that I could like her. Still, I very quickly learned to hate the boring, repetitive work. However, I lasted the three weeks that she had allotted for this particular sales drive. I felt pleased with myself and fulfilled, especially when I got high praise from Papa for my tenacity. It was a good lesson in perseverance.

13

The summer drifted along and I was becoming psychologically ready for fifth grade. Summer time was the best time as far as I was concerned. Sylvia concocted the most tempting double ice-cream cones and malteds for her little sister, compliments of "Engles Candy Store." Jack took me to the library regularly so that I always had a good supply of reading material. My baby brother was a constant source of fun and joy and I was permitted to play out of doors until twilight signaled that it was time to go upstairs. Very often my friends and I would wait for my father to arrive home from work at twenty minutes before eight o'clock, at which time he would present us each with that delicious piece of Nestle's chocolate with almonds. How I loved that generous, nurturing man. All the children in our family knew how limited his earnings were, but he could always be depended upon to supply small happy treats and act like the complete gentleman that he was. How lucky I was to have him for a father.

A new tenant was moving into the building. Aristocracy was coming to Marcy Avenue. The owner and landlord of our building was moving into our tenement! The difficult economic times had reduced him and his little family to what was definitely considered the lower strata of society and was forcing them to change their style of living and spending. They were going to occupy a first floor apartment that had emptied, due to the fact that the tenants could not afford to pay the minimal rental each month. The apartment was now being especially prepared for that special family. Painters, carpenters and decorators had been called in and their creative talents had been well utilized. All of the tenants of our building thought of the owners as nobility, and it was almost impossible for us to believe that they would be living in a six story, walk up, low class apartment house.

They moved in with expensive, authentic French Provincial living room furniture, gilt framed mirrors, elegant accessories and pink bedroom furniture for their little six-year old daughter. Many of the curious tenants were filled with wonderment as they surreptitiously watched the landlord's rich furnishings being removed from the moving van and carried into the four-room apartment on the first floor. We were filled with awe. We felt as though royalty had come to stay. How delighted and pleased we were when we came in contact with their friendly smiles and greetings. How sorry we felt when we realized that they unfortunately had to live with the likes of us. Much to our happy surprise, our handsome young landlord and his pretty gentle looking wife seemed to want to get to know their tenants, and even to offer their friendship.

One day Mrs. Kidman stopped me in the entrance hall. She was with her daughter and both she and her little six-year old Julia looked as though they had stepped out of the fashion pages of a book. They were dressed simply but elegantly. I thought they looked like movie stars.

"I know you live here," she said to me. "I've seen you with your mother and baby brother. I enjoyed watching you play with him and making him laugh. You're a wonderful sister. I thought perhaps that you might like to visit us occasionally and get to know Julia. I know she's much younger than you are, but she's very smart." She continued, looking down at her little daughter and giving her a brilliant smile.

"She's a lot of fun, too. She has many, many interesting toys and games that you can enjoy together. What do you think about that idea?" Julia, meanwhile, stood by listening carefully to what her mother was saying. She looked up at me and smiled broadly.

"Thank you." I answered. "I think I'd like it very much." I looked down at Julia's pretty little face. "It would be fun to spend some free time with you, Julia."

"That would be great," she responded in a high pitched voice.

I realized that my motives were mixed. I could imagine the wonderful toys, dolls and books that she probably had in her room and that I would actually be able to play with. I was also filled with tremendous curiosity to see their apartment, and this would be a golden opportunity. I would be happy to share all insights and information with my friends and family. I knew they would be very receptive and I would gain a feeling of much importance. "That would be very nice," I repeated. "Thank you very much."

"Would you like to come tomorrow at one o'clock?" I nodded my head and she said, "Good. We'll see you then."

Her apartment amazed and delighted me. I felt that I had entered a magical and beautiful palace that I had read about in one of my favorite fairy tale books. The rooms were meticulously painted in soft, varied colors and their walls were graced with impressive looking works of art. The floors were covered with thick carpets, and handsome draperies hung from those mundane, ordinary windows. What a complete transformation had taken place! Julia had her own bedroom, just like Goldie Engel, which seemed incredible to me. That had to be the height of luxury. The pale pink furniture, that we had watched being removed from the truck, was arranged and displayed in refined and graceful order. The far side of the room was set up as a play area featuring several dolls of different sizes clothed in rich colorful attire. One of the dolls strongly resembled a real baby. There was a toy crib and carriage, some games, interesting puzzles, books and lots more. What a treasure trove! I did not realize that I had gasped aloud. Mrs. Kidman laughed softly and said, "Before you and Julia get involved with any of the toys, I have some lovely dessert for both of you. Follow me."

My mind filled with delightful anticipation. I would have followed this lovely gray-eyed movie star image anywhere. She seemed to encompass all the attributes that I looked up to and admired. She was the epitome of gentility and her speech reflected her background. Her soft smile and clear beguiling eyes shone with superior intelligence and grace. She quickly became my ideal although my sister remained number one.

It was an interesting phenomenon that Sylvia and I were never permitted to baby-sit for a monetary reward. In the world that my parents had left behind when they came to America, people who took care of someone else's child or children were considered servants and that concept was something that my parents could not tolerate for us. Their children were never to be looked down upon as servants. No matter that the extra money would help the family. No matter that their economic class was not much higher, if at all higher, than the "servant class."

"Our families in Europe always tried to interest the children in learning," said my father. "Studying was a big part of our lives and still is. Mama's younger brother took violin lessons and played well at a very early age. Your mother has a voice like an angel, and we all enjoy our little Saturday family concerts. Those are the kind of interests we try to develop.

Baby-sitting is another pursuit. My children don't need to get paid for baby-sitting. Sometimes it's very nice to do it as a favor for someone who has an emergency. I guess that's all that needs to be said on that subject."

"I suppose it's alright to play with that little girl and have a good time together," my mother said when I told her that Mrs. Kidman had invited me to spend some time with her daughter. "Just make sure that she understands that you're not baby-sitting, just playing. And make sure that you never take any money from her." Discussion closed.

Time continues to reshape thinking. My parents' grandchildren and great grandchildren would think of baby-sitting, bird sitting and dog-walking as a worthy and meritorious moneymaking enterprise.

Mrs. Kidman led us into the kitchen that had been completely redecorated with simple but knowledgeable care and foresight. I intuitively knew that a good amount of money had been spent on this original sow's ear to turn it into a silk purse. The depression had obviously hit the Kidmans, but not too hard.

It was always fun to spend time with Julia. She was sweet company and possessed a genial personality.

Experiencing the variety of toys she had was exhilarating. My personal supply was practically non-existent. Everything that I looked at and examined captured my imagination and filled me with delight. We had a wonderful time together and I enjoyed the role of being a very young teacher to that receptive good-natured little girl. I could never figure out why I did not feel jealous and deprived.

14

Sylvia was now fifteen with a vivacious personality and a manner that attracted lots of boys. Every evening she and her best friend May, who also lived in our building, would congregate on the next block with several other girls and boys who were part of their group. My parents thought that this was fine and they were content when they thought of their totally responsible daughter having a fun time out of doors with a group of friends, and returning home at a reasonable hour. They felt that it was natural and healthy for boys and girls of that age to meet, spend time together, and learn to feel comfortable with one another. They did not reckon with my mother's close neighbor and more mature friend. Mrs. Gerber was outspoken and happy to express her extremely conservative views, which my mother listened to very respectfully.

Mr. and Mrs. Gerber were wonderful, caring neighbors. They had two grown children. Lilly was twenty, tall and slender. She wore silver-rimmed glasses that gave her the look of a natural born spinster, cool and distant, possibly due to her mother's restrictive influence. Davy was a seventeen year old irrepressible happy-go-lucky fellow well liked by everyone, including Sylvia and her friends. Mrs. Gerber felt that it was her duty to inform Mama that she had seen Sylvia outside with a bunch of girls and boys, and that it just did not seem to be a righteous pastime for a well-bred girl. There was too much laughter, noise and dashing about.

Mama listened with much courtesy to her older friend and good neighbor, but she and Papa made their own private decision to continue to gently loosen the ties and trust their daughter's judgment. Sylvia was practically a young woman, and by this time had probably internalized the stability, values and love implicit in our family's life style. She would do fine.

One day she was invited to a little get-together at a friend's house during a rainy afternoon. Our parents unfortunately had a doctor's appointment and no doubt much to Sylvia's chagrin, she would have to take me along to her little party. That was not the most ideal situation, but there was no remedy for it. My mother and father would take a bus to the doctor's office and even though it was raining, our carefully bundled up little brother would accompany them. I reached for an umbrella from the closet as my sister and I started out. "Button up your neck," my mother loudly called out to me as we walked through the door. "It's not such a nice day. Papa and I will be home before you, and you'll have a nice dinner later. Don't eat too much junk," were her parting words. Sylvia and I huddled together as we walked down the drizzly street arm in arm. She carried the umbrella and tilted it towards me to keep me dry.

Sylvia's friends knew me well and greeted me warmly. They knew I would not be any trouble. I was little "Goody-Goody-Two-Shoes." There were several boys present and they pleasantly greeted me. They laughingly attempted to engage me in conversation. "We're going to be playing 'Spin the Bottle' later on." they said. "You know it's a kissing game." I could easily tell that they enjoyed teasing me. They continued, "Would you like to play? We can easily include you."

I could feel myself blushing deeply but I coolly responded, "I don't think so. I'll watch." They thought the conversation wonderfully funny and laughed a good deal more than I felt necessary. They were trying to act very grown up and big brotherly and thought they appeared sophisticated by lightly joking with such a young girl. I could see that my sister was a little embarrassed by this dialogue, but I confess, I enjoyed their attention. It made me feel older, and I happily accepted the easy camaraderie. My sister put her arm around my shoulder and gave me a warm hug. Her smile gave me a sense of comfort and well being. I knew that I was being well taken care of. She would not allow me to grow up too quickly.

The teenagers had a good time and they did play a kissing game. It seemed relatively innocent, even to me, at the time. The most handsome boy in the group, Eli, attached himself to my sister and paid her a lot of attention. I felt proud of her since she had attracted the most important looking male present at the party. I remained very quiet and attempted to keep out of the way. I did not want to be a burden to my sister.

15

A few weeks later, Sylvia invited me to go with her and several of her girl friends to Prospect Park. She enjoyed giving me a treat, and what a treat that would be! Mama would prepare a delicious picnic lunch for us and Sylvia's friends would each provide their own lunches. I loved my mother's cooking, and for this particular occasion she would fry thick hamburgers with onions until the hamburgers were crusty brown. She would set them in fresh seeded Kaiser rolls along with little slices of sour pickle as a condiment. We could add a little ketchup if we pleased. The choice was ours. She also placed some of Papa's chocolate treats in our paper sack with an accompanying apple for each and lots of paper napkins.

I kept thinking that Sylvia was a perfect sister. Who else would put up willingly with a small undesirable chaperone? I could picture the fun I would have on this sun-filled day, included in games that the girls would play. The walking, running, dashing up and down grassy knolls in the park, lunch under a tree and best of all, listening to what I considered to be grown-up conversation, mostly about boys, was powerfully satisfying.

There was one little problem that loomed large in my mind. We would be taking a twenty-minute ride on a bus to Prospect Park. For me, it seemed to be quite a distance from where we lived, and I would have to display tremendous discipline and positive thinking in order not to get too bus sick. I also had to make sure that I did not eat any breakfast prior to our trip. I would ply myself with hard sucking candy to quell any inclinations towards nausea.

The day arrived and the sun shone encouragingly. With a mouth full of cherry-flavored "Life-Savers" and the rest of the package in my pocket, I felt reasonably reassured. It would be all right, and it was!

I sat quietly next to Sylvia and was distracted looking out the window observing the changing scene as we approached the park. I was also peacefully enjoying the lively conversation between the friends. May, Sylvia's very best friend, sat right in back of us on the bus. She and my sister seemed to have a special bond. May and her family lived in our building on the third floor.

The bus was a lot more comfortable for me than the trolley car. The ride was relatively smooth and the time passed quickly. We arrived in a happy frame of mind and the fresh green foliage and the tall graceful trees that lined the entrance to the park seemed to welcome us. The cottony cloud formations looked like a beautiful painting. My eyes responded to their soft beauty and kept reaching upward to perpetuate the pleasure that the scudding clouds freely gave.

I looked forward to seeing the smooth lake where many rowboats skimmed along the water. The boats could be rented by the hour and the girls planned to take advantage of that opportunity to spend time alternately rowing, relaxing, enjoying the sunshine and the cool breezes. I happily stepped into the boat and sat on the little raised bench-like surface opposite Sylvia. May sat behind her and opened a little umbrella which she carried to guard her from too much sunshine. I was delighted to be part of this pleasurable pastime. I put my hand in the water and felt its smooth silky coolness while my sister and May took turns rowing. The other girls were in another boat nearby. Sylvia then allowed me very carefully to exchange places with her. I attempted to do a little rowing with her clear and explicit instructions. I was not too successful, but it was a valiant effort and it was fun. What a great sister I had!

We later picnicked on the grass and the delicious juices of the fried hamburgers in their crisp rolls exploded in my mouth as I savored each bite. We shared our chocolate with all, and they in turn gave us samples of their treats.

A group of boys nearby started attracting our attention by throwing a ball from one to another moving closer and closer to where the girls were sitting.

They obviously meant to establish a conversational connection and without much difficulty, they did. The mood was light, pleasant and flirtatious. Everyone was having a good time. I enjoyed listening and observing and I found this interplay interesting and exciting. I thought to myself, "What an opportunity to learn from the big girls." In retrospect, I think I was already slightly, or more than slightly, interested in boys.

After the initial exchange of talk and banter, one of the boys suggested that we all run down from the grassy knoll where we had been sitting, past the statue of a famous by-gone general on a horse, to the bottom of the hill where we would all meet. We could proceed then to another lovely area of the park. Everyone thought it was a fun idea and we started out.

The cool breezes gently whipped our faces as we started running. Our speed increased as we ran downhill. When I approached the statue, which was surrounded by a low iron railing, I accidentally stumbled on a small stone and bumped my head into one of the slightly protruding points of the railing. When I touched my head to assess the damage, I was surprised to feel an opening in my scalp. I glanced at my hand and realized that it was covered with blood. I found it difficult to believe that such a small head wound would cause such heavy bleeding. I called to my sister who was nearby and I could see the sudden panic in her eyes. She swiftly approached me, took her handkerchief and the paper napkins that had been in the sack she carried, and tightly held them in place on my head to staunch the bleeding. It seemed to work and we were both relieved.

She quickly announced to her friends that she was going to take me home immediately and get our good druggist to look at my 'hole in the head' and put some medication on it. "Anybody joining us?" she queried. Much to my dismay, and most certainly to hers, none of her good friends offered to accompany us home. They allowed their consciences to lie deeply buried in exchange for the pleasant company of the boys. Sylvia pretended that it was of no consequence.

We huddled together on the bus and I could feel my sister's strong presence and protective warmth. I still recall, a lifetime later, how soothing and dependable she was and how she took care of me with no admonitions or blame for my possible carelessness.

After what seemed to be a bumpy ride we finally arrived home. I had been so concerned about my bloody head that I forgot to feel nauseated on the bus. We went directly to our friend and healer, our druggist Mr. Saper, who cleaned the relatively trivial injured area of my scalp with a secret disinfectant. "What happened to you?" he asked me. "Did an Indian shoot an arrow at your head?"

He chuckled contentedly and didn't seem to require an answer. He then very carefully placed and secured a small bandage on the bloody area. It was completely covered. "There. That's good. You'll be fine." His assurances and attitude reassured my sister and me. I knew that I would be fine and so I was.

Mama got a little excited when she saw the outcrop of white bandage on my dark head, but she calmed down quickly when we assured her that the druggist had said that it would heal very soon. When she saw my positive response to the whole experience, she absorbed some of our quiet acceptance and serenity.

May remained my sister's best friend, but was relegated to a lesser and more realistic station in Sylvia's mind.

16

My body was experiencing some unanticipated and unwelcome changes. I was not quite eleven and was surprised by the appearance of budding breasts on my child's body. How could this happen to me? I was embarrassed and ashamed. The little pressed pleats on my dresses that Mama ironed so carefully were pushed out of place, and no amount of adjustments seemed to remedy the situation.

Finally, I confided my distress to Sylvia who had not noticed anything unusual. After listening to my sad story, she suggested that I ask Mama to buy me a little bra. She then talked to me at length about the supposed rewards, privileges and responsibilities of becoming a young woman. I accepted my fate and continued to grow up.

I silently started noticing the good-looking boys in my class and Jack Macey stood out. Besides possessing a sweet face, which I really thought was too pretty for a male, his cleanliness shone like a beacon above the average, shabbily dressed boys in our class. He always wore a freshly ironed white shirt that gleamed with obvious attention and care. Our fifth grade teacher complimented him in front of the class for his excellent daily appearance and commented on the beautiful looking white shirts he always wore to school. His response to this praise was very simple and direct. "I only have this one shirt, and my mother washes and irons it every night." There was a muted sound of a general intake of breath. He was even poorer than the rest of us, but obviously, cleaner.

17

My eleventh birthday was rolling around, and June 20th loomed large in my mind. Sylvia was going to Coney Island that Saturday with her group of girls and boys and I was going to be permitted to tag along. It was part of her birthday present to me. I was ecstatic! Sylvia was well liked and her friends put up with me on the occasions when I tagged along. They were an easygoing group and I never heard any overt complaints. Fortunately they were too busy with themselves to be disturbed by my non-interfering presence.

We had to take an elevated train to get to the beach and I barely made it without heaving up my breakfast. However, when we finally arrived and walked out of the station, I immediately recovered. I took deep delicious breaths and felt cleansed and purified by the delightful salt-scented sea air of the Atlantic Ocean that played about our faces. I was completely happy and ready for the delights and pleasures that Coney Island had to offer.

We walked along Surf Avenue leading to our destination of 23rd Street. There we would take a left turn that would lead us to the hot sands that bordered the Atlantic Ocean. I trailed behind my sister and her friends on Surf Avenue and saw my full reflection in the large glass windows of the stores we were passing. A thought entered my mind and kept repeating itself.

"You'll never be eleven again. You'll never be eleven again."

I enjoyed deeply inhaling all the smells and fragrances that came from the different stores and stands that we passed. There was the mouth-watering aroma of hot-dogs and French-fries from Nathans.

Popcorn, chocolate, spun sugar on a stick, hot corn on the cob floating in huge pots of boiling water, salt and pepper containers placed next to bowls of butter to generously dab on the corn, and a myriad of other temptations of the palette were offered loudly to the passersby.

"You'll never be eleven again. You'll never be eleven again," reverberated in my brain.

Young men and teen-aged boys called "barkers" were calling to the pedestrians and potential customers to try their luck at throwing a ball at a particular target to win a prize. Another barker shouted, "Drive your own little electric car. You're in charge. You control it!" Kids were already lined up to buy their tickets and were soon rushing to seat themselves and test their power and skill. These small cars, that could seat two, were in an enclosed area surrounded by a chain link fence. One could bump his cushioned car into another and experience excitement, thrills and fun with no harm done, and only the loss of a few cents.

There were also entrances, for a fee, into a makeshift theatre to see a being with the head of a man and the body of an animal. For the same price, one could view Siamese twins, the fat lady or the sword-swallower. There were many thrills and much more excitement available for those who were tempted and had the price of admission.

The sun, sand and ocean beckoned, and we hurried down the hot streets anxious to reach the beach and remove our outer clothing. Our bathing suits were worn underneath and our bodies were ready to be enveloped in the cool, foaming waves that tasted so salty and burned the eyes. However, we were happy to overlook such minor inconveniences. We loved the strength of the surf and its power to knock us down if we were not on guard. We alternated between the hot sand and the cool lure of the ocean. We hated to leave this little paradise that we delighted in for the better part of the day, but eventually it was time to go.

After what seemed to be an uncomfortable and endless trip to me, we arrived home, weary, a little sunburned, and feeling the fine grains of the beach lodged in every crevice of our bodies. The warm baths that Mama prepared for us were a great comfort. When we were clean and shining, she splashed our sunburned parts with vinegar.

The evening hours rushed by and I was happy to fall into bed. The sheets felt cool and comforting. Later on, Sylvia would join me in our single bed. I would try to stay near the wall and give her a little extra room. I dreamed about the blue-green waves bordered with white spume rushing towards us with great energy, but allowing us enough time to jump up and out of its way, most of the time.

It was a wonderful and eventful eleventh.

18

My birthday had ushered in another summer. I would be entering sixth grade in the fall and I felt very grown up. Sixth grade was the graduating class in elementary school and upon completion, it was on to junior high school. There were two ways to get through junior high. One was a rapid advance program for supposedly superior students that they would complete in a special two-year track. The other, was the more mundane and usual three-year program before entrance into senior high.

The warmth and freedom of summertime was a gift. Gilda came with her elegantly dressed beautifully coifed mother to visit her grandma, who owned a rather large old house across the street from my tenement. Her house was near the glazier's store where I had addressed envelopes the previous summer. Gilda was a beautiful girl, and when she visited her grandmother she would join me and my friends for jump rope, jacks and lots of the things that eleven-year olds enjoyed doing. We were all a little jealous of Gilda and her status when she entered our intimate neighborhood. She seemed to come from a moneyed background, and her looks were special. I was particularly jealous of her mother's elegant facade and seemingly easy life style, especially when I considered my beautiful mother's face aging too quickly, day by day.

Gilda seemed to know a lot about boys, and her conversation always reverted to her favorite topic. She, and the rest of the girls, were still flat chested, and were very impressed by the grown-up changes in my very slender young body. I was maturing physically at an early age, and I did not let it be known that I was dissatisfied with this condition since I realized that the girls were quietly envious and could hardly wait for their bodies to mature. I, however, did not feel ready for this alteration in my appearance.

I never told anyone about the day that I went to visit a new friend that I had met at school. I strolled easily and contentedly along the familiar streets when suddenly I noticed several youthful teen-agers, whom I did not recognize from my neighborhood, walking very rapidly in my direction. The sun was shining brightly and my eyes were temporarily blinded. An occasional person passed by, but suddenly my pounding heart informed me that I was being threatened. I could feel the reverberating echo of their approaching footsteps. I walked faster, but was aware of the sound of insistent pursuit. My legs seemed to start running of their own accord, but the boys easily caught up and started shouting what I considered obscenities directed towards my vulnerable chest. They laughed, pointed, threatened and came closer. I felt faint. Fortunately their gesticulating and taunting yells seemed to fill their needs and satisfy them.

They finally ran ahead, leaving me trembling and overcome. I felt tremendous frustration. There was nothing I could do about this kind of incident except childishly mumble the totally unacceptable words under my breath, "Bastards... bastards... bastards." I could not easily or casually handle what had occurred. I was too young and bathed in inexperience. This kind of situation was totally out of my control even though I did nothing to evoke their mean-spirited sexual bullying. I was thankful that they had made no attempt to push me or touch me. They had gained power merely by intimidation and for them, that was satisfaction enough.

Gilda's grandmother, Mrs. Kulick, was certainly a grandmotherly type. Her soft, gentle voice made me think of my mother's Tante Lakie. However, her mind and what she considered prevailing practicality had a completely different focus. Mrs. Kulick was in charge of the prominent numbers game in our building and surrounding area. She had a colleague, a bookie, making his rounds and going from apartment to apartment to mark down the numbers on his little pad that the good ladies of the tenement wanted to play. Each day, this friendly, family oriented bookie consulted with the willing tenants. Every selection of the number to be played consisted of three digits. One could bet on a number with a few pennies or as much as one could afford. Generally, my mother and most of the women in the building would spend from twenty to twenty-five cents per day placing a few cents on several different numbers, one of which they hoped would be a lucky winner.

It seemed as though most of the staid, stolid "housefraus" invested in this undercover gambling business. Mrs. Gerber, my mother's neighbor and most conservative friend and self appointed advisor, would consult with Mama daily and suggest several good numbers. Mama, however, would follow her own instincts and occasionally hit a winner. Mrs. Gerber, that strong-minded lady naturally followed her own intuition and hunches.

The winning numbers were based on horse races and when someone in the building would hit a winner, there were loud congratulations forthcoming from the many neighbors who, no doubt, were probably disturbed that they had not picked the winning number of the day. They put on a good display of pleasure to mask what I believed was not complete sincerity. Their faces smiled, but not their eyes. It seemed to me, in my surprisingly cynical youth, that their reaction to other person's good fortune was based on their desperate basic need for a little extra money. That dire need bit into their souls.

Very often a woman would play the same numbers for several days and sometimes continue for weeks in hopes of a win that never arrived. Some numbers and some people seemed to be luckier than others. My mother favored birthday numbers and when my father's forty-ninth birthday rolled around it was a day of great celebration. 049 came in! It meant a badly needed coat for Sylvia.

19

A new family moved into the building. They had a daughter who was three years younger than I. She had a very pretty, vapid face that was framed by beautifully ...m. cared for blond curls. How I admired that lovely golden head! I hoped that with a little practice, I could duplicate those curls on my own dark wavy-haired head.

Her parents owned an upholstery and decorating business several blocks from where we lived, and although they shared the tenement mode of living, I recognized the fact that the apartment they occupied was on the second floor, not the fourth, and their life-style existed on a higher plane. Little Roslyn was the only child in her family and ate baby lamb chops and creamed corn for dinner! It was so luxurious to my way of thinking and so very American. My mother never ever served creamed-corn, and a meal of lamb-chops was indeed a rarity. Chicken or potted chuck steak and potatoes were much less expensive to serve to a large family and would go much further to appease the budget and the voracious appetites.

Mrs. Newmark, Roslyn's mother, was a good-looking woman with an attractive and authoritative personality. She spent a good deal of her time with her hard-working husband in their upholstering and decorating store trying to pull out of the depression syndrome, and I believe that very slowly they were reasonably successful. They too, had a piano and I was invited to listen to Roslyn practice. Mrs. Newmark felt that a listening audience was excellent motivation for her daughter who appeared to be completely uninterested in music and its accompanying discipline. She was only a little girl but she had a strong will, which she displayed negatively when her mother asked her to practice. She also unfortunately suffered from a case of weak talent, which was eminently apparent even to me, when she was coerced to play.

A male piano teacher came to her apartment and gave her a lesson weekly. I was present on one occasion and was very impressed with the teacher's ability and patience since Roslyn always looked as though her thoughts and concentration were elsewhere. She sighed audibly, rolled her eyes and glanced away whenever she could. I wished that her teacher could come up to the fourth floor and give me lessons. I believed that I would be appreciative and that our big, beautiful black player piano would be put to good use.

I enjoyed spending a little time with Roslyn, especially since she had American parents. I was always curious to see how they conducted their lives, and compare it with my own family.

One day Mrs. Newmark said to me, "Beulah, would you like to spend two hours a day with Roslyn? You could help keep her busy in a constructive way and we would pay you for your time."

Once again the thought of earning a little money during the summer months without putting forth too much effort was enticing. I also knew that I would be on the receiving end of some of the edible goodies that were always available for Roslyn. "That sounds very nice to me, Mrs. Newmark. I would like that very much, but I'll have to ask my mother."

"That's fine. Perhaps you could let me know tomorrow."

I vaguely remembered that both my parents did not like the idea of any of their children baby-sitting. A real job was one thing. Addressing envelopes was acceptable, but for them, baby-sitting was in a different category. I wasn't surprised therefore, when my mother reiterated with a definite, "No. Don't forget to say thank you, but no."

Once again Mama explained patiently, "This is not a regular job, Beulah. This is being a servant and Papa and I do not approve of your being a servant. I hope you don't mind too much. When you get a little older, you'll work plenty. Don't rush."

"I really don't mind. I forgot that you and Papa both felt that way. I'll have more time for my friends and myself. It's absolutely fine. It's great."

I hid my slight disappointment at what I considered to be their old-fashioned reaction. It was no doubt a deeply ingrained feeling brought over by them from the old country where the influences and prejudices were beyond my ken or comprehension.

I thought about the piano lessons that Roslyn was taking. I had been an observer on several occasions by this time, and I continued to be confounded by what I considered to be her complete lack of talent and enthusiasm. I was deeply envious of the fact that she had a special piano teacher. The need for more music in my life was a powerful force. My family continued its songfests, often on a Saturday or Sunday morning for an hour or two, and I knew and realized that my voice was very strong and very beautiful. No false modesty for me!

Jack and I loved to harmonize and one of our favorite selections was, "Silent Night." That was really a strange choice in a Jewish household, but my parents never stopped us or discouraged us from expressing our musical inclinations and pleasures.

They frequently volunteered my singing services at our numerous family functions such as Bar-Mitzvas, weddings and private meetings at their fraternal and burial society. The nervousness that clenched my throat at the thought of performing did not seem to be of great significance to them. They were proud of my voice as was I, and they wanted to share the pleasure and praise. Once I got past the gripping, tightening opening line of a song, I generally loved the sounds that were coming from my throat, and I certainly loved showing off.

The society that my father belonged to had been established by the men and family members who had been residents of the town in which my father had lived in Russia. This group had joined together as a support system for each other. They collected dues, raised a little money, and would give loans to those in dire need, and aid to those who might fall ill. They had meetings and get-togethers once a month, which culminated in the serving of wonderful homemade delicacies and baked goods brought by the wives of the members. It seemed as though each woman had a special talent for a special treat.

Perhaps the most important function of the society was the provision to supply a burial plot and religious services when one of the members or any other person in his family died.

20

Our player piano sat sedately against the wall in our dining room and begged for our attention. Sylvia had taken lessons for a while, but discontinued when her interest in music lagged and her interest in boys skyrocketed. She indicated that she had quite enough responsibilities to keep her occupied without any additional commitments. It was just as well. Money was still scarce.

However, at that time President Roosevelt established the W.P.A., which stood for the "Works Progress Administration." Its purpose was to take the multitudes of unemployed and put them into work programs of many kinds that would restore self-respect and give them the opportunity to work and earn some money. They cleaned and swept the streets, and cut down dead or diseased trees to make room for new growth. They built new roads and filled in the potholes of the old. They were pushed and pulled into various fields as one of the means that attempted to break through the depression, and many talented persons found a pathway into the arts. Those who were qualified could conduct classes in music and painting. There were classes to teach English to the foreign born. These adult students could also get a taste of literature, math and science if they had the time, the strength and the inclination.

Wherever a possible opportunity to get a job to teach one of these classes existed, an enthusiastic individual happy to be working once again, filled the position. A minimal wage was gladly accepted regardless of whether it involved day or evening hours.

This was the opportunity I had been waiting for. A piano class was being offered by the W.P.A. for young beginners who owned a piano. Each class would have six students who would share the instruction consisting of one hour. The cost for the weekly lesson would be fifty cents, and each student would spend a short time at the piano with the teacher while the other children observed and listened carefully.

The main difficulty was that in order to reach the school where classes were being given near Prospect Park, I would have to walk to the station several blocks from where we lived and take the elevated trains that loomed above. Would my parents be willing to allow their eleven-year old daughter to travel alone to achieve a questionable education, and an even more questionable goal in the study of the piano? Their other daughter had not been enchanted with the idea of practicing every day. There had been too many distractions and other interests in her young life, but now notably, one fine young teen-ager, Charlie, commanded her thoughts and time. He was a classmate of hers also attending Eastern District High School.

I discussed the matter of taking piano lessons from the W.P.A. with my parents, and I talked about the opportunity it presented. I made it clear that I did not foresee becoming a concert pianist. I just wanted the educational stimulus in order to increase my musical skills and pleasures. Much to my delighted surprise they appeared to be very receptive to my pretty little speech.

"I think that's a wonderful idea," my father offered. "It's very worthwhile. You should do it. The more you learn, the better."

Mama agreed. "Papa will make sure that you know how to get there. You won't have to worry about that."

Jack, at this point, was immersing himself not only in chess but in literature and music as well. He listened to the classical "Masterwork Hour" on the radio every evening and either pretended or sincerely loved everything he heard. Everyone in the family was a captive audience and he directed his particular attention to me as usual, encouraging and pressuring me to listen carefully and attentively. He was always lecturing me on the benefits and delights of becoming familiar with the renowned composers and he continued this nagging process by also strongly emphasizing the importance of literature.

He started mentioning the name "Anne" in our conversations, and told me that she was someone he knew who was seriously interested in listening to what he considered to be good music. "She can give you the name of practically any composer after listening to a short excerpt of a piece of music," he said very proudly, as though the accomplishment was his. According to his rather reserved manner and mild formality when he talked about Anne, I intuitively understood that Anne was actually Jack's version of an angel in disguise, and that this was Jack's first big crush.

I was delighted and slightly apprehensive when my parents definitely permitted me the freedom and responsibility to travel alone in order to start taking the piano lessons that were to be given by the W.P.A.

Mom, that was what I now called her at my newly acquired level of maturity, advised me in a rather light hearted little speech not to speak to any strangers on the train, and to be sure to get off at the proper station. I thought about what she said and according to my analysis at that time, I realized that the reason for her seemingly casual approach to a serious subject was that she did not want to instill fear in me. What keen insight and wisdom she showed.

Pa, no longer Papa, gave me explicit directions from the train station to the school where the lessons were being given. He drew a map, which showed clearly and exactly where I was to go. All I had to do was to glance at it to feel secure and reasonably safe.

How grown-up I had become. I could feel my self-esteem expanding as I worked hard to allay any remaining insecurities that rumbled about in my mind. I thought about my immigrant parents. How come they seemed to know just what to do to guide their children towards self-dependency?

I skipped down the four flights of stairs with my new music notebook held tightly in one hand. The other clasped a pocketbook in which I carried important items such as carfare, the fifty cents fee for the lesson, a little extra money that my mother had given me for any emergency that might arise, a pencil and a handkerchief. My mother loved pretty things and she often allowed herself the pleasure of buying a special inexpensive handkerchief that was particularly appealing to her. She had a beautiful collection of delicate looking handkerchiefs of various shapes and fine fabric and I would watch her on occasion ironing them lovingly. I had one of her dainty favorites with me that she had tucked into my pocketbook. I considered it a good luck omen.

It was a lovely balmy day and the sun and sweet breezes softly stroked my face. It was exciting to embark on a new adventure. I knew in my innermost being that I had no extraordinary talent for the piano, but that self-knowledge would not spoil the pleasure of enjoying the sounds and harmonies that I would be amateurishly creating and forming in the future. My instrument was the voice, and the voice was considered by many to be the most beautiful instrument of all. I also knew that I would never become a successful singer in spite of the strong recognition that I possessed tremendous raw talent. I lacked the essential resources to succeed. Money was needed for training, and an aggressive and ambitious temperament was necessary to pursue the goal. I possessed none of these prerequisites or qualities.

I loved the power, sound and timbre of my voice and I innately knew how good it was, but I suffered deeply and profoundly from stage fright. I continued to sing often at family functions, but I was barely able to breathe until I had sung the first few notes. The encouragement from my family was strong, and the high praise from guests and friends was satisfying and even exhilarating, but it did not calm my intense nervous reaction prior to performing. I sadly missed eating the delicious dinners that were served at family weddings and Bar-Mitzvas. I could not swallow a morsel because I knew that I would be called upon to sing. My reaction was strangely ambivalent. I ached to sing and allow my voice to soar and be heard, but I lacked the nerve. I was a coward. I realize now in retrospect that if I had persevered, I might eventually have overcome my fears. "Too late, too smart."

The train ride to the WPA music school was surprisingly delightful. I did not experience the usual nausea that always accompanied me on my limited travels. Perhaps I felt fine because I stayed on the open platform that attached and secured one train car to another. It was like a ride in the open air on a magic carpet.

I followed my instincts and my mother's precautionary instructions and felt shielded from harm. I was delighted to be approaching a new adventure in learning. My father's well drawn map ushered me to a park-like area where I spied a small building with a sign that proclaimed that various classes were being held inside. Room numbers were listed. I picked out the piano class for beginners and hesitatingly entered the room. The teacher was a young woman who was seated at a large upright piano. She welcomed me warmly and said, "We'll wait a little while for the others who registered for the class. They should be here very soon. Have a seat."

There were two other girls about my age waiting patiently with a keyboard constructed from heavy cardboard balanced on their laps. Mrs. Letterman handed me one and I took a seat next to the girls. They flashed a welcoming smile. Two boys came into the room and that completed the roster for our class. The presence of boys lent a degree of added stimulus and excitement, and increased my interest in learning to play the piano.

Only one student at a time could sit at the piano with Mrs. Letterman while the rest attempted to follow her instructions on the cardboard substitute. It was not particularly satisfying. However, when it was finally my turn to sit next to the teacher on the piano bench, it was wonderful. I listened attentively and did everything I could to show how cooperative I was and how anxious I was to learn. My private lesson with my esteemed teacher was much too short.

However, I tried to remember and absorb everything she taught us, which, of necessity, was quite limited, but I was intensely satisfied and looked forward to the next lesson. I practiced daily and my parents were pleased with my very modest progress.

21

Great changes were coming! Goldie's mother was selling the candy store, and they were planning to move to a better neighborhood. I already began to miss this person, this pseudo friend whom I never really liked. How was it possible for me to feel a sad emptiness when I contemplated a life without Goldie and her obnoxious personality? Was it possible that I had misjudged our relationship during all those formative years?

When I discussed these thoughts with my mother, she commented, "Things change and people change. Nothing stays the same. We know that and have to be prepared. You'll miss Goldie because you became very used to her, but you'll adjust. As you get older you'll make some new friends in school and keep some of the old." Her sensible comments always helped me put things in their proper perspective.

Mrs. Engel was selling the candy store to Georgie Balter who was a forty-five year old bachelor. He was a tenant in our building who had lived with his father for many years. When his father died, he remained alone and lonesome. He was ready for a change in his life. He was going to become a businessman. However, he knew that he would require a helpmate for the long hours and hard work involved in running a successful candy store. He thought about the possibility of finally acquiring a wife after all those years of remaining single. The more he thought about it the more he liked the idea. Not only could a wife be a tremendous help in the new enterprise sharing the long hours of the working day, but he would not have to cook his own meals anymore. He was getting so tired of preparing makeshift meals that were making him fat. He studied his expanding waistline and reasoned that a good woman would take good care of him. Besides, he was tired of eating solitary meals. He was a genial fellow and basically liked company. That was one more important reason for buying the candy store from Mrs. Engel. There were always people entering, hanging out, and leaving when they were ready. He knew that he would like that aspect of the business. There was also the possibility that he would really enjoy having a wife. He had been alone too long.

Two sisters who were spinsters shared apartment #23. They had lived together for many years and neither had achieved the desired or expected goal of marriage. Their status, they believed, was slightly diminished by this unfortunate failure. The younger, Ida, was approximately the same age as Georgie, and Ilsa the elder, seemed conspicuously so.

Ida had a peppy personality and a homey, lilting smile. Ilsa was a tremendous grouch with a face to match. I always preferred to avoid meeting Ilsa on the stairs, in the halls or in the lobby. She invariably had some little unpleasant or sarcastic remark on her tongue. She was not a well woman, and this no doubt contributed to her unpleasant disposition. She died a year later and I confess that I always had some feelings of guilt since I did not wish her well when she was alive. Could my negative thoughts have contributed to her demise? They had never before or since traveled that unknown and mysterious distance.

Georgie started the ritual courting procedure and Ida was thrilled beyond measure. What a great opportunity to achieve the status of married woman, to be called Mrs. Balter, and to have the kind attention of a good humored man. Ida's strong nature was generally no match for her sister's stronger dominance, but Ida preferred life with Georgie and she chose him, giving in to her better judgment.

Ilsa having no alternative, bitterly accepted Ida's decision. She would stay on in apartment #23 alone.

Most of the tenants in the building, however, would happily celebrate this joyous decision. Everyone thought it was a perfect match. The wedding would take place in Georgie's apartment and some of the women in the building offered to bake some cakes and help to set out other food and deserts that Georgie would supply.

There was great preparation and when the wedding day finally arrived, Ida, the elated middle-aged bride, was radiant in her beautiful lacey white dress. Her groom was dressed in a dark blue suit with accompanying bow tie looking eminently pleased and cheerful.

Everyone invited felt as though they were watching a modest little miracle. Georgie and Ida seemed so well suited to each other. They gazed fondly into each other's eyes and seemed so satisfied, happy and content. They understood that they were a refuge for one another. They were solemnly pronounced man and wife. Georgie lifted Ida's face veil and warmly and solidly kissed the bride. What a good combination they were!

Georgie and Ida took over the store and their customers were completely satisfied with the cleanliness, the service, friendliness, and the change in the personality of the store. The establishment seemed fresh once again.

Goldy's parents did sell their house and they did move. It broke my heart, temporarily.

22

It was back to the usual routine in the fall. I looked forward to being a senior in elementary school. This was a tall step up in self-esteem. This was a welcome elevation of status. All the children in the lower grades treated the seniors with deserved respect. They would be there some day and would be treated in this special way too. They patiently waited their turn.

Some of the teachers in the lower grades requested help. The seniors could apply and use their free study time as aides, tutors to the slow learners, or as secretaries to the teachers. Their services would presumably be listed on some kind of resume sent along with their records to junior high. I did apply, and every time I had dealings with a teacher whom I vaguely loved, I always thought she strongly resembled my sister Sylvia. I learned early on that "Beauty is in the eyes of the beholder."

Sylvia was doing very well in high school and was still working part-time in Georgie's candy store. Her boy friend, Charlie, was very welcome in our house. He came from a large orthodox Jewish family and was a good-looking, good humored and very bright guy. The family liked him a lot and Sylvia loved him a lot. Fortunately, the feelings were reciprocated and they were soon going "steady."

Sylvia was graduating from high school at the end of the year, and my father thought that the best thing she could do was to become a bookkeeper. Very few children of the depression were slated for college. Their working income was badly needed to supplement the family's survival needs. The family could move up a notch on the comfort scale when some extra money was forthcoming.

Even though Papa earned a regular, albeit limited salary, he felt important and needed as a salesman in his place of business. The firm had been steadily growing and people came in from many different parts of the world to ask for "Sam." They wanted Sam to sell them hundreds and sometimes thousands of yards of varied cotton goods. They asked for him specifically because he was trusted, accurate in his dealings with them and possessed good business acumen. This was an ongoing source of gratification for my father. His astuteness in the business world had earned him many friends. He was strongly aware of the fact that the bookkeepers were highly respected and relatively well paid, often earning more than the salesmen. He thought that this would be a fine profession for his daughter when she graduated from high school.

Sixth grade was going to be very exciting. For the first time, I was going to have a male teacher. Not only was he male, but he was very masculine looking and attractive. What a treat! All the girls were mad about him in spite of the rigorous academic program to prepare the class for junior high school. We were in the top exponent of the grade and groomed to make the "Rapid Advance." If we qualified, it meant that we would cover the three-year junior high school syllabus in two. Of course there were tests that had to be taken prior to graduating from elementary school. These tests would determine if we were acceptable for this academic challenge. We vowed to work hard for our handsome teacher. We loved his reserved maleness and we wanted him to be proud of us. We knew he was married, but that fact did not disenchant us at all.

Jack was doing exceptionally well in high school. He always got excellent grades and had a definite affinity for language. He studied Spanish, and with his usual intensive manner of concentration, proceeded to learn the language. He attended Spanish movies on a regular basis and read Spanish books that he borrowed from the library. He became fluent in the language.

At this time, he was captain of the Boy's High School Chess Team. My father was delighted when this honor was awarded to his son. They still played chess very often on the kitchen table after dinner. Pop seemed to retreat into the deep concentration and diversity of the game, and continued to take tremendous pleasure in being beaten by Jack.

It was understood that Jack would probably attend college. After all, the general assumption at that time was that it was more appropriate and important for a young man to continue his education than for a mere female to do so. The prevailing logic, no doubt, was that the male would be supporting a family some day and a college degree would be of tremendous benefit. The wife would be staying at home raising a family.

One afternoon a doctor visited the principal of Boys High School and asked him whether he could possibly recommend someone from the chess team, which had a fine reputation and had won many competitions, to teach him the game. The next day Jack was summoned to the principal's office. No one was there. He waited patiently for the principal to show up and enter this sacred retreat.

When the door opened, Jack stood up from his seat and respectfully waited for Mr. Mazur to speak.

"Sit down, Jack. Sit down." he said, as he walked into the room. "I have something to discuss with you that I think might please you. We've had a special request from a Dr. Elman who is very anxious to learn to play chess. I thought about our best player in the school and naturally, you came to mind, Jack. Do you think that you would have the time and the patience to teach Dr. Elman the game? He's looking for someone competent and reliable. I know that you can do a good job and you'll earn a little money. What do you think?"

"I'd like that very much, Mr. Mazur," was Jack's immediate response. As he spoke he felt a little pocket of pleasure explode in his chest. "It sounds great. I'm sure I can find the time."

My brother was chosen for the job and he happily tutored Dr. Elman for a year. He received a small monetary compensation and gave most of it to Mama.

Meanwhile, Jack and I continued to visit the library together quite regularly. He was always taking out books for me to read that were beyond my literary comprehension. I enjoyed pleasing him and I read those books word for word, not always understanding them or the full subtleties and nuances of classical writers. I can still feel those tremendous influences transmitting from Jack's mind to mine.

23

One day during line-up, before the classes marched from the gym into their respective classrooms, we happily noticed our teacher approaching. The routine for today was to be a little different. Our class was going directly to the auditorium this morning because a special early assembly program had been scheduled. There were going to be speakers from the police department to address all of the sixth grade classes. A film would also be shown. Since our teacher was in charge of the sixth grade assembly program, he had to be there a little earlier than the other teachers to greet our distinguished guests and attend to the technical details of introducing them properly and in the correct order.

The girls were delighted to see our teacher's handsome face, but a sharp tremendous feeling of doom slowly settled upon the entire class as one of the boys noticed that Mr. Martin's fly was unzipped. The news was quietly and quickly passed from one student to another until it finally made its way to our delicate female sensibilities. We were aghast! It was horrific! What could be done? Who could bell the cat?

The quiet whispering and tittering of the class did not seem to disturb Mr. Martin. His thoughts were elsewhere. He was completely unaware of the existing and embarrassing emergency. After all, he was not a petty female teacher. He allowed his students a little freedom of expression and therefore unwittingly, the news of the minor catastrophe had spread up and down the line.

Finally, the boys who admired and always looked up to Mr. Martin decided that he would have to be informed. We all knew and completely believed that though he might be a little embarrassed, he would be so appreciative, so grateful, that he would probably reward the brave fellow who would bring him the much needed information.

Jack Macy, he of sparkling white shirt, he of the cherubic face, he who was the epitome of good-natured courage, volunteered. We all watched intently as he quietly approached our Master. We saw his lips moving but could not hear his words. We respected his discretion and valor.

Mr. Martin looked shocked when he heard what Jack had to say. His face changed color and two red spots appeared on his cheeks. His eyes slowly glanced at his lined-up class and he realized that everyone was aware. He looked at Jack with overwhelming anger and hissed, "Mind your own business," loudly enough for everyone to hear, and swiftly walked out of the gym. We were startled and overwhelmingly disappointed by his reaction. Our teacher, our hero, had failed the test miserably!

It took us a long time to forgive Mr. Martin's harsh response to an innocent, courageous boy who had tried to do a good deed. We could all understand the embarrassment that had formed his response, but we all thought that our teacher owed Jack Macy an apology and a "Thank you," but he received neither.

24

My friend Ramona was moving. I felt terrible! I knew I would miss her greatly and that there would be a void in my life when she was gone. I still enjoyed playing jacks with her on the landing between the fourth and fifth floor even though we had become so grown up. The game of skill kept improving as we aged and practiced, but now we also had a good time talking about so many things that we had in common although we came from different worlds. Her skin color, her eyes, her speech patterns, her background and her general demeanor were so different from mine, but in spite of these external contrasts, we were soul mates.

We particularly loved talking about the boys in our respective classes as well as playing games, perhaps more so. I told her about the Mr. Martin incident and we tried to treat it as a serious happening, but we could not help but give in to much salacious laughter. Mr. Martin had acted like a fool, we decided. "Poor little Jack Macy," we both agreed.

I loved Ramona's somewhat prissy manner, her speech patterns, her plain outspoken analysis of our friendship, our mutual friends, and the daily happenings in our lives. My mother liked her a lot and thought that she was such a well-mannered and well-bred girl. She was a "mench"! She admired her capabilities and the way she handled very difficult responsibilities, creating a home for her father and herself. This was no small accomplishment for an eleven-year old.

"My father is determined to move," Ramona told me one day as we sat on the cold little tiles between our floors. "He says that the makeup of the building is changing, and too many Puerto Ricans are moving into our tenement. He also told me that there were some Filipinos that had moved into our building with white women and he doesn't like that at all," she confided.

"Are the men married to the women who live with them?" I questioned, feeling a little breathless at my audacity.

"No," Ramona responded. "Those white women are mistresses of the men and that means that they sleep with them even though they're not married, and on some nights they play loud music, and there's a lot of noise coming from those apartments on the fifth and sixth floors. Don't you and your family hear any of it?"

"I don't hear anything like that," I answered. "I'm probably asleep by the time they start playing their music, and my parents never said anything about it to me. Why would these men want to live with them?" I innocently questioned.

"Well, they're probably impressed with their blond hair and pale skin. My father says that they are stupid men and he disapproves of their life-style. Those couples are not married and the men buy their ladies lots of presents and try to show them a good time. My father says that the women would look for other men if they were dissatisfied with their presents."

Ramona seemed a lot more knowledgeable and mature that I regarding these matters. I was amazed that a man and a woman would and could live together without the benefit of wedlock. It was unheard of in my small world of rules and regulations.

Our Puerto Rican neighbors were very polite and friendly. Our encounters were brief and accidental. They never engaged us in conversation but I eventually learned that "Buenos dias," meant, "Good day," and "Adios," meant "Goodbye."

One day a teenager passed me in the hall, looked me over appreciatively and mumbled something unintelligible in my direction. I could not make out what he said and pointedly showed very little interest, paid very little attention, and overtly ignored him. However, my mind raced ahead and deeply noticed that he was darkly handsome and very attractive. I realized that he was a new Puerto Rican tenant. I had seen him on several occasions as I hurriedly dashed down the stairs in order to get to school on time.

Each morning every one in the family had to wait, patiently or impatiently, for the bathroom to be free so that we could take our turns using the facilities and get washed. There were inevitable intolerant remarks and retorts charging along the sound waves. My mother and father were the quieting influences. To help ease the situation in the morning, my father, whom I was almost ready to call Dad, always shaved at the kitchen sink that had a large mirror hanging above it on the wall. During his lifetime he always tried to do his best for his family and hopefully turn minor difficulties into positive actions and reactions.

I can still clearly visualize from this distant realm of time his rather small manly figure clearing the table of the breakfast dishes. He would invariably give my mother a hand by holding, feeding or keeping an eye on my two-year old brother before leaving for work. He always dressed formally and meticulously in a suit with matching vest. This benign, tender person possessed a knowledgeable look and an authoritative presence that evoked our respect as well as our love. What a good man he was!

I passed my Spanish Lothario once again one rainy, misty morning. I felt relaxed since it had not been a hurried morning, as it usually was. Once again he seemed to pause, look deeply into my face and murmur his little phrase. This time I vaguely heard the soft-spoken syllables, "Yo te amo."

I looked down and did not respond. I knew that my parents would be displeased and even worried if I displayed any interest in him. I was almost twelve and regarded myself as quite grown up. I kept repeating his words over and over to myself so that I would remember them. I could ask Sylvia, who studied Spanish in senior high, what they meant. She probably would know. I did not care to discuss this private matter with Jack although he was the Spanish scholar in our family. It always seemed to me that Sylvia was wise and had mature, good, grown-up judgment. She would give me proper advice and conversation that I might not be able or want to share with my mother, and certainly not with my brother. I was now intensely interested in boys, but was still completely capable of curbing my baser instincts.

Sylvia told me with decided emphasis, "It means I love you. You had better ignore that kid. He's trouble. He's Puerto Rican. He can't speak English and he's not Jewish. Keep away from him!" I wasn't sure I appreciated or liked her comments and advice, but I knew that she was right.

25

A new world was opening up! I, and many of the kids in my class had made the "Rapid Advance" or R.A. as it was commonly known. We would be entering a new school, a junior high school, in the fall. How stimulating and exciting it would be, and how grown up we all felt to be leaving elementary school and starting the next phase and level of our lives. We would be graduating in two years instead of three and at that time, we would enter senior high school's third term. Mr. Martin had been a great teacher in spite of what the class thought of as minor aberrations. We felt that he cared about us, and the girls continued to love his manly handsome face, and strong leadership. We tried to expunge from our minds the incident of the "unzipped fly."

I visited with my cousins at a family get-together and spoke with Jakie Joe's. He suggested that I was now old enough to attend a Zionist organization that he belonged to, where groups of pre-teens and teenagers had great fun. They did all kinds of Hebrew singing and dancing when they got together. The participants provided the accompanying music for their dances by singing the Hebrew lyrics in unison. My cousin was a member of this storefront Zionist organization that promoted Palestine as a homeland for the Jewish people. Persecution had always run rampant in Europe, and the Zionists felt that there was no hope for the Jews without a country of their own. They believed that it was their destiny to return from whence they came and fulfill God's promise to them. This group was one of many that collected and raised money for the Jewish National Fund in order to buy land in Palestine. The year was 1936.

The idea of spending two or three evenings a week, mostly on weekends, dancing and singing was very attractive. Music was such an integral, important part of my life. I knew that I could learn the songs with the strange sounding language without too much difficulty. My cousin had talked about his experiences at this meeting place and told me about the young people who attended regularly.

"The atmosphere," he said, "is always one of fun and friendship, of singing and group dancing. You'll love the music and you'll love the people you meet. All the kids go because they enjoy the singing and dancing so much. The leaders also arrange for us to have lots of outdoor activities. We go to parks once in a while on Sundays for picnics and games, and sometimes different groups go on hikes'."

"How old do you think the leaders are?" I asked.

"They're probably in their early twenties or less, although they do have a few who are older. A number of the leaders are planning to go to a farming community in Palestine, which is called a kibbutz. Their goal is to take the sterile land that was bought by the Jewish National Fund and turn it into fields of lush produce using irrigation and back breaking idealism."

"That sounds like a special group." I responded. "I think I'd like it but I'll have to check it out with my parents. I'm sure that they'll say that it's okay for me to come, especially since you're a member."

Jakie Joe's always appeared to have a serious demeanor, and the family, no doubt, based on his unsmiling face, felt that his judgment could be trusted. I always felt that he was a little pompous but reasonably pleasant and moderately sincere.

When I asked my folks about my joining this organization, they both expressed the idea that they liked the idea of supervised activity with Jewish kids from all over the neighborhood and beyond. "Besides," said Mama, "Jakie Joe's will be there."

That settled it. I thought about with whom I should go. Dorothy Krasner, whose mother had invited me for that delicious cholent lunch was a good choice. The taste of that exotic delicious meal still lingered in memory on my tastebuds. Perhaps she would invite me again. Dorothy had remained a sweet amiable friend, always pleasant and open to suggestion. I knew that her mother, whom I admired so much for her "American" look as well as for her fine culinary talents, liked and trusted me. She was pleased that Dorothy, who did not seem to make friends too easily, would be accompanying me in a social situation. I was all set to go.

That Friday evening instead of visiting the aunts, uncles and cousins with my parents, Dorothy and I excitedly walked the several blocks to our destination. Upon our arrival we saw my cousin Jack waiting to greet us. He was the second Jacob in our family. My brother was the first Jacob, named after my father's father whom I had never seen. There was one more Jacob in the family, born a few years later to my father's sister, Aunt Clara. It seems that Jews name their children after a respected, loved and deceased member of the family. The three Jacobs were all named after the same man, and in order to differentiate among them, they were known within the family as Jakie Sam's, Jakie Joe's and Jakie Chaikie's. Chaikie was Aunt Clara's Jewish name and was used exclusively by all in the family. She was well loved by my mother who had unexpectedly found a sister in Chaikie.

My grandfather, Jacob, had died in Europe never making it to the golden land of America. His wife, my bubbe, my grandmother, was a widow long before she arrived in the country where the streets were supposed to be paved in gold.

Dorothy and I felt very grown up and excited as Jack ushered us past the huge glass windows that bordered the wooden entrance door to the interior.

As we entered the tremendous store, which extended all the way to the back entrance, we could see a large group of teenagers and a few leaders already forming a great circle. They were all holding hands, moving to a rhythmic Hebrew melody sung enthusiastically in unison. Two young teenage couples with hands clasped were inside the slowly moving outer circle. They appeared to be gliding along in the opposite direction to the rhythm of the music. The persistent underlying beat of the melody softly pounded itself into my welcoming, receptive brain. The music captured and delighted me.

A break in the singing occurred and sent a signal. Each of the dancers within the circle dropped their partner's hands and selected someone else of the opposite sex from the outer ring. Those who had danced twice rejoined the circle. The singing resumed and slow movement of the circle made its way once again. It looked like great fun and appeared to be slightly complex. Suddenly, the outer circle stopped moving while the singing continued on an upbeat with everyone eagerly clapping his or her hands in time to the music. The two couples within the circle danced a brief, spirited, Hebrew dance. It was wonderful to behold. The grace and enthusiasm was contagious.

Jack whispered to me that he would later introduce us to a few people of our age. He then pulled Dorothy and me into the large circle for the next dance. The original partners returned to the outer ring and the new people who had been selected to dance remained in the center and repeated the entire procedure.

Dorothy and I were delighted, and Jack, assuming his usual authoritarian manner said, "I knew you'd love it. I told you." We thanked him politely and did feel grateful for this ongoing fun-filled opportunity.

He was happily chosen for the next dance by a pretty little girl, and I hid my inner laughter as I watched him, his feet banging the wooden floor harder than others, with great enthusiasm and joy. He did not relate to subtlety in his dance or his dealings with people. However, I was happy to see that he was well liked and I realized that he was a good reflection of my family.

Dorothy and I continued to attend the dances and minor social get-togethers at every opportunity. We could hardly wait to involve ourselves in the singing, dancing and interesting activities that were provided for us. We congregated in front of the storefront at every opportunity and waited patiently along with others for the doors to open. We did not want to miss out on the fun and camaraderie that invariably was offered.

I was enchanted by the charm and quality of the young leaders who hoped that one day they would be called "Young Pioneers" in Palestine. We looked up to them. They were special and dedicated in their beliefs. We watched as they danced and felt that their dancing had been elevated to an art form. When their arms were entwined and they circled around, we were enthralled by their grace. Their welcoming friendship was a continuing source of pleasure.

They knew and let it be known with deep conviction that Jews would always be persecuted. They felt that the only possible solution to this devastating problem would be a homeland that had been promised to them by God. They never forced their ideas, but enveloped and immersed us in the warm sea of Judaism and the possibilities of Zionism.

26

The summer weather was upon us with its concomitant gifts and what some parents might have considered mild disadvantages. At that time of my life it was my favorite season of the year. It was great not having to think about school for two full months. What a relief! What a joy! I was practically free to pursue any dream that I might envision, although most of my dreams were concentrated unceasingly and increasingly on the opposite sex. Boys were the most interesting idea I had ever encountered. My thoughts were innocently filled with them. I could absolutely visualize and imagine the ecstasy of being kissed and having a young man's lips upon my own. It would be the most thrilling moment and experience of my life.

I took Sylvia into my confidence one evening. She was putting on some lipstick and combing her beautiful hair in preparation for a date with her boyfriend Charlie. She had already graduated from Eastern District High School, and was working as a bookkeeper in an upholstery and drapery fabric shop. The owner, who had been a friend of my father's when my father was in business before the "twenty-nine" crash, was kind enough to take Sam's young, inexperienced daughter into his business. He would train her to be an efficient full-charge bookkeeper in his very busy wholesale and retail establishment, which was located on the East side in New York City.

Sylvia, to no one's surprise, adapted well and after a while, handled the very responsible job pleasing her boss, his very bright personable salesman son who possessed a strong and likable personality, and all the workers in the place. It was a union store, slightly red-tinged, and

Sylvia, as young as she was, began earning more money than several of her co-workers as she gradually acquired the skills that were necessary for her particular job.

Within the family, we knew that her new existence was filled with stress, and that she initially suffered from strong feelings of inadequacies and inexperience, but we also knew that she was very smart and had a strong mind-set. Sylvia slowly overcame her fears and gradually began to enjoy managing the complex bookkeeping system as it became more familiar. Daily she handled large sums of cash and the quantities of checks that arrived regularly in the mail. She answered the phone that seemed to be constantly ringing, and ably juggled numerous other responsibilities. She was a capable and dependable asset to the company. The quality of her work was acknowledged and she was shown respect and a good deal of affection.

The store was open every Sunday for the retail trade and she had to work on that day. As a result, she did not have to go in on Friday. Saturday the business was closed. Most of the money she earned was donated to the family, leaving her with an allowance that covered her expenses. Financial pressures had eased up a bit and the grocery debt was slowly decreasing.

I told Sylvia about the redheaded boy Walter, whom I had seen many times, dancing and hanging out in our Hebrew club. He had a serious almost fierce demeanor, which seemed to match his fiery hair. He danced with strength and purpose, and with arm upon arm he twirled his partner around in time to the beat and melody of the music being sung. Very often when he was selected to be a partner by one of the dancers, who was in the center of the circle, he would flash an intense self-satisfied smile. His hair was a beacon of light that drew the girls like a magnet. It was easy to see that he had a strong sense of self-confidence and was well aware of the fact that he clearly attracted the young teen-age girls. He carried himself with a slight air of impudence, which only served to make him more engaging. Dorothy and I were timid pre-teens who longed for his glance in our direction.

Meanwhile, however, I had learned the songs and dances, and after a while was often chosen to enter the inner circle and dance with a partner while everyone on the outside sang and clapped their hands. I felt as though I were releasing energy mixed with pure joy! When Walter picked me as a partner one rainy afternoon, I was convinced that the skies blazed with sunshine through the sparkling drops of the rain swept windows.

Walter lived in a tenement around the corner and down the street from where I lived. The grocery store, where we ran up our food bills on credit, was right next door to his building. A candy store was located on the other side. That candy store was a hangout for some of the kids who lived in the building. Walter and his exceptionally pretty younger sister were part of that group. Occasionally when I went shopping for Mama at the grocery store with my little three year old brother tagging along, I would stop in to buy a bit of candy to please him, or myself. Mostly, however, I would stop by in the hope that I would possibly get to see that redhead who would give me a whimsical superior smile of greeting.

I became somewhat friendly with his beautiful red-haired sister. Very often she accompanied her brother to our club where she loved to join in the singing and dancing. Her red hair was magnificent, with soft curls surrounding her delicate complexion, drawing everyone to its luster and tender beauty. She was easy-going and sweet tempered, and I was flattered that she confided in me.

"You know, Beulah, I've always done very poorly in school, but it doesn't bother me at all. I was held back when I was in the fourth grade. The teacher was ugly and I could tell that she didn't like me. I know that I have all the "smarts" that I need in the real world, the more important world, and not the school world. I'll do fine."

It seemed to me that with the "smarts" and the beauty she possessed, she would no doubt end up being a huge success and marry a millionaire. We little bookworms should be so lucky!

Sylvia listened carefully to my thoughts and feelings about boys and the overwhelming, exciting possibility of being kissed. "If Walter tried to kiss me," I told her, "I would say, 'Yes. Yes. Yes'."

She assured me that my ideas and feelings were not only perfectly normal, but she knew that I had very good judgment. That subtle statement about having good judgment was meant to put a brake on my juvenile emotions.

"Sylvia," I questioned hesitatingly, "what should one do if a boy gets fresh?"

She thought for a moment and answered in a slow reassuring voice. "You can tell him, 'I don't go in for that sport'."

27

Junior high school was only a few blocks from where I lived, but I felt as though I had been transported into another world. The school seemed so large and the new entering students felt so small and insignificant. The sense of security of spending the entire school day in one class with one teacher was gone. We had different teachers for different classes. Bells were rung at the end of each period to signify that we were to proceed to our next class.

Initially, we felt insecure and unsure of ourselves, but in a short period of time we learned our way around the building and considered ourselves at home. As a matter of fact, we decided that it was considerably more interesting than elementary school. Now we had a variety of teachers. If one were bored with a particular teacher, there was always another to look forward to when the next bell rang. We were starting to feel quite grown up even though we were freshmen. We were freshmen, it was true, but there was a strong undercurrent of respect that was granted us because we were members of an elite group. We were the "Rapid Advance" students who were going to graduate in two years instead of three.

My strongest recollection of junior high school, for the most part, was of trying to stay awake in some of the classes. That was often a struggle. However, in addition to some inevitable boredom, I also experienced the dramatic impact of some of my talented teachers. The subject that was most intriguing for me was literature, and I generally looked forward to the bell that propelled me to that class.

I would rush down the narrow hall, open the door expectantly and see Mrs. Smith, our English teacher, standing near her desk. Her clothes and general outward demeanor was definitely dull and drab. Reading glasses were perched on the tip of her shiny nose and her fat arms were crossed and folded over one another resting on her sizable stomach as she waited for the class to arrive and take their seats. With a slight smile on her face, she leisurely surveyed her captive audience as they slowly entered the room. One or two of her students were actively yawning. Mrs. Smith repressed her smile.

After taking attendance she stood up from her desk and was ready to recite and dramatize poetry that unexpectedly came forth as music. Her plain round face lit up with electricity as she spoke the lines of the masters. She brought life to the written word and held us enthralled with her literary power. My brother Jack had instilled in me a potent love for what he considered to be good literature. He had bullied me, nagged me and pushed me into reading and hopefully appreciating his idea of good writing.

I fell completely and unreservedly in love with Mrs. Smith. I recognized the power and beauty she possessed and generously lavished upon her students. I finally understood what "Beauty is in the eyes of the beholder." really meant. To me, she was the ideal, a guide for the uninitiated into the world of the written word and works of art.

I made some new acquaintances and a friend or two along the way. Anna Ashkinazy was very unlike me in appearance. I was a little girl and knew that I was destined to remain little. Fortunately, the proportions were favorable for attracting the opposite sex. That was a great source of satisfaction to me even though I seemed outwardly reserved and somewhat timid at that immature stage of life. Inwardly, I had already developed a profound, but silent interest in the surrounding male population.

Anna was a large robust girl who had a round cherubic face.

She had come from another elementary school and had also made the "Rapid Advance." Somehow, in spite of our unmatched physical appearance, our relationship developed and mellowed creating a deep feeling of comfort when we were together, especially when we shared time during our lunch hour.

We would carry our paper sacks that contained our heavily filled sandwich that our mothers had prepared early in the morning before we left for school. It was wrapped in heavy wax paper to prevent any possibility of leakage and was securely tucked into a brown paper bag.

When Anna and I finally got through our morning classes and were ready for our lunch hour reprieve, we would head for the candy store located near the school. There we would comfortably take our seats at a little marble-topped table that had black wrought iron chairs surrounding it and order a most delicious chocolate malted. This drink, this nectar of the gods, would accompany our most delicious sandwich. It was a favorite and fortuitous combination. The fulfilling fragrance and aromas that emanated from our sandwiches always increased our appetites.

I can still remember our lively talk about our favorite foods, which was Anna's preferred topic of conversation. "What's in your sandwich today, Anna?" I asked.

"Well, I have some of the leftovers from last night's meal. My mom is really a great cook. That's why it's hard for me to watch my weight. I've got chicken with a little ketchup on a seeded roll. She also put in some pieces of pickle. I really like this combination a lot and it will taste even better with the malted. I've also got some cake in my lunch bag. What do you have?"

"I've got one of my favorites, chopped liver. It's one of my mother's specialties. She's got a lot of those." I thought about the food and love that was packed into our brown paper bags and once again the realization that I was guilty of breaking the Judaic law by eating meat accompanied by a milk drink entered my mind. The mixing of meat with milk products was strictly forbidden in the Jewish religion and tradition. At home, Mama ran a kosher kitchen, but since orthodoxy was never crammed down our throats, I felt free to occasionally take a different route as long as I did not discuss it with anyone at home.

We sat there contentedly waiting for our malteds to be served. We could hardly wait to bite into our sandwiches. It was the best part of the school day. Anna's full, round, guileless face beamed with anticipated pleasure. It gave us both a good feeling of satisfaction to like each other unequivocally, to enjoy each other's company, and be part of a smooth, understanding and undemanding relationship. Our friendship made it easier and more comfortable to deal with the general pressures of home and school.

We were the happy and satisfied confidants of one another.

Waves of excitement permeated the school building and flowed through the halls. We breathed its pervasive, heady essence as we made our way from class to class and bells to bells.

A big production of "The Mikado" was in the works in our junior high and daily auditions were being held. My friends and family kept urging me to try out, but I resisted. I knew that I had a better voice than Clarisse who might be slated for the lead part. Her prognathic chin jutted out even more than usual, displaying her willingness and enthusiasm. She exuded the confidence and the courage that I lacked. I felt an inner rage and contempt for my inadequacy. What held me back? I had high praise from the people who mattered in my life. My teachers pushed and encouraged me to go for it. They had heard me sing a number of times at class parties and minor school entertainments.

Why did my heart pound and my throat tighten with fear whenever I stood up to perform? I loved the accolades and craved the enthusiastic approval of my severest critics, but perhaps I could not handle the possibility of failure. Was my ego so fragile and insecure? Was I doomed to carry this not quite fatal flaw with me throughout my life? Could I overcome it, or was its destiny written in my genes?

Clarisse got the part and she did a fine job. I suffered from a great dose of jealousy, and relief. I obviously needed to be surrounded by inner peace and calm rather than by stimulating excitement. I loved the sweet feeling of success obtained in a relaxed environment, which I invariably received from teachers, friends and family. "Perhaps as I get older," I thought, "I'll develop a stronger ego and be able to show my talent and joy of music without an overwhelming sense of fear, and allow my inner voice to express its power and beauty."

School days kept rolling by quickly and inevitably. I came to the realization that since we are not in control of the passage of time, and it proceeds with or without our approval, we might as well try to accomplish what we can within its framework. My mind dictated and repeated, "Fill some of your hours with important and worthwhile pursuits."

For me, reading, listening to music, and perhaps learning a skill, fit into this scheme. My brother Jack reinforced these feelings regularly, and his words and influence resonated through my malleable brain. I greatly admired and looked up to my handsome big brother. I wanted to please him and reward him with my perseverance in pursuing what he considered worthwhile. It was the way in which I could best show him how much I appreciated and loved him.

28

The daily routines were pleasant enough if not particularly interesting. The acute pleasures came from other sources. During the continuing warm weather, a horse pulling a wagon carrying huge cans of home-made lemon ices plus a few other less popular flavors arrived daily at the school during lunch hour. The horse was directed and led by a large, rather fat man who sat inside the wagon and sold his half-frozen, moist delicious wares. A paper cup filled to the brim with one's choice of flavor cost two or three cents depending upon the size of the cup. The students, who lounged in front of the school, loved this refreshing treat, and "Kishka" as he was known because of his impressive size, did a good business. The sound of his loud musical bell announced his presence, and the sight of a large gray horse pulling a cart that sat securely above huge wooden wheels, signaled the welcome approach of "Kishka" to the pearly gates of our junior high. He was happily greeted by the very young impatient smiling teen-agers who clutched a few pennies in their hands. They were ready and waiting to give an order for the cold, reviving delight that "Kishka" generously doled out on a warm sun-filled day.

When I slowly walked home from school late that afternoon, my thoughts turned to the previous evening. I had gone to the Hebrew Club after dinner and spent two hours singing and dancing. It was much more satisfying than doing homework. I had made short work of that, not paying too much attention to fine details. My priorities were shifting. A dance with Walter was beginning to mean much more than a teacher's praise. Happily, my parents were satisfied with my moderate progress. My grades continued to be reasonably good, and I continued making modest improvement on the piano.

Jack was spending some of his time drawing large faces on sheets of drawing paper that measured twelve by sixteen inches, and our entire family thought he was remarkably talented. Everything that he did seemed to be imprinted with his great ability and skill. A series of his pencil-drawn art decorated our kitchen and each drawing of a face was tacked on to the molding that surrounded part of that homey room and extended down about two feet from the ceiling. Those countenances above us, one next to another, seemed to proclaim lives of their own. Each face was completely individual. Each face appeared to exude a benign existence. When I occasionally glanced up and looked at any one of the drawings, eyes seemed to capture mine and hold them momentarily. I often felt that they were observing me closely and knew what I was thinking. My imagination took flight and gave them human traits. Their eyes followed me when I was in the kitchen and appeared penetrating, albeit benevolent. I always appreciated the effort, skill and thoughtfulness that went into their creation, and I began to care for the faces of the people looking down upon my family. When I told Jack what I thought about his work, he laughed and said that he always felt that he knew each one personally.

29

I was almost finishing my third semester of junior high. Six months more and I would be entering senior high school. My Uncle Joe and his family had moved from Williamsburg where we lived in Brooklyn, to another Brooklyn section called Brownsville. He considered it to be a real step up in the world regardless of what anyone else believed. He urged his brother, my father Sam, to move to an apartment in that area as he had, thereby bettering himself and his family.

At this time, my father was thoroughly disenchanted with our present location and residence. Uncle Joe had reached out to Papa at a vulnerable time. More and more of our neighbors were moving out, and my father thought that the Jewish environment that he wanted for his family was rapidly diminishing. Several more Filipino men had moved into the vacated apartments with Caucasian women who did not give the impression that they were married to these men. Music was still heard too often late at night emanating from these apartments. I remembered my brother Jack seriously frightening me several years before, when I was completely naïve and impressionable, telling me imagined or invented tales.

"During the playing of loud music and drum-beats," he informed me, "these men are injecting drugs into the women to make them completely dependent upon them. You can't hear the women scream or cry out because of the sound and intensity of the music."

Of course I was duly impressed by this fanciful misinformation, and Jack was no doubt was duly impressed that he was able to get a huge reaction from his little sister.

Quite unexpectedly my parents made the exciting announcement that they had not only been looking for a larger apartment in a different and more stable neighborhood, but that they had found one consisting of six rooms instead of our four, in a three family private home in Brownsville. We would occupy the top floor, which was two flights up instead of the four flights of stairs that we were accustomed to in the tenement. It was within walking distance from my Uncle Joe's new place, and that knowledge supplied a modicum of added security for our family. There would be relatives nearby.

It sounded like heaven, except for the fact that I would be leaving behind some good friends. Most of all I would miss the weekend pleasure of singing and dancing at the Hebrew Club. That indeed, would be a great loss for me. I loved the participation and spirit of the group and had become quite proficient at doing the varied dances with its complex steps and swinging turns. The collective singing was a joy that I always looked forward to. My voice loved its release. But even more, I loved the mildly flirtatious looks that were artfully exchanged and the exciting awareness elicited when the boys chose me to dance with them within the circle. Walter, that dashing red-head that all the girls could barely resist, was the most masculine of all the boys in my age category, and I recognized the fact that I had a mild crush on him. However, I philosophically accepted and felt an inner reserve of pleasure when I thought about moving. A change was always stimulating and I expected to experience new and interesting times.

There was one important problem that I would have to handle regardless of how difficult it would be. My final semester of six months would have to be completed in my present junior high school. Subsequently, I would enter third term senior high in my new area. Meanwhile, I would have to take the trolley car from our apartment in Brownsville to my junior high in Williamsburg every school day for this last semester. This would entail a thirty-minute nausea-inducing ride each way. I still suffered severely from the effects of carsickness, particularly on the trolley, which always seemed to display a wicked, malicious, lurching, jerking motion when it stopped and started at each corner. I never mentioned my fears and trepidation of this unchangeable and unavoidable development to my family. They had enough to worry about without added difficulties. Everyone had to make serious adjustments and I surely did not want to dampen the happiness and upbeat enthusiasm that we all felt about moving. Change of this kind, no doubt, would be good for all of us. Besides, I would still be able to enjoy my old companions in school for six months longer in spite of my suffering to get there, while hopefully, I would be making different friends in our new neighborhood.

30

The eagerly awaited moving day finally arrived. It was a lovely benevolent spring day in May and the sun shone brightly making our spirits soar. We thought about the positive changes that this move was bringing into our lives. We were moving into six rooms in a three-family house! We would have a back yard! We were getting out of the six-story tenement building! Our street was lined with trees! It was just too good to be true.

The perfect weather supported our high spirits. However, we all nervously held our breath, watching once again as our huge, black upright player piano proceeded on its reversed journey. It had to be painfully eased out and moved with excruciating slowness through the removed bedroom windows. It had been wrapped in heavy blankets to protect it on its precarious journey, and was supported by heavily thickened ropes for its descent down the side of the tenement from our fourth floor apartment to the ground. It had come up, following the same route, when we had moved in many years before, and now it seemed as though this impossible feat was being accomplished once again, albeit with much difficulty. What a world we lived in! Anything was possible!

The huge moving truck carried all of our furnishings and belongings to our new address. My family followed in the trolley car and despite my constant complaining, moaning and threatening that I was going to throw up, we finally reached our destination. We quickly rang the bell, which signaled the conductor that we were ready to get off. What blessed relief it was to once again breathe the sweet fragrance of fresh air. Once again I was able to resume what I hoped was my normal stance of behaving like a good-natured, non-complaining, even tempered, cooperative human being, a tried and true member of the family. I felt positively euphoric when I considered all my virtues. Fortunately, I was completely ignored. My family had more important things to think about.

We had to walk three long blocks from the trolley to our new home, and our little four-year old Murray never complained. His small feet covered the distance with eagerness. He was happily excited by the family moving to a new area, even though he was not quite sure of its meaning or consequences. As a matter of fact, none of us were.

The three family house that we reached and would call home was attached on both sides to another three family brick house, and this pattern continued its architectural similarity for most of the block. Seven extended concrete steps led up to the small square outside entrance area where thick concrete slabs provided sitting space on each side of what was called the "stoop".

Our new landlady, who occupied the first level of the house that was called the ground floor, was outside sitting on the stoop and she rose to greet and welcome us as we arrived. She was a short, well-rounded middle-aged woman with eyes that viewed the world through a veil of experience. She allowed those eyes to rest on each one of us quickly, and with the insight and quick intelligence she naturally possessed, formed some initial judgments. Our first impression of her was one of good manners, basic kindness and sensitivity with which she related to our family. In the following years she never disappointed us in our immediate evaluation.

In a low-pitched voice that hinted strongly of her European roots and background, she greeted us. "Hello, I'm Mrs. Gensburg and I'm happy to see you. Your moving truck hasn't arrived yet. Why don't you come into my apartment for a little refreshment and then you can go upstairs and decide where you want your furniture to be placed."

My mother thanked her warmly and we all marched gratefully into her large immaculate kitchen, which sported a shiny new looking linoleum floor and an attractive looking table and chairs. There was an old beautiful vase on the table filled with real fresh flowers resting on a small doily. I was tremendously impressed. This was like a scene from a movie; fresh flowers in a vase! This large old kitchen was furnished not merely with a kitchen set, but rather with a junior dining room ensemble! I realized that we were two floors directly above her apartment and that we had the identical layout, albeit different furniture.

There was a husky looking boy who looked about my age sitting at the table drinking milk from a huge glass. He had a large chunk of delicious looking chocolate cake on a napkin set in front of him.

"This is my Bernard," Mrs. Gensburg volunteered. Her face was wreathed in a smile of pride. "He loves my chocolate cake." Bernard looked up with a friendly grin. He directed his gaze at me and much to my surprise said, "I'll be glad to show you around the neighborhood."

It took me a moment to absorb his generous spontaneous offer. His amicable thirteen-year old face still had traces of baby fat.

"Thanks. That would be very nice," I responded in what I hoped was a ladylike manner. My parents had always stressed good manners. Good manners; that was a big part of acting like a "mensh!" This important Yiddish word, which has been in many English dictionaries for years, has always had a special meaning for Jews. A "mensh" is literally a benevolent person, a human being. However, the real connotation describes a person who is ethical, compassionate, loyal, and possesses other wonderful attributes all rolled into one. I always considered my father to be the epitome of "menchiichkeit". He was a caring, generous man with somewhat courtly manners. He quietly proceeded to make a good impression on Mrs. Gensburg. After some pleasant conversation and after we had eaten some of the lovely delicacies that our hostess had served, she commented on our little Murray's sweet behavior. We happily and profusely thanked her again and again, and made our way out of her apartment and up the rather dark, dimly lit two flights of stairs to our new home.

Papa used his brand new key to open the door and we all crowded quickly into a bright, large kitchen. The sunny May day streamed into the room and warmed the air with the fresh fragrance of spring. We were delighted. The apartment had been newly painted and smelled very clean. The kitchen linoleum would have to be changed, but Mama assured us that it would be no problem. We walked through the six empty rooms that seemed palatial to us after having endured living in four crowded rooms for many years. We were enchanted and duly impressed by the idea of having a living room as well as a small separate dining room. My mother's heavy beautiful mahogany dining room furniture would be squeezed and pressured into its limiting borders.

There was a sturdy iron fire escape outside of my parent's bedroom window that looked down upon a partially paved yard and a rather trivial, neglected garden.

Beyond that, appeared an uncultivated green belt. We did not realize it at the time, but that unexpected bonus of greenery would become a great source of pleasure during the summer. The open windows and cool breezes that always came from that direction would invite Jack and me to occasionally sit on our comfortable fire-escape on a hot day sipping some cold lemonade, enjoying the spectacle of lush plant life and the huge trees that grew wild and splendid beyond our enclosed boundary.

This leafy, verdant outside environment would transport our mind and eye to a faraway sylvan country. Conversation took second place to sight and sound.

My family waited patiently for the moving truck and it finally arrived. Painfully, piece by piece, the heavy mahogany dining room furniture that was my mother's hidden pride, was delivered. Each unwieldy piece was turned and gently twisted to fit into the small middle room. The piano, that huge entity for which we had the most respect, was arduously and distressingly hauled up the narrow stairs one difficult threatening step after another. It was manipulated, turned, mishandled, dragged and finally set down heavily in the empty living room, which was the most beautiful room in the house with its three large windows granting us light and sunshine. This room faced the front of the house, and looking down from its modest heights, one could see occasional automobiles, a few people walking by and some children contentedly playing together.

Just across the street facing us was Eastern Parkway with its lavish display of many trees filled with their new soft spring foliage lounging in front of tall apartment houses. The house we had just moved into was located at an intersection of Park Place and Eastern Parkway where a gasoline station was situated unobtrusively on one side. Large surrounding trees lent its gift of benevolence and softened the look of its purpose. The entire area looked green, clean and most welcoming. I felt as though we really had moved up in the world.

It was a proud moment the day before we moved when Mama sent me to pay our total grocery bill to our patient and consistently helpful grocery man. He had always behaved like a complete gentleman to our family. Through all the dark difficult depression years he had accepted the fact that we, and so many others like us, were not always able to give him more than a few dollars on account each week to pay for the food we were consuming.

He greeted me with a particularly pleasant smile. "So you're really moving! I'm glad for you and sorry for us. The neighborhood is beginning to change, and my Missus and I are not happy to see you go."

"Tomorrow is the big day, Mr. Gelber, and I'm here to settle our bill," I happily replied.

He nodded and reached under the counter where he kept his thick pad and slowly lifted each page until he finally came to the particular paper that was headed by our name. His makeshift pad of records held together by a huge safety-pin looked worn and frazzled. He took a fountain pen from the pocket of the hand-knitted sweater he was wearing under his large white apron and carefully wrote, "Account Paid" across the entire page. He thanked me warmly and said, "It's been a real pleasure to have known you and your family."

"My mother told me to thank you too," I answered, "for everything you've done for us. She told me that you and your wife are special people and she wanted you to know what she thought. I want to thank you too," I added, "for your patience in waiting for our bills to be paid. That was very kind of you." Little nervous palpitations beat in my breast as I spoke but the words had to be said. He had earned my family's gratitude. I felt very courageous.

Once again a smile lit up his tired looking face. "Listen, I know that you really like those delicious mallomars in that cardboard box near the wall. They just came in today and they're very fresh. Please take three. Here's a little bag to put them in. They're a small goodbye present from me to you. You were always a good shopper for your mother and I liked how you took care of your little brother." His words and gesture of continuing kindness affected me deeply. I could already taste the crisp chocolate topping surrounding the moist creamy filling of the little cake.

Our conversation brought to mind Papa's comment stated on more than one occasion, "It's no crime to borrow, but it is a crime not to pay back." I knew in the deep recesses of my relatively immature and unsophisticated mind that we had had dealings with certain noble people from the tenements, and that our kind grocery man and his wife were of that assemblage.

I stopped into our candy store for a last malted from those familiar shiny, "Hamilton Beach" malted machines that Sylvia had so often used in the past to treat me to a doubly rich drink. I was happy to be greeted by the welcoming smiles of that relatively newly married couple, Georgie and Ida looking contented and pleased with themselves. My old playmate Goldie Engel came to mind and a mist of nostalgia emerged, lingered, and was slightly painful. I longed to sing "Goodnight Sweetheart" once again with my little friendly enemy from the past.

Georgie and Ida made a good team, and maintained a clean, pleasant environment in the candy store for all their neighbors. How good it was to see them happy and working together. Georgie put an extra scoop of ice cream in the mixture, just as Sylvia used to do, and refused my payment. "It's our treat," he said, with a huge smile on his face. "Enjoy the malted." Ida was profuse with her good wishes. "Go in good health, you and your family. You're such sweet people."

Mrs. Gerber, my mother's neighbor and friend who had always acted like a surrogate mother or elder sister, cried when she embraced Mama in a final good-bye. I was deeply affected by that scene, as was Mama, since Mrs. Gerber had always worn a cool reserved demeanor on her slightly wrinkled face. Since no one in the building owned a car and transportation was always difficult, we knew there would be very few get-togethers in the future, if any.

It was much easier to say "so-long" to my friends. I would be traveling by trolley car from Brownsville to Williamsburg every school day after the summer vacation, and therefore would continue to see them for another semester in junior high. We all would then move on to high school, and go our separate ways.

31

Everybody chipped in to help unpack. All the furniture was in place. Even little Murray was helping and would very cautiously bring us one dish at a time from an opened carton that we would place in our newly painted kitchen closet. It seemed as though there was so much more room for everything. In spite of the advanced age of our new apartment and its mostly old-fashioned accoutrements, our family thought that we were now in the lap of luxury.

We settled in after a few days of hard work unpacking all those cartons that Papa had packed so meticulously and responsibly. He was an incredible packer. Not a dish was broken. Mama dearly loved pretty pieces of china and crystal. She had slowly accumulated some choice objects that she had obtained by fierce economizing, and she placed them lovingly around the house. We were home.

It was time to explore our new neighborhood. Bernard had scooted up the two flights of stairs and knocked at our door. He addressed his remarks to me. "Would you like to take a walk? I can show you where the movies are, and the best place to buy ice-cream."

"Go, go," chimed in Mama. "It's a beautiful day, and it's very nice of Bernard to show you the neighborhood. Maybe you'll meet a few nice friends, also."

I flashed Bernard a big smile, grabbed a jacket and followed him down. Bernard kept up a running chatter as I walked along beside him. He pointed out the candy store, first in importance in his mind. It was located down the block from where we lived, on the side of the gas station, and it was part of the accompanying row of stores across the street where Mama would visit the butcher for delicious cuts of inexpensive protein. Near the end of the block there was a large sign which announced "Green-Grocer for the Best in Vegetables". As we passed, I could see and smell the variety of the out-of-doors display of fresh, well-watered soup-greens, carrots, lettuce, tomatoes and a host of other fruit and vegetable offerings. The aroma was clean and fragrant.

We crossed the street, turned the corner and there was the grocery store where Bernard told me his mother did a good deal of her shopping. It was a Mom and Pop store, reminiscent of the one that we had left behind. My family would continue to get hot rolls, freshly baked bagels and bialies every morning for breakfast. Butter and cheeses were stored behind the counter in large glass windowed refrigerators. The chilled butter was removed from a huge wooden tub with a metal scoop, placed on a piece of wax paper, and immediately transferred to a small scale that rested on the marble counter. The customer decided on the amount desired. But, ...did they sell chocolate-covered Malomars?

We passed a girl on the street who appeared to be about my age. Bernard stopped and introduced us. "This is Pearl Becker," he said to me. He turned to Pearl and continued. "Beulah just moved into our house a few days ago and I'm showing her around." We smiled at each other and a spark of friendship was ignited. "We're going for a walk," I said. "Would you like to come with us?"

"That would be great," she answered. "If you could just wait a minute, I'll just tell my mom that I'm going."

"O.K.," agreed Bernard.

I was happy to see that he was such a good-natured kid. I knew intuitively that Pearl could become a good friend. It showed in her amiable and welcoming smile. The three of us walked all over the neighborhood on that bright shining day in May and I absorbed the pleasure and warmth of the sun and the establishing of new relationships. Later we all went home feeling satisfied with one another. We had our dinner and we looked forward to the rest of the weekend with its reprieve from school.

Inside the small downstairs entrance hall to my house was a wall dressed with three brightly shined brass mailboxes. Above each mailbox was a button that rang a bell in each individual apartment when it was pressed. This was a little luxury to which we were not accustomed. We had never had this amazing convenience, or anything that resembled it, in the tenement from which we had come. It seemed magical to be summoned to our door by the musical sound of a bell coming from an electrical signal downstairs.

That very evening to our surprise, the bell rang. We all looked at each other wondering who it could be. I quickly opened the kitchen door leading to the stairwell and I called down in my most elegant Brooklyn drawl, "Yes?" I was delighted and surprised to hear my new friend's voice spiraling up the two flights of stairs. "It's Pearl. Is Beulah home?"

"Yes, I am," I quickly answered.

"Can you come down for awhile?" she asked.

"Yes, I can, but please wait a minute. I just have to tell my mother that I'm going out."

"It's Pearl, Mama. I met her this afternoon when I was with Bernard and she just called for me."

I think that my pleasure came through clearly. It was reflected in my mother's face. "Be back by nine o'clock, Beulah."

"O.K., I'll see you all later," I responded as I grabbed a sweater and disappeared down the stairs to greet the bell-ringer. My self-esteem rose a notch when I thought of Pearl seeking me out. It was going to be good living on Park Place.

The following morning, Saturday, dawned clear and warm. I looked out from one of the windows in the living room and saw that it was going to be a beautiful May day. The fluffy cottony clouds slowly and gracefully danced above high in the sky, and the trees below, lushly adorned in their spring greenery, clearly called to me. Daddy, as he was now intermittently called, did not work anymore on the weekend. What a tremendous improvement and gift it was in our lives to have him home. A number of years before, he had to go "in" on most Saturdays, but when the business was unionized, it became a five-day workweek. It was a blessing for our family and it was special having him around.

This cotton goods business, where he was one of the top salesmen, had grown and become a large money-making and successful enterprise. Even though he had started with it and had helped build it into the kind of business where buyers from all over the country and indeed, various parts of Europe came to make their purchases, he remained a salaried salesman. However, he continued to feel greatly pleased and perhaps a little proud that the most important and respected buyers continued to ask for "Sam" when they came in, rather than for the newer, younger American born salesmen that had been subsequently hired.

Daddy was a heavy smoker and had been one since he was a very young man in Europe. He was eminently pleased that we had moved and were now living in a pleasant Jewish neighborhood. He was well aware of the fact that there were a number of residents who were orthodox Jews living in some of the adjoining houses. My father explained to us that although he was not orthodox in his beliefs and disposition, he would never smoke outside of our apartment on the Sabbath because he thought that it was a sign of disrespect for those who had strong feelings and commitments to Orthodox Judaism. He was always sensitive to the needs and feelings of others. He was a true gentleman.

The orthodox Jews followed the strict dictum of Jewish law and were completely and unequivocally kosher. They would not eat certain unacceptable foods that were adverse to their religious views under any circumstances. They did not cook, smoke, hold money or travel on the Sabbath.

Mama kept a kosher home, but the family and most of the people with whom we associated maintained more liberal behavioral patterns as far as religion was concerned. In our opinion it did not make us less Jewish, but rather less rigid. Jews are well known for their diversity and differences of convictions and ideas. However, my parents always instilled in us the concept of having and displaying respect for one another's varying views.

Pearl called for me often after that first night. I would rush down the stairs to where she would be waiting. The warm spring evenings called to us. They were beautiful and mild and Pearl and I were both happy to be together and out of doors. One day at dusk, she said, "I'd like you to meet my family. They're a little different from yours. You'll see what I mean when you meet them, but they're really wonderful."

We strolled along together to her apartment at the end of the block. Our conversation was pleasant, friendly and relaxed. I thought she was a lovely girl. Pearl said that we would only stay for a little while, and then we could take a walk on Eastern Parkway towards Lincoln Terrace Park. There were lots of benches along the way where we could sit and chat.

Her parents were at home and greeted us warmly. Pearl had two older sisters and one younger. The only male in the family was her father, and he was extremely quiet and reserved. I assumed that it was difficult for him to enter any conversation with so many females around. It was a close knit family and much to my surprise, I was immediately made aware that they were totally immersed in communist ideology. The "Daily Worker" was displayed and spread out on the kitchen table. Her father had been reading it when we walked in, but looked up and welcomed his daughter and me. The sight of that paper was a little shocking to me since my family never seemed to delve into that aspect of politics or philosophy.

My parents listened daily to news programs on the radio and were always interested in world affairs. They regularly read a Jewish newspaper as well as one in English. They were very well informed of world happenings and occurrences but they had never turned to the left. I suppose they could have been called moderates. They seemed to prefer reading the more conservative Jewish newspaper "The Tag," rather than the very popular more liberal Jewish newspaper, "The Forward." Their choice might have originally been casual and accidental.

Pearl was not at all politically minded and it was very satisfying and natural for us to become friends. She was always there for me with her easy-going pleasant ways. We were compatible and comfortable in each other's company. We regularly took long walks to Lincoln Terrace Park, played jump rope with a few of the kids on the block and stoop-ball with others on a regular basis.

We could only play stoop-ball when none of the mothers would be sitting at the top of the steps which led into the entrance of my house. This was a sitting area that was provided with a raised length of flat concrete on each side of the stoop that could comfortably accommodate two sitting adults. Since our house was on the sunny side of the street, some of the ladies from Eastern Parkway would cross over to sit and chat with one another. They enjoyed the pleasant conversation and the warmth of the sun.

The six or seven steps that led up to the top of the stoop were utilized in our stoop-ball game. We would throw a good rubber ball called a Spalding against the steps, allow it to bounce and catch it, thereby gaining points. If we caught it on the fly, it was worth even more points. If we missed, our opponent took a turn. It was a fun game of skill.

I was particularly successful at a simple competition of hitting a little ball that was attached to a paddle with a strong rubberband. I could hit the ball several hundred times before I missed, and it became an ego building pastime when the kids on the block gathered around me and started counting the hits. While engaging in this skill, I surreptitiously noticed a small group of boys who seemed to be watching. I had seen them often on my side of the street and had discovered that one of the boys, Barney, lived in the middle of the block and his friend Leo, lived across the street on Eastern Parkway. Leo's apartment house faced my house from across a large double street divide. He seemed particularly attractive to me because of what I considered to be his unconcerned masculine demeanor. Barney was better looking, but his head seemed to slightly precede his body, thereby reminding me of a turtle. After some serious concentration, I decided to reserve and restrict my overt attention to the girls who lived nearby, and attempt to ignore and set aside the intense and secret interest that the boys awakened in me. This seemed appropriate as I approached my thirteenth birthday.

The girls who lived on my block were openly friendly and welcoming. Hilda, one of the girls that I was drawn to, was good company. I was greatly impressed by the fact that her parents owned the three family house in the middle of the block. It was similar to the one that we had moved into. Her father owned some kind of factory and her mother went to work with him every day. She had straight iron gray hair in a stolid, plain looking face. Hilda's father was also gray haired, but good looking. Hilda was my age and the youngest in her family. She and her older college age sister were pretty, and they had a brother who was a doctor! They were an impressive family and I imagined that they had lots of money and lived a life of luxury. Imagine having a sister who attended college, and a brother who actually was a doctor. Having a doctor in the family was the epitome of success for Jewish parents. Education, ethics and a worthwhile profession that commanded respect contributed to the Jewish ideal. Hilda was as nice as Pearl and so it was very easy to like her a lot. We became good friends.

I later discovered that her life and daily routine were not too different from mine except for the immense emptiness she experienced and lived with. It was created and prolonged by her mother's daily absence from home until dinnertime when she returned with her father from their factory. Good meals were an unusual luxury for her family, served infrequently.

"You're really lucky to have your mother around all day. We hardly ever get to eat a decent meal. By the time my mother gets back from the factory with my father, she certainly doesn't feel like cooking, and my sister and I scrape something together to eat. We do eat a lot of tuna fish." Hilda continued, "I sometimes feel sorry for my mother, but I mostly think that she probably wants to get out of the house and be around my father."

"Well, I guess there's always a balance." I responded. Maybe you get to go to restaurants more often. That would really seem great to me." As I spoke I knew that I much preferred having my mother at home.

"As a matter of fact, we don't get to go out very often," Hilda answered. "My mother generally cooks up a storm to last for several days and she's not exactly a gourmet cook, but what I really mind the most is that the house always seems so empty. As a matter of fact, I hate it."

I did not know what to say.

32

Getting to school in Williamsburg every morning, and back home again to Brownsville every afternoon five days a week was very difficult for me. Fortunately, we were in the middle of May and only a month and a half remained till the end of the term. The tortuous traveling by trolley would continue until the arrival of the welcome summer vacation in late June. I decided that I would not allow myself to think about the problem of commuting back and forth for the last six months of junior high until that time rolled around. It would be easy for me to postpone these negative thoughts until the beginning of September when the new term would start.

I had to get up quite early in the morning in order to get to school on time. I walked the three long blocks from my house to reach the trolley car that attempted to deliver me reasonably close to my destination. I found that I was developing strong leg muscles along with my accompanying weak stomach muscles. When I climbed up the entrance steps of the trolley, nausea, my companion, would follow me, sit next to me and breathe heavily upon me. I mustered all the strength and determination I could gather and stayed the course for five, ten, and sometimes fifteen blocks. At that fragile, repressive moment, I urgently and forcefully rang the bell in order to get off quickly at the next stop. I weakly descended and breathed deeply of the life giving fresh air. Strength and good spirits would return as I gathered my schoolbooks firmly in my arms and started the long remaining trek to school. Most of the time the weather cooperated during the lovely months of May and June, but when it did not, I just suffered the consequences. It was better than the trolley. Anything was better than the company of that debilitating and nauseating monster.

The happy compensation for my difficulties was in finally reaching J.H.S. #148, not particularly for academic pursuits but once again to get together with school chums, particularly Anna Ashkinazy. She always greeted the world and me with a merry smiling face. I loved looking at nature's gift of generosity. Anna was large in every way. She towered over me. She exuded warmth, friendship and fealty. Thoughts of Anna make me feel nostalgic and slightly melancholic, and bring to mind the sweet relationships that have touched my life briefly and disappeared.

Anna and I continued to lunch together every day and enjoy our chocolate malteds at our favorite candy store. We savored each other's company as well as our edible treats. She seemed so innocent and pure as opposed to those girls who always appeared to be trying too hard to elevate their status in the scheme of things and make a strong favorable impression on those they thought counted. Their sense of personal ego had not yet been firmly implanted or established. Perhaps they would never change but would wander down the path of life attempting to be seen as someone other than themselves, someone better.

Anna told me one day that she was thinking about becoming a nurse. "I think I'd make a good nurse," she said. I'm big, I'm strong and I like the idea of helping someone get better. I know that I could handle the job. I've been told that the training can be rough, but I don't think it would be too much of a problem for me. My mother thinks it would make a great career."

I thought that it was an eminently suitable career for her to pursue. I intuitively knew that she possessed many of the necessary attributes for that kind of profession. She was a hard worker and was filled with a sense of sensitive and tender compassion. I had no idea as what I could or should evolve into, but it would be a long process of decision making, and a slow one.

33

My long walks to and from school were arduous and somewhat difficult. I did not possess the legs, strength or stamina for a two-way hike. Nevertheless, I did what I had to do since there was no alternative. I buoyed up my spirits by stopping at a candy store each day on the way home. I looked forward to buying a raft of two-cent candies, which I happily munched as I strolled along. My favorite purchase at that time was a strip of chocolate licorice. I would buy at least three of them at two cents per strip. What sweet pleasure they supplied as I walked along and relished the little bites that entered my mouth slowly, filled it with delicious chocolate flavor, and eased the way home. My legs felt stronger and the heavy burden of books lighter as I consumed my treats.

As I finally approached my house, I became impatient for my mother's warm greeting. Murray, with his funny little mischievous four-year old face, would be waiting to give me a big hug and kiss that I relished and returned. It tasted better than the chocolate licorice. If it was Friday, our big kitchen floor would already have been scrubbed on hands and knees by Mama, and newspapers would have been spread around to keep the floor particularly clean for the Sabbath.

Generally, there would be wonderful smells and fragrances issuing forth from the oven and stove. Friday night was reserved for chicken and chicken soup served with matzo balls, fluffy and delicious Jewish dumplings. Fine noodles further enhanced this wonderful dish that was deeply imbedded into our psyche for a lifetime. All kinds of side vegetables and dishes were cooked to Jewish perfection. I loved

Mama's cooking, which was creative and reminiscent of East European flavor.

She had special recipes that she used for baking wonderful huge sponge cakes that were frosted and served with real hand whipped cream. The whites of the eggs used in the preparation for the cake had to be whipped to a frothy consistency, and I well remember my father helping her beat them to perfection. A dozen eggs were used, and occasionally eighteen. Mama's sponge cakes were so light and flavorful, the word ephemeral would come to mind when they were being greedily consumed.

She also baked special rolled up concoctions that included raisins, walnuts and luscious strawberry jam. These delectable ingredients were spread out over delicately rolled out dough that embraced all these magical, fragrant and delicious ingredients.

The main purpose of her life was the nurturing and life-giving force that she dispensed easily and naturally to her husband and her children. However, in spite of creating a loving and caring family that gave my parents so much pleasure, much sadness and tension regularly invaded my mother's difficult life. She thought about her family in Poland that she was not able to help. She thought about her husband working very long difficult hours earning a salary that displayed a lack of appreciation, and her children who had never experienced even simple luxuries. What she neglected to realize was that her children did not feel deprived. They were surrounded and enveloped by the security of love and total and undivided interest. That not only sustained and satisfied them, but also gave them a strong feeling of self worth.

Our financial status, and much of the rest of the country, seemed to be slowly pulling out of what had appeared to be a hopeless depression. Our situation was improving slowly but surely. Much to our delight and joy, Mama and Papa had purchased a three-piece French Provincial living room set consisting of a couch and two chairs. The silky-looking fabric that covered the furniture and the delicate graceful legs that held them up appeared to guarantee a short life span, but to our surprise it held up for many, many years and continued to look reasonably unspoiled. The furniture provided an ambience of modest luxury, pleasure and a sense of modest extravagance that the entire family relished. My parents had also purchased at that time a French Provincial coffee table and a small beautiful round companion side table. The latter has been ensconced and treasured in my home for the last thirty-five years.

How lovely our living room looked with our respectable tall black upright piano on one wall and our treasured large radio standing on its long legs occupying a convenient corner. It generously gave forth beautiful music that always managed to lift our spirits. We loved its elegant and resonant splendor. It was a great gift for our family. It also fed us dramatized stories that were known as radio serials dealing with ghosts and gargoyles. We looked forward to being delightfully frightened by these episodes. We always listened to them in the dark.

Our new living room furniture gave the family a tremendous feeling of heretofore inexperienced bourgeoisie opulence. We felt so foolishly proud.

I know now that all this elegance provided by my parents was purchased at a relatively minimum cost, and was paid off over a long period of time. My parents attempted to insert beauty and a semblance of elegance into our lives, and somehow or other, they succeeded. Mama, long before, had developed a special love for beautiful objects. She had a need to be surrounded in her home by a few pretty delicate dishes, a lovely piece or two of crystal, decorative ornaments and anything else that could bring beauty into her deprived lifestyle. She had great difficulty with the idea that some of her neighbors strongly held which was that the only worthwhile items in life were utilitarian.

34

Big excitement was coming our way! Sylvia would be eighteen years old on June fourth. At that time, not only was the arrival of sweet sixteen celebrated, but also those who had reached their eighteenth birthday were entitled to a "wild" eighteen party. Everyone knew that Sylvia was far removed from any wildness. Her nature and personality epitomized responsible, mildly conservative and fun-loving actions. However, she definitely deserved a big celebration in her honor, and my parents were going to see that she got it.

They were very pleased with our new location and modest apartment. With our French Provincial ensemble and what we all perceived to be an elegant setting for a party, Mama proceeded to invite many of my sister's friends from the old neighborhood. Of course, Sylvia's boyfriend Charlie was at the top of her list. My parents realized and acknowledged the fact that Charlie and Sylvia were deeply in love. They knew that Charlie was a real gentleman and everyone considered him to be a "mensch". Sylvia had shown not only young passion in setting her cap for him, but inordinate good judgment. Fortunately, their attraction was mutual. He and Sylvia made up the list of invitations. What a party it would be!

Our landlady, Mrs. Gensburg, continued to be a friend and good neighbor. She struck me as a cool, clever and sincere person, always treating my family in a kindly and helpful manner. Her husband was an affable man who lacked her good sense and grace. She allowed him to think that he was the power in their home but even in the midst of my inexperienced youth, I could tell who actually was in control. Bernard, who was a sweet boy, looked like a young clone of his father. His earthy dimensions and plodding gait always announced his innocent presence. He was a very likeable boy.

Our first floor neighbors, who lived in the apartment beneath ours, had the identical apartment, as did Mrs. Gensburg on the ground floor. They seemed rather elderly but they had a son Eddie who was only a year or two older than I. Eddie's personality vaguely conflicted with mine and I avoided him whenever possible. He was a very small boy, and perhaps to compensate for his lack of size always seemed to have the need to dispense a trivial bit of authoritative information to demonstrate what he considered to be his innate superiority. I found his manner and personality slightly abrasive. However, that did not make him a bad person, did it?

At any rate, the night of Sylvia's big bash arrived. She was the star of the evening and her eyes gleamed with its reflected light. She looked absolutely radiant, aglow with youth and beauty. Neighbors dropped in, and Sylvia's invited friends all arrived in high spirits ready to enjoy the celebration with music, enthusiastic conversation and copious quantities of delicious delicacies, food and desserts. Sylvia was a warm, delightful hostess and once again my family perceived her to be the blessing that she was. The young revelers rolled back our beautiful new domestic Oriental rug, and enthusiastically danced to the music of a borrowed record player.

Later in the evening my sister asked me to sing to entertain her guests and I was glad to please her in spite of my terror stricken pounding heart. However, in spite of my fear, I knew that I really wanted to sing. I looked forward to releasing the sound and power of my voice and I looked forward to the probable accolades that would come my way. My parents were delighted. Their pleasure and muted pride was strongly evident to me and that was my best reward.

The first few notes of my song floated nervously from my mouth when I started singing "There Goes My Heart." Breathing was difficult. I felt faint. I knew that everyone was looking at me and judging me, but suddenly my nervousness disappeared and my throat relaxed. My spirits soared with the rich sound issuing from my throat. I loved the strength and control that I evoked. My young thirteen-year old body was capable of producing this magical gift. I knew that I would never become a professional singer, but it was all right. I realized once again that I lacked the drive, stamina, and personality to achieve that particular goal, but I also knew in my inner being that I had a deep talent and that it would help motivate me to the knowledge of self-worth. I was profusely and loudly congratulated by our guests at the end of my song, but the most meaningful commendations were in the eyes of my sister, brothers and beloved parents.

35

School was out for the summer! No more trolley rides until September, no more long tedious hikes to and from school for a while, and no more chocolate licorice sticks until then. I once again decided that I would not think about that last semester awaiting me in the fall. All things come to an end, and that too would pass. I would concentrate my thoughts on entering high school as a sophomore in January. My junior high school days would be over and that was a pleasing thought that I could look forward to.

Friendships with girls on the block and across the street expanded, but most of my free time was still spent with Pearl. I was always a little shocked at the vehemence and almost fanatic political dedication that Pearl's mother displayed. Her leftist views consumed her and her emotionalism was always in evidence. Her husband, who was a quiet well-spoken man, probably shared her ideas, but he was calm and reserved. Rosie, the eldest daughter, was a smart, good-looking young woman married to fanatical Maxie. Maxie's eyes gleamed and glowered when he spoke of his political views. He pierced the air with his sharp, oft repeated communist slogans. His needle-like glances skewered his quarry with his relentless gaze. His idealism was never in doubt, but I thought that his judgment was. He and Rosie were both exceedingly idealistic and faithful to the cause. Their leaders could do no wrong. Pearl paid no attention. Her head was filled with other ideas and images. It was easy for us to get along.

She and I would sit on my stoop in the late afternoon until it was time to go in for dinner. We would surreptitiously watch the boys from the immediate neighborhood playing punch ball or stick-ball in the streets. The year was 1937 and there was very little traffic. Occasionally a few cars were parked where the boys played, but that was no deterrent. Sometimes, if the boys knew the owners of the cars, they would ask them to please move them so that they would have a completely open area for their important games. We were fascinated by the maleness and muscled talent of these young athletes that we so dedicatedly observed. We silently yearned for their attention, but always directed our eyes innocently elsewhere when they passed. However, slowly but surely after the game, they started gathering around us on my stoop like honeybees seeking pollen. It was inevitable!

Manny was the butcher's son. He was fifteen years old and he and his family lived in the apartment above his father's store. It was located next to the candy shop on the other side of the street. My mother bought her weekly supply of meat there, and I had the golden opportunity of picking up her order on occasion. Manny was a big handsome boy with a football hero's body. His voice and personality was gentle and sweet. I could tell that he liked me a lot and found me attractive. My mother's meat order would sit on the raised marble counter while he attempted to engage me in mild and inane conversation. He knew that my family had recently moved in and he indicated in an innocent manner, lacking any hint of subtlety, that he and a friend would be passing my house after lunch. I knew that I did not want to miss that chance of a lifetime. I gave him a happy smile, picked up my mother's order, and planned to be sitting on my stoop at precisely that time of day with my friend Pearl. If Hilda joined us, that would be fine too. Manny was mine!

Summer progressed slowly, happily and hotly. Manny became a regular feature hanging around my house. He smilingly showed me how easy it was to pull a leaf from Mrs. Gensburg's bushes, place it in the upper part of his palm and separate it evenly by pressing and slightly turning his other palm against it exerting a little pressure. I was not particularly impressed by this simple, artless demonstration but pretended that it was quite a feat. I knew that Mrs. Gensburg did not appreciate anyone tearing the leaves from her bushes, but I said nothing. This activity seemed to be a necessary, somewhat less than intellectual, pursuit for Manny. It was a mild form of showing off for my benefit. I could do nothing less than show my approval.

Another young cherubic suitor wandered over from across the street. He was funny, clever, and more importantly, attentive. Albert

Cohen was delightful company and he was welcomed. My limited social life was growing and eminently satisfying.

Albert surprised me, actually shocked me one afternoon, by asking me to go with him to the movies the following day. He would take me to see a double feature at the Loew's Pitkin, the best movie theatre in the neighborhood. At that time some of the movie houses were built like minor palaces with elegant statuary distributed in the huge entrance foyers. As one entered the spacious darkened inner sanctum where the movies would be shown, an usher would quietly guide you to your seat using a flashlight to light the way along the lush red carpeting. The ceilings were about fifty feet high with myriad settings of soft blue lights to emulate the stars. Sitting there before the film started was like experiencing the vastness of space. The impressive stage up front boasted a beautiful large organ for occasional live performances.

Albert called for me early in the afternoon. It was my first real date and I was intensely happy and excited. My family's reaction was always supportive and fun. Jack seemed to derive a great deal of pleasure teasing me and giving me lots of good, unusable advice.

"You can let him hold your hand and buy you some candy. I know that he'll enjoy that a lot."

"I think that I'll enjoy it a lot, too," I responded. "Albert's a really nice kid."

Mom and Sylvia smiled and allowed Jack to have the final word.

"Have fun."

Albert did hold my hand as we walked several blocks to Pitkin Avenue where the Loew's Theatre was located. I could feel my palm starting to sweat with apprehension as it remained temporarily locked against his. What was I doing? Perhaps I was not yet ready for a real date. However, I willed myself into believing that I was indeed grown-up and responsible. I vaguely wondered where Albert had gotten the money to pay our way. I sensed that his family had a lot more money than mine. Perhaps he had an allowance and had saved some of it. I vowed that I would only have one candy bar. I felt self-satisfied and gently virtuous.

Our conversation was slightly stilted, a bit forced and strained at first.

"Hot day, isn't it? It's a good day to go to the movies to cool on."

"Yes," I answered. "The air conditioning will feel great and I've been told that it's a really good movie."

We smiled benignly and uncomfortably at one another. However, once inside and seated, the conversation barrier broke down spontaneously and I enjoyed laughing at Albert's clever dry wit. I was an appreciative audience and Jack's advice to have fun was an easy order to follow.

The summer was passing pleasantly and Pearl and I spent a lot of time together. We took long evening walks along tree lined Eastern Parkway to Lincoln Terrace Park and felt safe and secure. The word "mugging" had not yet been invented. No doubt there were occasional hidden dangers, but we were totally unaware of them and oblivious to any possible threat that life might present.

The only apparent exception to this feeling stemmed from our weekly Saturday afternoon visit to the movies. There we knew from prior experience that one must be on guard. Not too infrequently a man would take the empty seat next to a young girl and slowly and furtively edge up to her a little too close for comfort. The next step would invariably be the real or imagined slight movement of his hand in her direction. Inner alarm bells would go off and seat changes were promptly made.

One Saturday afternoon Jack and I went to the Stadium Theatre to see a film in which we were particularly interested. It was very special for me to have my handsome seventeen-year old brother accompanying me. We leisurely walked to the movie house and Jack bought our tickets at the box office. We entered and stopped off at the candy counter. Jack and I selected several favorite varied bars of chocolate and sat down in the uncrowded theatre. We looked forward to watching the feature film, and the inordinate pleasure of slowly devouring our candy bars.

I immediately felt threatened when a middle-aged man took the seat next to me. There were lots of other empty seats around that he could have occupied. I decided that I was not going to jump to any conclusions and would remain calm and serene, but my pounding heart refused to listen to my good intentions and it continued to send harsh warning signals to my brain. My brain proved itself to be correct. I leaned over to Jack and whispered my dilemma.

"Let's exchange seats," he strongly urged. "That should solve the problem."

It was a great idea and we quickly followed through on it. Imagine our dismay when Jack realized that the situation had not changed, and that now he was being threatened. The two of us rose and quickly found seats on the other side of the theatre. We made our swift escape from the evil and perversion that afflicts some human beings. I felt frightened and knew that our special day had been damaged.

36

A colorful street fair was being held near Lincoln Terrace Park. It attracted young people from all over the neighborhood. It contained all the necessary attributes and accoutrements such as a medium sized Ferris Wheel and several different kinds of rides. Some were swift and some a little less challenging to those who were not so adventuresome. There were lots of appetite provoking, fragrant foods being offered for sale to the hungry pleasure-seeking, always ready to eat, public. Corn on the cob simmered in huge vats of boiling water, frankfurters, ice cream and all kinds of attractive and addictive junk foods and candies were being hawked and sold.

Pearl and I meandered along to our destination of lights and excitement, but we were not too enthusiastic because we lacked the money to participate in the fun. We walked along the grassy pathway outside of the tennis courts in the park when suddenly my eye was caught by a metal gleam on the ground insisting on my attention. I bent down and discovered a bonanza. There to my surprise and delight was a mound of coins half- hidden by the grass.

"Pearl," I shouted. "Look at this. We've struck it rich!"

"It's too good to be true," she cried.

We counted two dollars and sixty-five cents and knew that we would have a great time at the fair. How did it get there? We did not waste any time thinking about it. We quickly gathered our riches from its earthy resting-place and spent every penny going on rides and filling our greedy bellies. Truth, indeed, is stranger than fiction.

There was a boy who looked, walked and appeared a little different from the others. He lived in the same apartment house that Albert Cohen lived in on Eastern Parkway directly across the street from where I lived. He was a year older than Albert and seemed to possess a darker more serious side. His friends called him Leo. Often after school, he and a group of neighboring boys would get together and play stickball in the street. It appeared to be a very serious game. The stick substituted for a bat. Two teams were drawn up from the boys who were available on that particular day. They felt that the street was theirs since there were very few automobiles parked or driving by at that time. There were not too many people living in the area that had enough money to own a car.

I had seen Leo pass by my house many times when he went to visit his friend Barney. Barney was better looking, but he lacked the subtle almost hidden secretive personality that created a charismatic appeal. I would sit on my stoop and watch Leo's reserved unwary swagger as he moved. I would watch him hit the ball and run the bases. I would watch his smile of reticent delight when he hit a home run. We never acknowledged each other's presence but I intuitively recognized his interest in me.

I had become acquainted with several girls shortly after I moved into this new neighborhood. They lived on Leo's side of the street in adjacent three-story apartment houses. They confessed to me that they had crushes on him and were drawn to his reserved, albeit strong personality. Their judgment and inclinations made him more attractive and valuable in my eyes.

37

One hot summer day, Pearl and I decided that we would spend the afternoon at the newly constructed nearby Betsy Head Pool.

It was a huge city subsidized enterprise, and boasted an Olympic sized swimming pool which progressed from shallow water to a deeper area suitable for the enjoyment of real swimming buffs. There was also a separate large diving pool for the experts, with varying heights for the boards.

Upon paying a quarter when we entered, we received a key that was attached to a thick elastic band that comfortably fit on the wrist. We were then ushered into an area that separated the sexes and led us into a huge space filled with small individual brass lockers that were set into shelves. Belongings could be stored there until needed. There were benches in every aisle in front of each row of lockers. We had worn our bathing suits under our clothes. It was easier and more convenient and comfortable to sit down to remove ones shoes and outer clothing that covered your bathing suit. The compartments, which were secured with individual keys, held one's pocketbook, unneeded apparel and all extras easily and safely.

I stepped out in my virgin white skin and one-piece bathing suit into the blinding sun, which had fully cooperated and said yes to our prayers and wishes. Our keys were firmly established in place hanging from our wrists signifying that we belonged here for the day. Pearl's lovely skin possessed a beautiful natural bronze tone unlike my pale, colorless exterior. I glanced at her, noting her carriage and perfect posture. She was two or three inches taller than my straining five feet. I admired the queenly look that was part of her artless demeanor, but mostly I enjoyed the quietness and sweetness of her personality. How was it possible for this soft-spoken person to come from such a fanatical family of screamers? These screamers, however, were basically good people who were caught up in the political injustices and difficulties of the times and perhaps over-responded with their strong emotions. In spite of my inexperienced youth, I judged that they were the kind of people who could be, and were, easily led and influenced by powerful demagogues.

Pearl and I walked slowly around the Betsy Head pool observing the different areas and their offerings. Snacks could be purchased here, and ice cream there. There were groups of young people already clamoring to buy refreshments, but Pearl and I were ready to sample the inviting calm, clear water of the pool.

We walked to the area that indicated that the water was four feet deep and we slowly immersed ourselves in its cool beneficent embrace. I had never really learned how to swim properly and I vaguely paddled around a bit savoring the refreshing delight of partial immersion. Pearl was no better at swimming than I, but we both did a lot of smiling to express our pleasure. I did not dare to put my face in the water. That would certainly lead to the sputtering, spattering ingestion of the chlorinated broth, a most unpleasant experience. Eventually, as I relaxed, my swimming ability improved slightly, and I felt secure in water that did not reach over my head.

After we had spent a good deal of time gently splashing and pseudo-swimming, we were ready to emerge and sit on the ledge that encircled the pool and rest. Pearl was no better at swimming than I, but that had not stopped us from having a good time and releasing much of our pent up accumulated energy. We were warmed gently by the sun and were in a totally relaxed frame of mind. My very young womanly body was carefully and beautifully enclosed in a form-fitting bathing suit and as far as I was concerned, all was right with the world.

Suddenly we noticed that serious looking introspective fifteen year old Leo who lived across the street, walking in our direction followed by his ever present sidekicks and cronies. From a short distance away, I could furtively survey the scene and note his handsome, manly body in his well fitting swim trunks. He had a distinctive walk that separated him from his friends. They were slowly approaching us, and we silently held our breath and waited for them to go by.

Leo and I had noticed each other in the street but had overtly pretended complete lack of interest. By this time the boys were directly in back of us and Pearl and I waited silently for them to pass. Without warning, Leo reached out as he went by, giving me a gentle but firm obviously pre-planned push into the water. I dropped like a log into the four-foot depth, sputtering, swallowing and attempting to straighten up. It was an indelicate and clumsy process and I was mortified. When I finally cleared my chlorine soaked eyes and glanced up, I could see the small group of boys in the distance with their backs to us.

After wiping my face with the towel that we had brought with us from the locker room, and a little thoughtful consideration, a feeling of complete satisfaction and even joy descended upon me. I knew the reason for the ducking, as it was called. It was a certainty that Leo was strongly attracted to me! This was the foreplay of an innocent teen-age relationship. Those were the rules of the game and his actions reflected the times. That was my analysis and happily proved to be correct.

38

The hot weather continued and lots of ice cream treats were greedily consumed. My friend Hilda and I made daily trips to the ice cream parlor where homemade ice cream was dispensed quickly and with a flourish. It was the big treat of the day. An even bigger treat was getting a glimpse of Leo as he crossed the street and made his way down the block to his friend's house. No comment was ever made about the ducking at the pool, but now when he passed me he would nod his head or casually murmur, "Hi." I liked the low sound of his voice. It had a distinct timbre that matched his quiet intense look.

Other boys still gathered regularly around the front of my house, pulling leaves from Mrs. Gensburg's bushes and respectfully ignoring and accepting her not too friendly comments, "Don't tear the bushes," which was repeated at regular intervals. Mrs. Gensburg was a nice lady who commanded my respect and affection, and I certainly would never want to antagonize her. However, I loved the attention of these young virile males and did little to discourage them. The few leaves that they collected to demonstrate a minor trick would not injure the bushes in any way. At any rate, Mr. Gensburg was always cutting them back since they grew so rapidly. These boys were determined to enjoy the exuberance that a sunny day and female company would provide in spite of Mrs. Gensburg's muffled objections. After a while, she got used to them and accepted their quiet antics with good grace.

Vacation time was drawing to a close, and a case of mild depression set in when I envisioned having to use the trolley once again for that last semester of junior high school in Williamsburg. I felt saddened and disheartened when I anticipated the nauseating daily routine that demanded that I step down from the trolley a short time after boarding and walk the rest of the long way to school. The same routine awaited me coming home. It was a double dose of hiking to relieve and offset the results of that terrible, sickening trolley ride every school day. There was also that initial walk of three long blocks to Ralph Avenue to reach and wait for the arrival of my nemesis.

The weather was often another obstacle that had to be accepted and overcome. I did not look forward to the rain or snow that might accompany me on my trip to school. The trolley would bear down on its tracks resembling an ugly monster stalking its prey, me! I would ascend the two or three high steps to its interior, knowing that in a very short while I would have to leave my antagonist and plod the rest of the way to school. The trolley was always the winner! However, it obviously did me no lasting harm, and perhaps strengthened my body in spite of ingesting all the junk candy that I could afford on the way home.

Once again I was back in "memory lane" in junior high school with all the persons I had gotten to know so well through the years. I had started in elementary school in the first grade with many of them. There were all those long pleasant associations that I would be compelled to give up now that my family had moved to a different area. All the accumulated experiences and the relationships that I had built up through the years that were so meaningful would begin to recede when I would leave junior high at the end of that semester. Memories would slowly fade, evolving into gentle nostalgia, edging into an inner sphere in my mind for fond reconstructing.

Life was moving along and I was inevitably caught up in its momentum. I did relish the thought of change, which I anticipated would be exciting and stimulating. What would senior high be like? Would I fit into that sea of strangers and would I be able to make new friends? Was I a little too young and perhaps a little too immature to cope with the elevated requirements of a different level of education?

My mother made it known to me in many subtle ways that she considered me to be a special person with a superior intellect. That secretly worried me. Perhaps I could not live up to what might be her unrealistic expectations. Fortunately, my father and mother never seemed to pressure their children in any particular direction. There was just this air of gentle pervasive encouragement, which generally sat lightly, but steadfastly, on our shoulders. We could do it! There was, therefore, that underlying innate desire on our part to please them and make them proud of us. That in itself, exerted a subtle form of pressure to do well and succeed. They were so hard working. They deserved to reap a little "nachas" which translated to mean pleasure and pride in their children.

39

Sylvia was still very much involved with her full charge bookkeeping job and doing very well at it. It was a great responsibility for a very young woman, but responsibility was a concept with which she was familiar. She did what had to be done. She worked hard and with great competence in the wholesale upholstery and drapery fabric store on the Eastside of Manhattan. They also did a brisk retail business, particularly on Sundays, when the store was always kept open. They were very receptive to private orders for draperies, slipcovers and upholstery fabrics. There was a lot of money to be made on retail sales. Sylvia, of course, had to work all day on Sunday and had Friday off instead. This was a hardship since she did not have the pleasure and opportunity to spend the full weekend with her friends, and more importantly, her boy friend Charlie. If she had any complaints, and I'm sure she did, she mostly kept them to herself. It was a good job and fortunately, she enjoyed it. In addition, all the sales people and the boss liked her a lot and provided good fun-loving company during the day. Most importantly, she was in love, and the world was a beautiful place.

Papa continued to play chess every evening even if it were only for one game. Jack was his powerful opponent, and the stronger Jack became, the more my father enjoyed the game. Papa had one disconcerting little habit while thinking about his next move. He hummed softly and sweetly to himself. Jack did not appear to notice this minor distraction at all. Nothing seemed to interfere with his power of concentration. I loved the mellow unobtrusive sound of my father's non-melodic voice. As a matter of fact, when he came home from work, his quiet humming preceded him up the two flights of stairs to our apartment. We always knew that Papa was approaching, even before the door opened. Perhaps this was the way his mind automatically buoyed up his flagging spirits at the end of a long, perhaps difficult, workday. Mama welcomed him and made the transition easier by providing wonderful home cooked meals that the entire family enjoyed and looked forward to. She was my father's comfort and satisfaction. She provided solace and cheer, and he was the pillar and support for all of us.

40

It was graduation time at Junior High School #148, and all of my classmates and I marched down the aisle in the auditorium to the measured sounds and rhythm of "Pomp and Circumstance." We felt inordinately proud and grown-up returning our parents smiles and loving looks as we passed them in their seats. We slowly advanced to the reserved section for the graduates located in the front of the auditorium and we listened to the endless speeches of speakers extolling the virtues and promise of our graduating class.

Finally, it was over! We were free to leave and greet our waiting families. We exchanged emotional and hasty good-byes with our classmates and friends with words that spoke of continuing relationships. However, we basically understood that that would not happen for many of us. We would be moving in different directions and I, surely, would be disconnected from them having moved to another neighborhood. I regretted the compelling separation from Anna, who had become such a faithful and sincere school chum and sincerely hoped that I would be able to visit with her on occasion in the future. I would sorely miss our shared lunches and confidences. I would miss her cherubic smiling face. I laughed to myself when I thought about how she always managed to increase my appetite when I observed her as she diligently and with great gustatory delight consumed her mother's thoughtfully prepared sandwiches. Her pleasure in food was profound. We hugged and exchanged warm kisses.

"Beulah, you'll have to make the effort to come to see me or meet me once in a while."

"I know," I answered. "I already miss those lunches that we used to have together. I can see myself losing weight without you. We had a lot of fun and the future won't seem the same without seeing you in school every day."

Tears were restrained. Our families were waiting.

We had to take the trolley home, and I was absolutely determined not to upset my family by getting off and walking home prior to our arrival at Ralph Avenue. I used all the control I possessed along with lots of lemon drops. The nausea was encompassing, but my resolute perhaps stubborn power and pride supported me, and I made it home, albeit with a repressed and silent demeanor!

To celebrate my graduation from junior high, Mama had made a special dinner that evening that included several dishes that I particularly favored. She had gone to the trouble of baking her special sponge cake for desert, which was heavily topped with real hand whipped cream. I could feel my love for the food transferring itself to my mother's mind and soul.

41

I was now becoming truly excited and a little fearful about the brand new experiences that would be coming my way. In my mind, high school was a grown-up domain. I was only thirteen years old, about to enter tenth grade as a sophomore and I felt extremely vulnerable. To add to my sense of insecurity was the surprising information that I would be attending Tilden High School as opposed to Thomas Jefferson. I was a little worried since almost everyone in my neighborhood attended the latter. However, having moved in from a different school area, I had been assigned to Tilden High, which my new friends in my new neighborhood considered a step up socially, economically and academically. I was advised not to make waves and create difficulties by requesting a change. They considered it a stroke of luck for me.

Both high schools were a bus trip away. It would take me about a half-hour from door to door in either case. After stop and go journeying to Williamsburg for those unending months by trolley, I felt like a seasoned traveler, and I knew that I would do much better on a bus. The lurching of a bus compared to a trolley was minimal, and the ride would be smoother. Unfortunately the same transit smell that I experienced on the trolley and subway also permeated the bus environment. However, it seemed to be less obnoxious and noxious.

The first day of my new life dawned early in February and was filled with good omens. The temperature was low, but the sun was high in the sky and its blue was punctuated with fluffy, floating white cottony clouds. The third and fourth term students, the sophomores, were on "late session" which meant that we started classes around noon and would not get out of school until five P.M. when the streets would be dark. The older, early session students were finished with their classes at one or two o'clock. The juggling and manipulation of courses and time were necessary and was caused by the overcrowding of the school population. The administration and the school board had made concerted efforts to fit everyone in, regardless of minor lapses of comfort. The students would just have to manage their schedules. There was not much of an alternative.

I had lots of time during the early hours to smell and enjoy the freshly perked coffee lightened with a touch of heavy sweet cream. The memory of its extraordinary flavor lingers still. I had lots of time to sample the big poppy seeded Kaiser rolls, still hot, spread with cream cheese and perhaps a touch of lox that Mama had hastily picked up from our local grocery store that morning. I had lots of time to relax with the family before most of them had to rush off to fulfill their daily obligations. I had lots of sweet time alone with Mama and little Murray who still was too young to attend school. However, I left the house earlier than necessary that first morning to make sure that I would not be late and would be able to find my way to Tilden High. I was wearing a brand new navy-blue skirt and a starched white shirt. I was ready! My dark blue felt hat with its roller brim, accompanied my well-brushed but not so warm coat. The clear, frosty air that greeted me as I opened the downstairs door made me feel happy that I had succumbed to my mother's repeated request that I wear a sweater under my coat.

I crossed the street and walked the long block on Eastern Parkway to Saratoga Avenue and there was the large corner candy store that was an assigned bus stop. To my delight, there was my bus, with its proper number posted on a front window, waiting for me at the red light. I held on to my hat and dashed across the street just as the light changed. I stepped up quickly through the opened door and smiled breathlessly at the bus driver. He offered me a welcoming hello and I was overcome with gratitude for his friendliness. I made my way to an empty seat and smelled that elusive but recognizable odor peculiar to motorized vehicles that had always embraced me in its slightly nauseating grip. I would handle it. The lemon drops that were stashed in my pocketbook would help. I would be fine. I had no alternative. I was getting older and hopefully tougher.

We traveled into a new area that was significantly more residential than mine, with its rows and rows of small private brick homes. The beautifully manicured bushes surrounded the pretty little lawns that were filled with wintry uncut grass. In front of every house was a tree or two, sans leaves. This neighborhood, I thought, possessed a touch of luxury and class with which I was not too familiar, and as I looked out of my bus window, I realized that most of the kids attending Tilden High would be coming from this surrounding environment.

Several students got on the bus along the way, and although they too were obviously on late session, they seemed older than I. Two of the girls were wearing darkly shaded lipstick, and I felt like a babe in arms with my bare, unarmed face and my juvenile looking roller hat that up until this moment had seemed so stylish.

I sat quietly in my seat while I continued to look out the window at the passing scene. Suddenly I saw this large new impressive looking high school looming ahead. The bus stopped and I quickly got off and followed the girls that preceded me. There was safety in numbers. "They must be in tenth grade," I thought. "They know exactly where to go." There were many entrances surrounding the school, but they made their way without hesitation to the main gate. I gratefully shadowed them and moved to the posted area for new entrants.

The day passed quickly albeit with great confusion, but my program was finally set and I was satisfied. The next day would be easier. It was five P.M. and dark when the late session students emerged from our educational prison, and what a huge crowd of noisy young people we were. I had become acquainted with a pleasant third-term student who seemed to be following my program. I felt comfortable with her even though I could tell that she came from a family that enjoyed luxuries that I could barely envision. Her elegant cashmere twin sweater set looked perfect when she removed her warm looking wool coat, and it blended beautifully with her softly pleated skirt. She wore no make-up and appeared completely unpretentious. She lived in one of those lovely little brick homes that my bus had passed along Kings Highway and that had so impressed me. I felt pleased and a little proud when she quietly approached and greeted me. We exchanged names and pleasantries, and together carefully studied our programs. She stayed nearby as we moved from class to class. She later became a close school chum, but I always felt the presence of an economic distance between us of which she, no doubt, was completely unaware.

There were a number of men waiting for the kids to emerge in the cold dark street outside of the school. They were pushing little carts that contained heating elements that kept a variety of foods piping hot.

They were ready to sell all kinds of delicious aromatic snacks to starving kids. There were offerings of large heated pretzels that were heavily salted with coarse kosher salt, and portions of peppery chickpeas that we called "arbis." They were scooped up with a little metal shovel from a huge covered pot placed within the cart. The chickpeas were served in small brown paper bags and were wonderfully hot, pungent and mouth watering. The cost for this special treat was five cents.

Other delicious delicacies called "knishes" were also offered to the starving masses for five cents. They were made of hot well-seasoned mashed potatoes formed into large thick pancakes that were crisp on the outside and soft and flavorful in the inside. I believe that any of the offerings would have tasted great to the very young hungry multitudes, myself included, but I turned away from these temptations. I wanted to keep nausea down to a minimum on the bus ride back to Brownsville.

Doris and I met every day in school and we had a lot to talk about. She was a year older than I and her favorite topic of conversation, as expected, was "boys," with whom she actually had very little contact. Occasionally we would discuss school work and would share mostly negative opinions of our teachers, but every once in a while we would express our appreciation for our rather fat, middle aged, pasty looking English teacher who would read wonderful poetry to us with an actor's dedication. When she read "Bells" by Edgar Allen Poe, I could hardly wait to go home and read it once again for my own private pleasure, and then read it once again aloud to any one in my family who would be kind enough to listen. I tried to imitate and emulate my teacher but invariably settled for a lesser performance. When Mrs. James spoke to us or discussed any piece of literature that had been assigned, she would fold one soft fat arm across the other. Her eyes would be probing with sharp concentration demanding our complete attention. She remained in this position, her favorite stance, for practically the entire period until the bell rang releasing us to marvel at her expertise and her ability to hypnotize us. We would pause for a moment and then dash through the halls to our next class.

Lunch hour was relaxation time and the need to satisfy our hunger for food and conversation would be fulfilled. I always brought the lunch from home that my mother had prepared, and it was invariably delicious. One could purchase lunch for a nominal price at the cafeteria. Tempting desserts were always offered and they were very hard to resist. Very often, I did not. Doris bought her lunch daily but she never flaunted what I believed to be her riches.

One day during our lunch hour she confided to me that there was a boy of seventeen who lived in the house next to hers. She unhappily admitted that she had a powerful crush on him. "I think I'm becoming obsessive. I really think about him too much. I even dream about him occasionally, but he doesn't even seem to know I exist. Maybe I should start wearing a little makeup and tighter sweaters. That might make him sit up and take notice."

I offered my inexperienced expertise and advice that she eagerly listened to and encouraged. I made it up as I went along.

"Perhaps you can smile and say hello when you pass him on the street. That would get his attention."

"I'd like to do that but I don't know if I'd have the nerve. He may think that I'm very forward. His mother always gives me a big smile when she's around. He never even looks up when he passes. I can tell that she likes me. I wish he did."

I did not think that a smile from his mother would do her much good but I refrained from telling her. We talked and talked and our conversation went round and round in circles. We kept each other interested.

I told her about this blue-eyed boy with a thick crop of dark curly hair who lived across the street. He had that non-compliant look and an expression of thoughtfulness and introspection that I found engaging. I confided to Doris that I would sit alone on my stoop during the late afternoon before dinnertime, twilight descending, watching him as he walked away from the stick-ball game that had just ended down the block. I hoped that he would stop by for a few minutes to talk with me before crossing the street to his house. Our extremely casual relationship, nevertheless in my mind a relationship, had started the day he ducked me at Betsy Head Pool the previous summer. He had never apologized for his action that day and had continued to maintain a somewhat quiet, disinterested image. I intuitively felt it was all an act!

One cold day as I was sitting on my stoop surreptitiously watching him play ball, I felt the chill of the rising wind and the cold stone that I was sitting on getting colder by the minute. "Enough!" my mind ordered. "Get upstairs. It's time for dinner. You're acting like an idiot."

Twilight had already set in, and the streetlights were gently beginning to merge with the night. Suddenly, however, I went into a slight case of shock. I saw him heading towards my house after the game instead of crossing the street to his building as he usually did. He quickly ran up the steps leading to my stoop.

"Hi. I just thought that you might like to come out after dinner and take a little walk. What do you think?" His blue eyes flashed lightning.

I thought that I had just died and gone to heaven. He did not have to wait long for what I hoped was my restrained positive answer. "That sounds very nice."

"We can walk down Eastern Parkway and head for the library. It's a little more than a mile away, but if you get tired, we don't have to go that far."

"That sounds fine," I answered.

The center promenade of Eastern Parkway was laced with trees that had lost their leaves for the winter. "There are many benches along the Parkway, and if it's not too cold," Leo responded, "we could sit for a while and possibly talk a little if we chose to."

I thought about what he said and I rather hoped that he would take the golden opportunity that could easily present itself, and attempt to kiss me. I considered that possibility a good deal. I had never been kissed by a boy before, and I could hardly wait to experience this thrilling event.

When I agreed to see him that evening, Leo suggested that warm clothing would be the order of the day. It seemed as though he cared enough to be protective, and I was flattered and delighted.

I was almost too excited to have dinner. Fortunately, it was Saturday and my school and home responsibilities were minimal. I was free to go and hopefully have a good time. My parents maintained a slightly loose rein and trusted my judgment. They also felt secure in the knowledge that Leo came from a stable Jewish family from across the street. Mama knew Leo's mother who often frequented our sunny stoop, and they had a pleasant rapport.

I would have preferred doing without the sweater under my coat. I would have preferred a svelte, not bulky look, but comfort was a necessary priority. I wore the accepted "babushka" or scarf on my head that covered my ears, which certified that I would be warm and comfortable in the cold night air. Much to my surprise, Leo wore his very light leather jacket that seemed to be his uniform. It probably was the only jacket that he owned. He was waiting for me when I got downstairs at the appointed time. When I passed Mrs. Gensburg's ground floor apartment, her door was wide open and she greeted me with a big smile. "Have a good time. I saw through the window that he's waiting for you."

"Thanks, Mrs. Gensburg," I answered. There was something so open and forthright about her. I found it endearing.

We greeted one another quietly. I felt a little shy. I knew that he was different from the other boys, less open, less friendly, more introspective, more interesting. His manner was cool, strong and attentive. He did not seem to have much to say, and I sharpened my conversational skills against the chasm of possible silence. He was the antithesis of Albert, who was so overtly funny, clever, conversationally adept and never at a loss for words.

We crossed the darkened street and the cold, silent, frosty air whispered about our faces. Leo took my hand in his and I felt a shock of electricity pass through my arm. We walked hand in hand not saying very much until we reached the main tree-lined thoroughfare of the center promenade of Eastern Parkway. The trees were bereft of their beautiful summer foliage, and their bare branches gracefully moved in the dark, obeying the impulses of the chilling wind, lending an eerie shadow to the dimly lighted streets.

We sat down on a cold bench and Leo moved very close to me. I could feel the side of his body leaning strongly into mine. "Perhaps," I thought, "he's just trying to keep warm."

We noticed several other young persons gathered about other benches in the distance. The moon emerged from the darkened mists and shed its gentle rays of soft light. I was overwhelmed with the youthful romantic emotions that were evoked at that moment. They powerfully invaded my mind. We sat there quietly, his hand in mine for a short period of time. The icy cold penetrated our innocent facade and we decided to proceed quickly and directly to the library. I was not kissed that night, but a little flame had been ignited, and it refused to be doused.

That library became one of my favorite places to visit. There were always the rewards of reading materials to be gratefully gathered. My brother Jack had succeeded in instilling in me a love and appreciation of literature. What a lasting and loving gift it was. My library card was one of my most prized possessions.

That evening was the beginning of many such walks with Leo and it created the start and opportunity to get to know each other on a deeper level. Very often after dinner, we spent much time sitting closely together leaning into one another on my dark cold stoop.

Eddie, who lived on the first floor, would pass us too frequently and give us a sly smile. He was a great irritant to me and his expression belied his friendliness. Leo ignored him completely as though he did not deserve our attention.

Perhaps my new love interest was shy or a closet coward. He acted like a perfect gentleman and his attention was focused and centered on things that seemed to be more important to him, and less important to me.

One dark night, however, when the moon did not emerge from behind the clouds to light the way, he drew me closely to him and gently placed his lips on mine. The cold air surrounding us sizzled with its newly discovered source of heat.

42

School became an unimportant and insignificant backdrop to my significantly more important youthful social life. I had by now acquired a number of friends in addition to Pearl and Hilda. There were the girls from across the street on Eastern Parkway who lived in the buildings adjacent to Leo's. They were all attending or planning to attend Thomas Jefferson High School. I was on my own in Tilden High. From what I had heard, it gave me a little more status and I almost enjoyed the separateness and the life away from too much familiarity. My attitude did not seem to interfere with the slowly budding friendships and relationships where I lived. There was a happy balance.

Frances was a small girl, my age, my size, but not of my temperament. She was strong, consistently opinionated, bright and friendly. I found her company and personality attractive and somewhat compelling. She lived with her sisters and her twin brother in an apartment that held very little furniture except for the necessary beds to sleep in. Both parents had died some time before in some obscure manner that was never discussed. It was hinted that their father had run out on their mother a long time ago, leaving her stranded with seven children. The next to the oldest sister, who was in her early twenties and very lovely looking, took charge of this remaining parentless brood of four girls and one boy, and maintained a strong control and a positive influence over them. There was also the older married sister who looked in on them frequently, and she and her husband always offered solid encouraging support.

Their apartment was immaculately clean consisting mostly of beds, and always well taken care of. Each member of the family was assigned a responsibility, which they knew that they had better fulfill. It worked! They were all destined to live a proper and law-abiding life.

Frances reminded me of my long lost unloved buddy, Goldie Engel, who still came to mind after all those years. They were cut from the same sturdy cloth of the same pattern, and I had a sense of their strong connection. Frances had a good self-image and ego in spite of her almost homely, squashed in little face. What she lacked in looks, she made up for in personality. She was a popular girl. She confessed to me that she really liked Leo a lot. She did not realize, or care to acknowledge the fact that Leo and I were spending a good deal of quality time together. He certainly seemed to have a number of female admirers. That, no doubt, made him more valuable to me. I would see big gawky toothy Ina most days on the Kings Highway bus that took us both to Tilden High. Ina was in my literature class and one day I overheard her talking to another girl about her boy friend, Leo Brown. I laughed inwardly. I knew that she and Frances didn't have a chance!

When the change in season started to bring us the soft gifts of spring, many of the students began walking home instead of taking the crowded, airless bus. I had become acquainted with Henry, a pleasant personable boy who was an exception to the rule, who attended Tilden High. He lived in Leo's and Albert's building, and he worked in his father's herring store every day after school. We often walked and talked together on the long, long path home, and my hunger pangs inevitably and invariably increased with each step. Henry smelled faintly and deliciously of pickled herring. Our conversation always started on a high plane and descended gradually and happily to food.

He extolled the virtues of the different kinds of herring that were available in the market place in his father's store. It was located several blocks from where we lived. I loved all the different kinds of herrings that Henry described and planned on asking my mother to buy some. His fragrance was irresistible. I thought that Henry would have a fine career as a herring salesman.

43

My family had now been living on Park Place for one year, and we all enjoyed the change of environment from Williamsburg. The relative spaciousness of our little domain, the friendly and cooperative neighbors, and the tree-lined streets all contributed to our sense of well being and improvement.

The warm spring weather and the approaching school vacation time was delightful to contemplate. The windows were opened wide, and the cool breezes flowed through our apartment creating an airy and comfortable setting for family life. Papa and Sylvia had to take a bus every day for about ten or more blocks to get to the subway station. Much of the time they would walk, even during the cold harsh winter weather. It was better than waiting for the bus that always seemed to be crowded and late. The underground subway trains would transport them to work on their screeching and pounding electrical tracks and bring them back at night accompanied by the same din and clamor. Sylvia got home an hour earlier than Papa. It was a long day and they were both happy to be home.

The healing weather was a wonderful reprieve. On warm languid days Papa would sit on a chair at the open window in the bedroom next to the fire escape and smoke a cigarette before dinner was served. That small routine brought a modicum of peace and relaxation after a hard day of work. At that point in time it appeared to be perfectly acceptable to be a heavy smoker. The medical profession did not seem to have a clue or an interest in the devastation that could result from that deadly addiction.

The large bedroom faced a small lush green belt that brought fragrance and a sense of repose into the room. Papa needed that little bit of quiet time to balance the daily stress. We all intuitively knew that through that bedroom window, past the fire escape, lay the little bit of greenery that transported our minds and spirit into the serenity of a country scene. Sometimes Jack and I would sit on the windowsill with our legs resting on the sturdy little iron deck of the fire escape, and feel that we had moved into another realm.

Charlie was a steady visitor on Saturdays, and he faithfully showed up every Sunday evening after Sylvia got home from work. In addition, he also visited her several evenings during the week. They had a hard time staying away from one another. Charlie had bought an old jalopy that he was able to fix up mechanically and it supplied a regular, albeit somewhat unreliable means of transportation. However, love conquers all, it is said, and Sylvia and he were able to meet with great frequency. In our household, they were considered a beautiful couple. We all regarded Charlie as a loved member of our family. He was such a mensch!

About that time, Jack became intensely interested in learning to speak Spanish fluently. He had been studying it for several years in high school and he intended to continue in college. He started attending Spanish movies, and listened attentively and assiduously to the occasional Spanish programs that were on the radio. He became completely familiar and proficient in the use of the language. He continued to play chess with my father regularly much to Papa's delight. He read a great deal and insisted on guiding me in my choice of reading material and musical taste. He never seemed to comment about my choice of friends. He did not think that they were of any great significance.

One of his friends, David, started paying attention to me when he was supposed to be visiting Jack at our house. He often directed his casual conversation to me. "How do you like high school?"

"I much prefer vacation time," was my quick response. David thought that was very funny, and laughed heartily. I thought to myself, "It wasn't that funny."

He looked into my eyes and surprised me by saying, "Do you have a boyfriend?"

I was at a loss for words, temporarily. "I have a few friends who are boys. Why do you ask?"

"I think that I'd like to be one of them," he quietly responded.

I tried to cover my embarrassment and lack of sophistication by saying, "That sounds fine. You can be a friend of mine. I'm sure that Jack wouldn't mind."

As a matter of fact, Jack seemed completely unaware of his younger friend's interest in me, and I certainly made no effort to enlighten him.

A few weeks later David showed up at our house ostensibly to visit Jack, but he sought me out. I was sitting on the couch in our French Provincial living room, reading. The radio was turned on to the Masterwork Hour and the incredibly beautiful music of Mozart was flowing into the room surrounding me and enveloping me with its delicate loveliness.

I was startled by David's sudden appearance. "I have a little something for you," he said.

I nodded my head politely and waited curiously. He took a small jewelry box from his pocket and handed it to me. I opened it quickly and inside, resting on a white fluffy piece of cotton, was a large red shiny Lucite heart attached to a delicate silver chain.

"I can't accept this," I stuttered. "You're just a friend."

"I know," he answered, "but I'm only giving this to you in friendship. Please accept it."

I didn't know what to do. I did not want to hurt his feelings. He was so likeable and he was my brother's friend! I fully realized that he was a sensitive young man, but my conscience would not permit me to take the gift without expressing my inner thought.

"I'm already thinking about one boy in particular," I said, "and I kind of like him. I don't think that it would be fair to you if I accepted this lovely gift."

"That's all right. It would just make me happy to think of you wearing it once in a while."

His flushed face raised the level of my guilt. "Thanks. It's really beautiful. It's very generous of you."

He smiled politely and started edging out of the room heading back towards the kitchen where Jack was engaged in a game of chess with Papa. I knew that David would sit down and watch them play. He enjoyed that. I felt a premature grown-up sadness for him. I knew that I could never think of him as anything but a casual friend, a friend of my brother's. He was good-looking in spite of his slightly protruding eyes, but to me he lacked some salt and pepper in his personality. He was just too nice, unlike Leo,

44

The firm that my father worked for, that he and the owner had started from scratch when Papa's business failed in 1929 became hugely successful. It now occupied a tremendous building on Broadway in Manhattan that contained thousands and thousands of yards of varied kinds of cotton goods. Buyers came in from all over the United States and the rest of the world to ask for Sam and they purchased huge quantities of these fabrics. He always took good care of them, and they trusted his judgment.

However, my father always worried when other new salesmen were hired. They were invariably younger and more aggressive. They spoke American English without an accent and my father, no doubt, felt that he had to try harder to retain his place in the scheme of things.

Papa's boss had several sons who had become successful and accomplished professionals. One was a doctor, one a lawyer, and the other had become a dentist. Since education was so highly prized by most Jewish immigrants, my family was in awe of my father's boss and his prestigious family.

We were expected to be filled with respect and gratitude when we used their beneficent services. If we were having dental or medical problems, it was anticipated that we would use their services, free of charge. No doubt there was within us an element of strong discomfort and a restrained, perhaps unacknowledged sense of discontent. A strong sense of pride resided in our family and we did not take kindly to charity, even when dispensed with kindness and subtlety.

One day our friendly tooth puller cheerfully and politely extracted two of my teeth. Even at age seventy-four, I still feel a mild sense of anger knowing that he probably could have saved them. He took the easy and expedient way out. We realized that we probably should have been filled with deep appreciation since we knew that he performed this service gratis for my father's sake. However, all the sons were well aware of the fact that my father had helped establish and build their flourishing business that had paid for their education and luxurious life-styles.

At this time the doctor came in for a good portion of my business. It started with the unexpected appearance of a little boil on my forearm. Mama went to our relatively new druggist at the end of the block and talked with the gentlemanly Mr. Greenberg, who dispensed the special headache powders that she still required on occasion. He gave her a little container of black salve, which he highly recommended. I was to apply it directly on the boil several times a day and cover it with a bandage. I was also advised by him to use hot compresses every few hours. However, my stubborn boil refused to cooperate in spite of all the attention it was receiving. It remained inflamed, hard, swollen and very painful. The redness seemed to be spreading. Finally, Mama insisted that I see a doctor, and it was natural for me to take a long ride on the subway to reach the office of the doctor who did not charge us a fee. Mama accompanied me and she tried to bolster my failing spirits. She carried hard candy in her pocketbook to help alleviate some of my nausea. The potent subway smell invaded my nose and throat, but my apprehension as to what the doctor would do to my arm outweighed my nausea.

He was charming and treated us with welcoming respect. I could feel his great liking for my father whom he had known since he was a child. He spoke kindly and attentively to us. My spirits rose accordingly after he examined me in spite of the fact that he indicated that it was necessary to lance the boil. He promised that I would feel practically no pain and that afterward there would be positive relief and healing. He was a charming and likable man just like his brother, the dentist.

He spoke the truth and the entire procedure was not alarming and reasonably pain free. When we got home, Mama thought that I should be rewarded for suffering the discomfort of the train ride and the minor operation, which I secretly did not consider so minor. She was going to buy me a black and white ice-cream soda, one of my favorite treats, at the local ice-cream parlor located on Pitkin Avenue. The black and white soda consisted of a large scoop of vanilla ice cream eased into a tall glass of fizzy seltzer that had been amply flavored with delicious chocolate syrup. How delighted I felt to be alone with my mother, not sharing her company with any one else in the family. I loved having her all to myself. She exuded a soft love and sharp interesting conversation.

Our mutual sense of humor coincided and connected and we always found something to smile at and perhaps laugh about. She questioned me about school and wanted to know whether I was enjoying the grown-up change to high school.

"It doesn't seem so different from junior high," I said, "but the students very often look like adults. There's one girl, Mom, in my English class, who has a face like a kewpie doll and dresses her very full lips in bright juicy red lipstick. Her face is like a magnet for me and every one else in the class. She's really very pretty. Her mouth looks as though it has a life of its own. All the boys can hardly keep their eyes from looking in her direction and landing on her red mobile lips. What do you think about that kind of girl, Mom?"

"I think that you should not get too friendly with her. She's not your sort."

Mama thought that this little story was kind of funny, but perhaps a little sad too. She felt sorry for the girl who had such a strong need for attention and to stand out. We both thought it over as we quietly sipped our ice cream sodas through the double straws that I delightedly drew upon.

We walked home from Pitkin Avenue. The day had been a success. I had been well cared for and felt secure that the area where I had been lanced would heal rapidly. I did, but I did not anticipate that there would be a reoccurrence. Two weeks later, I became aware of an uncomfortable swelling under my arm. "G-d, it's starting again," I thought. I hated to tell my mother. I knew how much it would upset her. A day or two passed and I had to speak up. Nothing that I was doing was making it disappear. I applied the black salve assiduously several times a day that our pharmacist had initially prescribed, and I covered it carefully with a bandage to no avail. The boil and its accompanying redness under my arm was increasing in size and getting harder to the touch. It was more and more painful with each passing hour.

Arrangements were made once again to visit the "doctor." My best friend Pearl said that she would be happy to go with me. Mama thanked her profusely and insisted on paying her carfare. Pearl's mother responded to her request for permission to accompany me with kind gracious words.

"Of course Pearl will go with you. That's what friends are for."

While she was thus speaking displaying her integral generosity, a picture of her came to mind. She was standing on a street corner near the Loew's Pitkin with a collection can in her hand calling out to passers-by to please contribute money for China. The Japanese were massacring the helpless Chinese people. She and her family were hopelessly idealistic during very difficult times, thereby leaning far to the left hoping that their radical views, perceived by most as egregious and presumptuous, would act as a partial remedy.

Pearl and I left my house with a bag of delicious fruit and candy for the long train trip. It took us about an hour of eating to reach our destination. I found that I was becoming slightly less affected by the noxious odors of the subway. Filling my stomach seemed to influence me in a positive manner.

The kind and friendly greetings of my doctor put me at ease once again, and once again the boil had to be lanced. The first lancing was almost acceptable. The second was becoming a hateful habit. The doctor indicated that my problem, unfortunately, might keep repeating itself and boils might continue to erupt periodically. It was almost as though a pattern had been established. His judgment sadly proved to be correct and after many visits and many lancings through the next few months, a course of vaccine inoculations was strongly indicated and recommended.

I considered it a great hardship to make those long trips to his office on a regular basis to receive the injections. It was an unwelcome and difficult trial, but my parents and I realized that these trips were unavoidable and would hopefully cure me of this painful condition.

My steadfast friend always went with me and our girl talk was always enjoyable. The weeks and months rolled by and we found ourselves in the midst of summer weather. The vaccine finally proved successful after I received an ongoing and extended period of injections.

45

Pearl and I regularly frequented the Betsy Head Pool and loved the sun, water and the boys. We felt so proud of the way that we looked in our clinging bathing suits, and I was particularly happy with the attention that I was getting from Leo. We had continued taking walks together in the evenings several times a week, enjoying the slow changes of the seasons. It was lovely holding his hand and listening to his quiet, reserved manner of speaking. I was wrapped in an ardent palpable spirit of satisfaction.

Leo was an avid reader and seemed to gather and absorb so much information. I subjectively believed that he always formed a clever and insightful analysis of what he had read. I thoroughly believed in his intelligence and perceptiveness. At the other, perhaps more meaningful end of the continuum, I was completely impressed by his appearance in his bathing trunks when we were at the pool. He looked so manly. Even today, I can visualize his smooth well-muscled arms and legs, his flat tight stomach and his slightly arrogant stance. I found him very attractive. He was two and a half years older than I, and he seemed considerably more mature to me than the other boys who used to congregate in front of my house and who now camped out in other areas. I had become Leo's girl.

Leo hung out a good part of the day at Gellen's candy store just around the corner from where he lived. Mrs. Gellen, a widow, and her son Dave ran the little insignificant looking business. Georgie and Ida's candy store back in Williamsburg was much larger, lighter and more important looking. Dave was seven years older than Leo, and seemed to exert a mild influence over him, but I secretly believed that perhaps the reverse was actually true. They shared a camaraderie that was comfortable and interesting for them both. Often they would play checkers and talk. Their age difference did not seem to matter to them.

When Leo was not hanging around the candy store, he would spend his free time with his good friends Barney and Lefty. They were a faithful trio. Much time, however, was kept open for my company.

One hot summer night, Leo directed our walk towards Gellen's candy store. "How would you like an ice-cream pop?" he asked.

I was a little taken aback. This would be a first treat. "That would be very nice," I said. "I'd love it."

He appeared pleased and we strolled into the store that had a large refrigerated cabinet near the entrance. It held various kinds of ice cream and other frozen items.

Mrs. Gellen seemed very surprised to see Leo during evening hours. Dave was not there. He was out with his girlfriend Rachael who was eighteen and very plain looking. Her negative appearance was reinforced by heavy tortoise shell eyeglasses, which always seemed to be sliding down her nose. However, she and Dave had established a strong steady relationship and were practically engaged. In spite of her rather unattractive appearance, Dave seemed to love her dearly and treated her tenderly. I was impressed, and realized how little I knew and understood of the mystery of love.

Mrs. Gellen glanced at Leo and then looked hard at me. "What would you like to have, Label?" she asked, using his Jewish name.

"I'd like to have two vanilla ice cream pops, please," he politely responded. The pops consisted of a block of vanilla ice cream on a stick, covered by a delicious chocolate coating.

"Which ones would you like to have, Label, the nickel ones or the three cent ones?"

"The nickel ones, please, Mrs. Gellen."

A big smile turned the sour expression on her face to one of mirth and fun. She took aim and shot out her response. "Sport!"

Leo shrugged his shoulders and yielded a slightly embarrassed smile, while I laughed aloud. I could tell that he did not think that the situation was as funny as I did.

Several days later, Leo told me that someone had given him free tickets for "Steeple Chase" in Coney Island. If I were willing, we could go with another couple, the janitor's son Peter and his girl friend who also happened to be his cousin. Peter's family was German and his father was a mean anti-Semite with a perpetual scowl on his face. He was always complaining about "these people," which was a euphemism for Jews who lived in the building. As a matter of fact he displayed quiet hostility for the general population of the neighborhood. Peter on the other hand, kept his views to himself except for deprecating remarks about the British. It was 1939 and there were no negative comments forthcoming regarding Hitler marching into Poland.

Leo and Peter were casually and distantly friendly and occasionally rode their bikes together to distant neighborhoods. "It's an easy relationship," Leo told me. "We never discuss religion, politics or anything of importance. We get along O.K. and mostly talk about baseball and other sports."

"I think that a day at Steeple Chase would be a lot of fun," I said. "But I must tell you, I have this small problem sometimes with the trains. I get a little nauseated, but I think that I now have it under control."

"Good. I'll speak to Peter and arrange it," he answered.

Two days later, Mama packed a delicious lunch of thick fried hamburgers and onions on big seeded Kaiser rolls along with some sweet fresh peaches for the two of us. We started out early in the day with Peter and his companion whom I met for the first time.

"Steeple Chase-The Funny Place" was a huge concession in Coney Island. The tickets would allow us entry into a vast area that boasted Ferris Wheels, high roller coasters, all kinds of varied rides such as mechanical horses that moved swiftly on tracks, and rooms of mirrors that distorted one's shape and was supposed to make you laugh. There was also a huge variety of rides to choose from and enjoy, but unfortunately for me, most of them went round and round and round.

We took the elevated train to Coney Island and I arrived reasonably unimpaired by the trip along with my three other companions. When we got there, we had to walk several blocks from the train to "Steeple Chase". The welcoming fragrant salty ocean air had its immediate healing effect on my mind and body. I breathed deeply and contentedly. On the train it was necessary for me to remain rather quiet in order not to evoke the silent enemy, the nausea that always remained hidden and lurking on moving vehicles. I did not want to provoke the forces that I could not always completely control.

My spirits rose as we walked along, and I enjoyed the animated conversation taking place around me. Peter's girl was pleasant enough and Peter, whose expression was slightly surly, was polite and surprisingly talkative. I could foresee a fun day coming our way. Leo held my hand and guided me through the crowded streets of mostly young people who were buying and eating the multitude of offerings. There were delicious looking hot frankfurters, French fries, pralines, cotton candy and ears of fresh corn which were scooped up from huge vats of boiling water and offered loudly to all the passersby. Several barkers on the street called out to the people walking by to come into their tent to see the tallest man in the world, the smallest man in the world, the fattest lady in the world, the two-headed dog, the Siamese twins and other anomalies of nature. All of these fantastic sights could be viewed for the price of a ticket. What an exciting and festive environment! Many amusement rides were offered along Surf Avenue. The voices were loud and persuasive and promised much fun and pleasure. We passed them by on the way to Steeple Chase. We would have the opportunity to experience many of those same rides when we arrived at our destination.

Leo's tickets allowed us in without charge and we began to explore the numerous possibilities. There was a wait for the mechanical racehorses, but it was well worth the wait. The swift sliding forward movement of the horses was exhilarating and upon completion, I permitted myself to be persuaded to go on the roller coaster. That turned out to be a poor choice for me. I screamed hysterically, unwillingly, unwittingly, every time we descended at the speed of sound in our little open train-like cars. The screams seemed to find their way out of my throat of their own volition. A little six-year old boy, seated with his father in front of me, kept looking back and giving me tremendous looks of scorn as he observed my anguish. No doubt he was thinking, "What a chicken!"

We slid down what seemed to be a fifty-foot slide. I hated it! We went to "The House of Mirrors" and we looked at our distorted, completely unflattering images. I hated it! I was not bearing up too well. The paper bag of food that contained our lunch was beginning to show little fatty stains, but the rides beckoned to Peter and his girl and Leo and I obediently followed. I hated it! All the rides continued moving around and around and around. I suddenly excused myself and made a mad dash for the rest room. I just about reached the closed stall when my breakfast emerged. It was a tremendous physical relief but I hated myself and I certainly hated "Steeple Chase". I washed my hands carefully and rinsed my mouth many times. I dropped Mama's beautiful lunch into the garbage container.

My basic instincts informed me that Leo was aware of what had transpired and was not too pleased with my failings, and as a matter of fact, I was not too pleased with his. He did not appear to be particularly empathetic or sympathetic. We completed the day with few regrets that it was over. There were no goodnight kisses. For several weeks I did not bother waiting for him on my stoop or visually seek him out while he played ball in the street. My keen feelings of embarrassment lived with me for awhile and I unhappily embraced my disapproval and disappointment.

However, it turned out to be a good separation and it came at a favorable interval. Pearl had friends on St. Johns Place, a few blocks away, and she and I spent time with them and the boys they knew. We were welcomed into their group. Pearl liked one of the boys, Arthur, while I set my cap for a handsome boy called Sonny. It was a case of mutual attraction and I enjoyed his good looks and company. He kissed me lightly one quiet dark evening while we waited on Pearl's friend's stoop for Pearl and Arthur to get back from their walk. It was pleasant, but he was no Leo!

I clearly remembered that first kiss that took place on a frosty wintry night. It was bitter cold and Leo had walked me into the little entrance foyer, where the mailboxes and bells lived, to say goodnight. He courageously slid his arm around my waist, tilted my face up to his and leaned down to reach my expectant waiting mouth. The anticipation was agonizingly thrilling and the kiss justified my youthful feelings and expectations. Just then the little ubiquitous Eddie Krebs, he of the sly accusing smile, he of the bad timing, opened the door, sneered a "Hello" and walked up to his apartment which was one flight under mine. It was difficult to like him. He had a talent for showing up at the wrong time and creating unpleasant responses in the people he encountered every day. What an unfortunate personality!

46

The summer evaporated and it was time for students to go back to school. Tilden High awaited us and proceeded to remove our enthusiasm for academic pursuits. However, my brother Jack was there for me always pushing his agenda, tuning in the Masterwork Hour, and turning up the volume of the classical music until my parents would strongly insist upon controlling the level of sound. He kept recommending books for me to read that were classics, some of which were very difficult for me at my level of comprehension, but I did plod slowly through them just to please him rather than myself.

Since I was not slated for college, as was Jack, I took what was then called a commercial course to prepare me for a future as a bookkeeper to follow in my sister's footsteps. She was now a respected member of the business where she was employed, and she earned more money than several of the salesmen who were hired to sell drapery and upholstery fabric to wholesalers and the general public which was called the retail trade.

I was learning stenography, typing and bookkeeping. My program was filled in with a course of English literature, which I thoroughly enjoyed, history, which I should have enjoyed, and a foreign language. My choice was Spanish, no doubt because Sylvia and Jack had been there before me. I loved the musicality of the words, phrases and sentences, but I did not enjoy memorizing the vocabulary and attempting to absorb the apparently limitless rules of grammar. It seemed like mandatory torture. We never engaged in conversational

Spanish at that time, which to this day I still believe is the only way that one can really learn to speak and understand a foreign language.

Doris and I resumed our pleasant but superficial relationship in school, particularly in the lunchroom. We now felt comfortable and at ease since we had become well accustomed to the routines of high school. We laughed together heartily about Tilden High's football team that never seemed to be able to win a game against any other school. We attended the fiascoes and sang the school song mightily and with great spirit.

"For Tilden High
We will strive and try,
And we'll never yield,
When we're on the field,
For it's victory, or die, ...

One of the few exceptions to daily ennui in school turned up in the surprising guise of Leo's cousin, Ben Shepps. He was an important man on campus, sporting his special Tilden High blue and white sweater with the prominent letter "A" attached in a noticeable place. It was impressive. This indicated that he was a member of "Arista" which was a prestigious honor society that everyone respected and admired. He appeared quite sophisticated even though so young, with a special demeanor that belied his age. He was good-looking and always seemed to harbor an expression of semi-concealed subtle disdain for the general populace. Like his cousin, he exuded that delicate breath of arrogance that made him very attractive! He had a different look and his piercing blue eyes seemed to penetrate one's mind and thoughts that made communication exciting and delightful. He was shorter than his cousin Leo, but he had the compensation of a stockier frame. The girls liked his looks a lot. He was very popular.

I do not remember how he became mildly interested in me, but he did, and I was flattered. He amazed me by asking me if I would like to go out for some ice cream that Saturday evening. My inner response was "Yes! Yes! Yes!" However, I gathered all my innate restraint and quietly responded with a gracious affirmative. "That would be very nice."

I was still in a position where I felt perfectly free to occasionally date other fellows when Leo and I were in the midst of experiencing a time of temporary disillusionment with one another. However, Ben dropped an unexpected bombshell. "I'll ask my cousin Leo if he'd like to join us with one of his girl friends."

"Fine," I responded, while my delighted initial feelings plummeted into Hades. How ironic!

Leo's rotund choice for that evening was Esther, a very nice girl with a particularly beautiful complexion. She had a fair sized birthmark on her very pretty round face that was the color of light creamed coffee. It surprisingly enhanced her looks and her feisty personality.

I had met Esther a number of times prior to this get-together.

She was my friend Pearl's cousin, and she lived in a nearby neighborhood. I kept wondering while eating my ice cream and observing Leo and Esther carefully, whether he really liked her. I absolutely did not think so!

47

Ben's interest in me diminished after a while, as Leo's increased. Once again we were an item, and we both were the happier for it. Mrs. Gensburg, my landlady, nodded her approval as we walked past my house hand in hand. Mrs. Brown, Leo's mother, would share my sunny stoop with several smiling ladies and comment when I returned home after a school day at Tilden, "Here comes my little daughter-in-law."

My parents did not object to our youthful romantic relationship, but even without the benefit of stating what proper behavior was, the meaning of that term was implicit in the way that my family lived. The path of proper and respectable conduct was an integral part of their lives and deeply planted in their children's psyche. My mother and father brought these views and philosophies with them from the other side of the world and lived according to the rules of "Menchlichkeit."

A special treat was coming my way and I had difficulty restraining and calming my inner feelings of joy. Leo was taking me to the Loew's Pitkin on a real date! This obviously showed the world how much he cared for me since his finances were less than minimal. This was a powerful change from taking a walk together. We would be going to the evening show, which was more expensive than the matinee. Since money was scarce, it made our date even more important. We were going to see "Raffles" starring David Niven who was a great favorite, and "Congo Masie" with Anne Southern. All the movie theatres were offering double features to their patrons at that time in order to increase business. I have forgotten and blocked out so many memories during my lifetime, but I still remember the relatively insignificant details of these movies. They float around in my brain and conjure up innocent magical moments spent with a quiet, intense and sometimes difficult personality sitting next to me. I was aware of his strong, male aura and yet I also perceived a sense of youthful gentleness. There were many facets to this developing boy-- man.

He called for me, unhappily hesitating, before knocking at my door. He finally entered our apartment and greeted my parents politely and nervously. I did not introduce him since they had seen him often downstairs hanging around our house in my company. He appeared painfully shy with them and I felt a little embarrassed and disappointed. I had never witnessed this side of his nature. I wanted him to act proud and self-assured. My parents did not seem to pay any attention to his discomfort, which eased the situation.

Mama spoke to him quietly. "How are you, Leo?"

"Fine, thank you."

"How's your mother?"

"Good."

"You know she sits on our stoop a lot because it's the sunny side. She's a very nice lady."

"Yes. She's wonderful. Thank you."

I could see that Leo was beginning to relax. Mama offered him some refreshments, which he declined, and I said, "We have to go, Mom. The movie will be starting soon. I'll see you later."

Papa chimed in much to my surprise. "Take good care of her, Leo."

"I certainly will. Good night," he happily responded knowing escape was imminent.

Leo bought the tickets at the box office and we entered the lovely carpeted lobby with its beautiful statues and sculptures. It was just a movie house but its elegance and size impressed us inviting us into its beautiful interior. He held my arm at the elbow and guided me carefully into the welcoming darkness. We found our seats and settled into the togetherness that touched our young tender minds and hearts.

What laugh aloud fun it was to share the amusement and excitement that David Niven, jewel thief extraordinaire as Raffles, evoked. Ann Southern with her lively personality and lovely face was a well-rounded shapely star playing opposite handsome, well-built John Carrol in "Congo Maisie".

I never forgot our first real date! The double feature entertained us royally, and we left the theatre smiling inside. We walked home through the darkened streets and felt absolutely safe. Such were the times. The high street lamps were stationed at intervals and left small areas that were touched by the black of the night. I wished that Leo would stop in the dark, put his arms around me and kiss me with abandon. It seemed so appropriate. However, that was not to be. I put aside my childish romantic thoughts and we walked and talked about the films that we had just seen.

When we got home, he escorted me up the steps into the entrance foyer of the house. It was very quiet, warm, and cozy. We whispered, not wanting our voices to carry and announce our presence. Suddenly, the outside door opened and there was the ubiquitous Eddie, once again with that "I caught you" grin on his know-it-all face. I was learning to dislike him. We exchanged cool "hellos" and he walked up the one flight to his apartment. It was time for me to go up too. I looked at Leo and said, "I have to go. Good night and thanks. I loved the movies and I had a great time." I could see his light blue eyes gleaming in the semi-darkness staring into mine. He responded, "Good night," leaned down and lightly kissed me. That was the best part of the evening. I dashed up the steps and used my key to unlock the door. It seemed that everyone except Murray was up waiting for me and anxious to hear whether I had had a good time. My responses were all positive. It was a wonderful date! I told them all about the movies, but not about the kiss.

Pearl was still my best friend, but I was also spending a lot of supposedly free time with Frances from across the street, when perhaps I should have been studying. What was there about her that drew me? Why did I pick girl friends that reminded me of Goldie Engel? Did I really appreciate and prefer the company of strong mildly dominating females, or was it pure coincidence?

Pearl was a soft-spoken well-mannered person who nevertheless manifested a subdued strong will. She was obviously determined to follow her own ideas and destiny. One of the many ways in which she showed her independent streak was by remaining completely uninfluenced and uninterested in her family's radical politics.

Frances lived in the building next to Leo on Eastern Parkway and two buildings away from her was Esther, who became part of our group. Esther's parents were orthodox Jews who practiced our religion very seriously and faithfully. They carefully observed Judaic law experiencing great spiritual satisfaction. They kept a strictly kosher home using separate sets of dishes, pots and pans and separate kitchen utensils for meat and dairy foods. They did not hold money, drive or use public or private transportation on the Sabbath. Food was prepared well in advance of the Sabbath and was reheated slowly the following day on low burning gas stoves or ovens. They had been lighted before sundown on Friday, and allowed to remain untouched and unchanged until the conclusion of the holy day on Saturday when the sun set.

Esther's father attended religious services at the synagogue every Friday night and Saturday morning. He also attended the early morning prayer services every day.

Esther's parent's life style was quite different and set apart from ours. My mother maintained a kosher home and she bought meat for our family from Manny's father who had a kosher butcher store at the end of our block. She also kept two sets of dishes, for separation of meat and dairy, along with all the accoutrements that maintained a kosher kitchen. However, we were liberal in practicing our religion. My father always went to synagogue services on the high holy days of Rosh Hashoner and Yom Kippur. He loved listening to the beautiful liturgical melodies that the Cantor celebrated.

The feeling of spirituality that these holidays evoked elevated the family. We looked forward to the new clothes that accompanied the holidays now that there was a little extra income. These particular days were very special to us and filled us with a feeling of sanctity.

However, unlike orthodox Jews, we held money, used transportation facilities, turned on the lights, lit the stove when necessary and Papa smoked on the Sabbath. He would not smoke out of doors on Saturday, he made it a point to tell us, because he would not want to show disrespect to any of our neighbors that might be observant. He was a complete gentleman and always considered other's feelings thereby earning many loyal friendships.

I was celebrating my fifteenth birthday this June 20th with my friends Frances and Esther. The mint green leaves on the trees had darkened and filled the branches with their lush leafy foliage. The sun shone upon us and promised us the warmth and beauty of the day. We walked to Pitkin Avenue past Hoffman's cafeteria and were filled with the exuberance and the delightful promising thoughts of the young. We felt a pleasant bonding as we shared the perfection of this flawless June day. "What is so rare as a day in June?" especially for young teenagers.

Thoughts of school were acceptable especially since we were now free for the summer. "Joy to the world!" We relished our youth and high spirits and were well content with our looks and other concomitant attributes. We were becoming real participants in life and we were ready for it, we believed.

Esther stopped our walk and said, "I have a great idea. How about us having some lunch in Hoffman's cafeteria to celebrate Beulah's birthday? That would really be a treat. The food is the most, and we'd have a lot of delicious choices. We could always have some ice cream later in the day if we felt like it."

Fortunately, we all had a little extra money with us accumulated from various sources over a period of time, and we jumped at the unusual and exciting opportunity to have a real lunch in a real restaurant. We walked into Hoffman's Cafeteria as though we were young sophisticates that had eaten there innumerable times. We were favorably impressed with the varied selections at the huge counter where all kinds of foods were beautifully presented in individual servings. We selected a table near the dessert board that held our very favorite foods. We slowly made our way back and forth in front of the counter and finally enthusiastically made our selections and carried our filled plates, cutlery and napkins on a tray to our nearby table. We carefully placed everything we were carrying on its wooden tabletop and pretended it was an elegant setting. The little plastic rosebuds in its small glass container remained in the center.

"That was a great idea you had, Esther," said Frances, filling her mouth with heavily buttered corn bread and chopped herring. "My mother used to make chopped herring a long, long time ago, and it was one of my favorites."

Esther and I were at a temporary loss for words. Frances rarely mentioned her mother, and never her father. We realized that no doubt the subject was very painful and we were well aware that she and her siblings had been orphans for a number of years.

Esther quickly recovered. "I really love this egg salad, and I occasionally have it at home. These little onion rolls are the best. Oh.. I could make a meal of them with lots of butter."

"Me too," was my less than original contribution. I delicately placed some sautéed eggplant between my lips. It was completely new to my palate since my mother had never prepared it and I savored its delicate flavor. "Yum, this is good!" I proclaimed. "I've never tasted anything like it, and I really had not.

Suddenly, I felt a strong contraction in my throat. My heartbeat speeded up and I could feel hot blood rushing to my face. I spotted our old neighbor, Mr. Gerber, whose wife had been my mother's best friend and mentor when we lived on Marcy Avenue in Williamsburg. It was just two years before that we had moved from the sixth floor tenement building to our present apartment in a three family house in Brownsville. It was a great improvement in living quarters for my family even though Brownsville had never been considered an elite neighborhood. We occupied the six rooms of the second floor and thought that we were in heaven. We often thought about Mrs. Gerber who used to give us samples of her baked goods, particularly her incredible strudel. She had told us that her husband worked in a cafeteria as some kind of supervisor.

Here was this elderly gray haired man with bent back removing the dirty dishes from other tables. Mr. Gerber was a busboy! My young heart experienced the intense pain and pathos of the moment and a little scar formed and remained. He approached us and as recognition occurred, he gave me a wide sweet smile and inquired about my family.

He was completely at ease and without embarrassment. He had no need for false pride or pretense. He left that to his wife, the strong protector of his family's self-esteem. Even though I was quite young, I could easily relate to her delicate and protective sensibility. As far as I was concerned, she was the strength and core of that family.

I introduced him to Frances and Esther. "This is Mr. Gerber. His wife is a fantastic baker and she always brought us delicious samples when we lived in Williamsburg. She and my mother were neighbors and great friends."

Mr. Gerber's face was a study in elderly contentment. He beamed, "She still bakes wonderful."

"How's Davie and Lillie?" I asked.

"They're great," he answered. "Davie has a nice girl friend, and Lillie is still working hard."

I then questioned him about some of the other neighbors remaining in the building, particularly the candystore owners, the recently married Georgie Balter and Ida, that dyed-in-the-wool bachelor with his provocative mustache, and Ida, the former spinster. It was lovely to hear that they still "honeyed" and "darlinged" each other. The quality of their ice cream and their affection for each other had not changed or diminished. Our easy conversation eased my heavy heart. Mr. Gerber did not appear to be an unhappy man, and my birthday luncheon was a success and a celebration after all.

48

Leo was going to the country for the summer to work as a busboy.

Many hotels were located in the Catskill Mountains, and people who could afford a vacation rushed there with their families for a week or two to escape the summer heat.

Three very large meals were served every day, which the guests managed to eat with great appetite and gluttony. Leo was hired by his sister May's in-laws who owned a small hotel in Port Jervis, New York. His job was to clear the tables after the meal was finished and the guests had left the dining room.

May was ten years older than Leo, and pregnant with her first baby. She was spending the season at the hotel with her domineering and authoritative in-laws and in spite of their somewhat negative attitudes, she had arranged for her baby brother, who was now seventeen and a half, to work at the hotel for the summer and earn some money. There was a close bond between them.

No doubt Leo looked forward to a complete and diverse change from spending a hot summer in the city, and coming home with most of his earnings. He found the country environment to be intensely inviting. The dark, cool, clear air of the night allowed the stars to be viewed in their ostentatious splendor without the city lights obscuring their mystery and imaginative beauty. Leo wrote and described the surrounding grace and splendor of the countryside. The nearby flowing river created a stream of music for his mind and the lofty, reticent neighboring mountains sent his spirits soaring and brought him feelings of youthful joy. The singular discontent that he was experiencing, he wrote, was our temporary separation from one another.

I did not mind too much. Our minor commitment to each other did not completely exclude my seeing other boys, and I was not averse to this possible opportunity. However, I knew that I would be quite jealous if Leo found a substitute for me.

Dave Gellen, he of the candy store around the corner, promised his young pal that he would keep an eye on me during the summer, and so he did. When a young man, who resembled a big handsome gorilla, displayed a strong interest in me, Dave immediately proceeded to write Leo that he had seen me in his company. I received my first letter from Leo reporting that Dave had informed him about my supposed popularity with gorillas. He continued his tongue in cheek letter informing me in a non-too-subtle manner and terrible penmanship that there were many interesting girls and boys who were also spending their summer working at nearby hotels. I got the message. He led me to believe that he could be having a good time too. We both suffered!

49

Our kitchen window faced another kitchen window from the next house. We were separated by a very small courtyard. We could easily look into their kitchen and they could just as easily look into ours, and we surreptitiously did when no one was watching. Mrs. Weingard was a lovely older lady and she and my mother became great neighborly friends. Both sides of the court displayed great discretion and tried not to peek too much past the pretty curtains that dressed the windows.

Elsie Weingard, several years older than my sister Sylvia, possessed a fun-filled large voice that easily carried across the court into our apartment during the warm days of spring and summer. Two grown sons came to visit often and were always respectfully friendly to my family. The older son had what appeared to be a successful store in the Prospect Place market, which was located about three blocks away, where he sold all kinds of ladies and children's wear. There was always a stand in front of the store, covered by an awning when it rained, which displayed particular bargains for little children. The quality of this merchandise outside of the store was minimal, but the price was right. Mrs. Weingard's son asked me one day, through the kitchen window, whether I would consider working for him at his outside stand during the summer. It was an offer I couldn't refuse. It was an opportunity to earn some money that would help me, and possibly my family a little.

I started working the day that Leo went to the country for the summer and did not mind it too much. I stood next to the stand that neatly held the merchandise in separate little piles. There was a chair for me to sit on, but I rarely could take advantage of its invitation since there always seemed to be a customer or two who approached and carefully examined the little children's underwear, sunsuits, bibs, socks and bathing suits before making a decision. I tried to encourage them with a good dose of friendliness. That was an important part of my job. The most important task was correctly collecting the money for their purchases.

Above the stores in the market place were apartments that housed poor, mostly black families. No doubt the rentals were very low since the area was not too attractive. Outside the stores that lined both sides of the street were pushcarts that contained produce of all kinds and varieties. The streets very often displayed the remains and remnants of discarded vegetables on the ground under and around the pushcarts. The area had a littered and unclean looking appearance.

Above Mr. Weingard's store where I worked, lived a black middle aged man who spent a good deal of his time during the day lounging in his doorway that was situated next to my stand. Obviously he did not have a job but he did have lots of empty time, and after a while he felt free to engage me in friendly conversation. I felt a little uncomfortable but I responded, as I did not want to seem impolite. My discomfort increased as the days went by. He was just a bit too friendly. However, I did not mention this minor problem to anyone.

Some time passed and it appeared to me that he was hanging around more often standing in his doorway for hours dressed in his shabby clothes, which looked as though they could use a good washing. He generally needed a shave but was obviously quite satisfied with his appearance. He was now in the process of carrying on a mild verbal flirtation with me, and my responses were becoming shorter and shorter and finally monosyllabic. My cool and rather abrupt change of behavior did not discourage him and one day during a quiet moment at the stand, he said smiling widely, "I would really like to take you out to dinner. There's a little place nearby that makes the best chili. I know you'd love it. We'd have a good time. Of course, I would treat you just like a big brother. You wouldn't have to worry about a thing."

My young heart jolted in my chest. How do I make this person understand that I did not want to talk to him at all, much less become a little sister to his highly suspicious and dubious big-brother routine.

"I'm sorry," I replied. "I'm not permitted to go out with men. My family is very strict and I completely respect their wishes. Please do not ask me again. I'm also not supposed to speak to anyone except the customers when I'm working. I hope you understand."

He turned his face away, perhaps with embarrassment or anger. He opened the door leading up to his apartment and left without another word. The wild and powerful thumping in my chest continued for a long while. He never spoke to me again, and I felt thankful and sad.

50

Leo's return from his summer job in the country signaled a renewal of a warm hand holding relationship interspersed with frequent warmer and heated up kisses. We hoped to avoid Eddie, he who always seemed to turn up at the wrong moment in the little entrance hall near the brass mailboxes. We were not always successful.

A classical music appreciation class was being offered free of charge at a local junior high school located across the street from the public library that I frequented regularly. I loved that part of Eastern Parkway. Very often Leo and I walked there from our neighborhood. We followed that route regularly. Lincoln Terrace Park was located in the same area as the library and at that time was a beautiful, safe place to wander through. Evenings we would stop for awhile and sit on a bench under a tree or near the lighted tennis courts. It was delightful to be out on a warm pleasant evening, especially when the company was this good.

Jack encouraged me to enroll in the music appreciation class and I was happy when Pearl said that she would join me. We took the twenty-minute walk to the school and registered for the free class. We felt pleased and initially virtuous listening to excerpts of records that were played for our edification. However, concentrated listening to the music of Beethoven, Mozart and other great composers achieved its goal and I found much of the music thrilling. I experienced a deep appreciation for the gorgeous strains of melody driving a path into my inner being. The music surrounded us and we welcomed it knowing that we were in the midst of evolving self-improvement and a love that would last a lifetime. Jack had given me that gift of listening, recognizing and appreciating the great genius of those composers, and I offered a silent thanks to my caring brother.

The instructor talked to the class between musical selections and he was informative and interesting. I promised myself that I would attend as often as I could. Much to my disappointment Pearl lost interest and dropped out. The group met once a week in the early evening and I made up my mind that I would be there regardless.

The following Monday brought pleasant weather and I started out alone at twilight. The distance seemed long without company. When I arrived, I walked into the music class and noticed that there were about twenty people of mixed ages attending. One was a nice looking young man whom I had noticed the previous week. He was about eighteen years of age. He kept looking in my direction and every time I glanced his way, he averted his eyes. However, when the session was finished, he walked over to where I was sitting and introduced himself. I was pleased with his manners and interest. His good-looking face was appealing, but although I had barely managed to reach five feet, I was slightly disappointed to see that he was quite short. He was two or three inches taller than I. So much for built-in and perhaps learned prejudice. Height, too often, was equated with potentiality, power and masculinity, I sadly thought. His voice was surprisingly deep and resonant and very pleasant to my ears.

"I saw you here last week with your friend," he said. "Didn't she like it?"

"I guess not enough."

"My name is Eric, and I'm glad that you came again. The music's great. What do you think of the instructor?"

"Well," I answered, "he directs our attention to some interesting ideas and points out and explains harmonies that I might not be listening for without his knowledge and expertise. I think that he really knows his stuff and how to teach us in a way that holds our interest."

"I like that analysis," he countered. "Listen, there's a little candy store down the block that serves great ice cream. Would you consider having some with me? We could continue talking about the music."

I could tell that he was not an axe murderer or an overly aggressive young man. "Anyone who seems to be so interested in classical music couldn't be a bad person," insisted my fifteen-year old mentality. My thoughts centered on Leo momentarily, but my desire for ice cream and male company won out. "I'd like that," I said, and off we went.

The dessert was delicious and the conversation animated. Eric walked me home and said that he looked forward to seeing me and continuing our talk next week.

The weather was balmy and pleasant that fall and school days resumed with its constant routine. I was getting accustomed to my daily bus trip, but continued to walk home often during those cloudless days with my chum, little Henry, who still carried that wonderful herring aura and aroma from his father's pickle and herring store in the market.

Henry and I did not necessarily have the need to talk on the long walk home from Tilden High. Just having enjoyable company seemed to ease the weight of the books that we had to carry and the burden and tension of forthcoming tests that we knew were inevitable. When we finally reached home, we parted company. Henry crossed the street to enter the apartment building where he and Leo lived, and I stayed on the sunny side of the street that led to my house. I quickly noticed that Leo's mother was sitting in the sunshine on my stoop. I could hear her softly saying once again to the other ladies, "Here comes my little daughter-in-law." The ladies smiled and nodded their heads as I approached. I felt pleased to witness their obvious approval, but I was happy that my mother was not present. I would have been very embarrassed. I thought to myself, "How lucky Mrs. Brown is. Her son lives with her!"

I attended the evening music class at the high school across the street from the library on Eastern Parkway three more times. The music was wonderful. I recognized that Eric was a special person, but I knew that his beautiful resonant voice and charming personality were not sufficient to compete with Leo's unique and charismatic appeal that had completely captured me.

High school was becoming a little more demanding, but I was not paying too much attention. I was now on early session and had more time to pursue other more important interests, such as socializing with girl friends and spending more time with Leo. He was attending Alexander Hamilton High which was an all-boys school that was about three miles from where we lived. Much later in our developing relationship, he confided that he walked there very often in all kinds of weather to save the price of the carfare. In his junior year, however, he was able to purchase an old bicycle for five dollars. It served a good purpose providing convenient and pleasant transportation that contributed to his sense of well being and his need to save a little money.

His father had been one of the original organizers of the C.I.O., an important labor union of the time. He was a strong feisty little man with a tall degree of compassion and dedication to the needs of the working man. Unfortunately, he never seemed to earn enough money to make life a little easier for his family. The crash of "29" had made it a struggle for them to make ends meet. Previous to that ill-fated time, he had done very well financially.

Leo sold evening newspapers at a very early age to help bring in additional money to the family, but his earnings were minimal. His skimpy wages often fed the family a skimpy meal. He also acquired a shoeshine box, and gave a serious shine for five cents. Often he would receive a five-cent tip. Anyone who could afford having a shine, could invariably afford a tip.

Regardless of family circumstances his sister May, who was ten years his senior, was determined to go to college. She allowed nothing and no one to get in her way or deter her from her goal. All household problems, possible parental difficulties and any other hindrances or conditions were relegated to second place. As a result of her compelling self-centered desire for achievement, she arrived at a respected place in society. She became a teacher.

Next to the oldest was Rose, whose personality was as tart as May's was gentle. Surprisingly, that trait was part of Rose's attractiveness. Perhaps this made her more interesting than her sister. There was always a mood that prevailed of a special kind of excitement and tension when one was in her company.

Moe, Leo's brother, was only seventeen months older than Leo who was the youngest in the family, but he presented a more attractive and mature facade to the world. He was tall, good-looking and always fashionably dressed. He worked as a young salesman in a men's clothing store, a job for which he was eminently well suited. Leo, on the other hand, cared not a whit about his appearance or what he wore. However, his popularity was not diminished at all in spite of his complete lack of interest in clothes. His cool, quiet personality was admired by his friends and those of the female persuasion. He adopted several little key phrases for his own. "Don't get panicky," would be his reply in response to a question directed at him, which he obviously did not care to answer. This slightly rejecting stance attracted more female admirers. Girls, it appears, are naturally drawn to reserved, reticent guys who are slightly disdainful and mildly rejecting.

Leo confided to me that during his free period in school he had a job cleaning the tables in the lunchroom after the kids had eaten and left. For this professional service he was paid one dollar a day plus a slice of pineapple-cheese pie. Unfortunately, he never liked cheese in any form but was hungry enough to eat it regardless of his objecting taste buds. The lunch that he brought from home generally consisted of half a cucumber, which had been thinly sliced and placed into a roll. There were other fillers included but it was never enough to satisfy his insatiable teen-age hunger.

51

It was 1939. Hitler had come into power in 1933 with an appointment as chancellor of Germany, which was reluctantly given to him by President Hindenburg, the doddering old hero of World War I. He had bowed to the intense pressure of the industrial supporters of Hitler who clamored for his ascension as a possible means of controlling the communists, whom they were afraid might take over the country.

The occasional letters that my mother had received from her family in Poland came to a complete halt when Hitler invaded that country in 1939. England and France declared war on Germany within a few days. Prior to this event, Russia had signed a non-belligerent pact with Hitler. World War II had begun.

Young Americans were exempt from the terrors of European wars and did not give world events much thought. Life flowed on calmly and pleasantly bringing with it a gradual maturity for me, and a modicum of modest prosperity for my family.

I had been told about a woman that taught piano in her home on Eastern Parkway for two dollars a lesson. She had the reputation of being a good teacher in spite of the small amount she charged. I asked my parents if I could start taking lessons once again, and they happily agreed.

"I think it's wonderful that you would like to start again. The W.P.A. was hard to learn," Mama said in her broken English, which was always so sweet to my ears. "There were too many children in one class at one time."

"This would be a private lesson, Mom, and maybe I would be able to learn better."

"Good, good. You should do it, but remember, you must practice a little every day, more than before."

"I will, Mom. I'll really try to do a little better."

I walked into our fine French Provincial style living room and smiled happily at our big black upright player piano and I imagined that it was smiling back at me.

Leo created a welcome routine of walking with me each week to the piano teacher's apartment, which was located on Eastern Parkway. We strolled as usual, hand in hand, along the silent dark tree lined streets. The cooler weather had emptied the parkway and Leo would occasionally stop our slow loitering stride. He would quietly embrace me, hold me tightly against his taut body, place his face close to mine and gently kiss me. I loved taking piano lessons.

Miss Marks, the piano teacher, was a sharp-faced middle aged woman with a soft yet firm voice. I felt saddened when I learned that she was unmarried and lived with her elderly mother. The noisy bustling activity of my home was the antithesis of her life style. I, perhaps foolishly, jumped to the conclusion that our way of living was superior to hers. I supposed intuitively, without real knowledge, that her life was sterile and half-empty. I did not take into account her serious love and interest in music and her deep involvement in literature manifested by bookcases filled with varied classics and many renowned modern writers. Of course I had no way of knowing what her social life was like, but I did know that she would never experience the joy of having children.

At any rate, she encouraged, insisted and nudged me into practicing and playing some exciting music. For a while I cooperated though never with great constancy even though I enjoyed hearing the sounds and harmonies that I could manufacture with the help of my beautiful piano. I had always considered it to be a non-verbal but supremely articulate member of the family. It made me feel so elegant, virtuous and worthwhile to be sitting at this lovely instrument gently showing off when Leo called on me. My act worked since he was obviously not in a position to judge my talent, or lack of it. I could tell that he was impressed.

Now that I was on early session in school, every Friday afternoon I took over the job of washing our large kitchen floor in preparation for the Sabbath. I liked the idea of trying to conserve my mother's strength, even minimally. The job had to be accomplished on hands and knees with a soft soapy scrub brush and a big rag like an old torn tee shirt for wiping up the suds. These old-fashioned housewives, like my mother, never owned a mop and looked down on the incompetents who thought that mops were efficient and a good idea. I worked up a good sweat and barely had time to wash my face. I laughingly thought to myself that Leo would not have been deterred by the sweat of my brow. He would shortly be knocking at my door. He knew that I would be alone because Mama would be free for the afternoon. Her morning session of cooking for the family, dusting, changing the bed linens, hanging out some wash, and doing other chores would have been completed. She was finally free for an hour or two.

When my hard work of scrubbing the kitchen floor and then applying a layer of liquid wax with a clean damp tee shirt was finished, I looked forward to my deserved reward. Leo was coming and he was excellent company. When he arrived, we visited in my French Provincial living room, turned on some soft romantic music on the radio, and necked.

52

Time slipped by like water gently streaming down a riverbed, flowing easily and immutably over smooth stones but occasionally pausing and breaking against sharp rocks that temporarily impeded its flow. Weekend afternoons were generally spent with the girls. Frances and Esther were now bosom buddies of mine, and we were a threesome. There was always a lot to talk about. Pearl was still a good friend, and Hilda was busy with school and a boy friend called Mickey. Leo knew and liked Mickey, but we spent very little time together since he was from another neighborhood. We certainly did not double date since no one really had any extra money to spend on "dates". Our winter evening dates continued to consist of long walks and sitting on my cold stoop trying to keep each other warm. Once in a while we would ease into the entrance foyer and exchange a few sweet kisses before saying goodnight.

I was growing up and other good things were happening, too. At last, spring was beginning to send its early message of warm and soft fragrant breezes. We welcomed the lovely change of seasons, and were charmed by the appearance of little green leaves that pushed their way out of the dry branches of the bushes and trees.

School was progressing satisfactorily, and I was looking forward to the end of the school year. My sixteenth birthday was coming up in June and I would be graduating from Tilden High the following January. At that time, I would be entering the adult world working five days week at a full-time job, if I were lucky enough to find one.

I did not give my future plans much thought. My immediate concerns were relegated to all the tests and "Regents" that would be coming up shortly. The Regents were specific all-encompassing tests given in one area such as history, English, foreign language, math and other subjects that students had studied for several years in high school. New York State mandated these exams in order to evaluate all the high schools in the entire state. New York City was concerned only with its own image. It craved a superior status. I could not neglect the necessary additional studying that was required if I wanted to do well. Strangely, I felt a stronger responsibility to my parents rather than to myself. They deserved to be proud of my latent talents, if any existed.

The last of the Regents had been finally given and had been completed successfully, albeit nervously, and "joy to the world," the semester was over! Henry and I walked home together on that last hot day of school. His delicate herring aroma caught by the gentle breezes evoked a nostalgic response and encouraged my lagging appetite for lunch.

Our apartment was delightfully cool in our mostly railroad flat. The bedroom windows were wide open and they overlooked the casual green belt that boasted many tall, wild and uncultivated trees. Some of them were known to be poison sumac, which would cause a rash if touched. We ignored any negative aspects of our delightful view of the back yard, which was our landlord's domain. We never visited, but observed and enjoyed it through our bedroom windows. We appreciated the shaded breezes that danced through the bedrooms, kitchen, and dining room and also cooled our sunny French Provincial living room.

Mama was home alone. Murray, who was seven years old and in the second grade, had still not returned home from school that day. He was a sweet little fellow who brought a lot of joy to the family. He was good-natured and easy to be with. His antics very often created a fun atmosphere that kept us laughing joyfully and spontaneously.

I made a small meal out of Mama's home made filled "Mandelbread". It was fresh out of the oven and still warm. She had rolled out sheets of dough and decorated them with dollops of pure strawberry jam, coarsely chopped walnuts, golden raisins, and sugar carefully mixed with cinnamon. The delicious dough was then rolled up and baked. When the loaves came out of the oven, lightly browned and fragrant, they were allowed to cool. At that time they were sliced and stored. What a rare treat it was when it was accompanied by a glass of cold milk. What a Mama!

Unknown to me, she had told my friend Frances that she wished to make me a surprise sweet-sixteen birthday party, and she asked her to please invite all of my friends. Frances responded that she would be happy and pleased to do that. My mother felt that responsibility had been given to the proper person.

The big day arrived and what a tremendous surprise it was for me! Sylvia and Jack had decorated the living room with what appeared to be hundreds of balloons of different colors, and trails of silver and varied colored streamers. How festive the room looked and felt. What a wonderful celebration it would be. The rug was rolled up for dancing, and a phonograph and accompanying records were in place to provide lots of music. My eyes filled with tears of gratitude and pleasure when I unsuspectingly walked in with Frances and was greeted by ringing and enthusiastic shouts of "Surprise!" I looked around and quickly searched the room. There was no Leo in sight. My mother wondered aloud, "Where's Leo?"

Frances, with a "Goldie Engel" look, replied, "I didn't invite him. I thought that Beulah might prefer having other boys."

My gentle Mama gave her a look that would have destroyed a lesser personality. "That was a terrible thing to do," she said.

I said nothing but would never forget Frances's treachery. I now understood with whom I was dealing. The party was a great success for my guests who enjoyed superior delicacies, ate fully, drank tons of soda pop and danced to a small record player. The rug had been rolled back as it had been for my sister's eighteenth birthday party and it provided a smooth dance floor. For me, there was a void that ached. The party was a complete failure. My family and I suffered. Leo was not present. How could Frances do that? Why would she want to cause me pain? I did not sever the relationship, but I no longer called her "friend."

Leo attempted to minimize the affront, but he had warned me about Frances in the past. He had always seemed to be able to judge people and their motives accurately. I intuitively trusted his incisive judgment, but had preferred to set it aside as it applied to my supposed friend.

"I told you what to expect from her," he mildly stated. "She's never been dedicated to your happiness. It was an easy way to spoil your party and it obviously gave her a little pleasure."

"I can't believe she would be so mean and devious," I answered. "Why would she want to act that way? My mother trusted her to invite all my good friends, and you're certainly one of them."

"Thanks a lot," he laughed. "That sounds like faint praise."

I stood on my toes, reached up and kissed him lightly on the cheek. "Actually, you're my favorite friend," I laughingly answered. He smiled, and leaned down to return a warm response to my waiting, welcoming mouth.

Leo bought me a golden round Coty compact for my birthday. I loved the elegant smooth feel and look of it and I considered it to be a treasure. Unfortunately, I lost it at a high school football game the following season. My heart was mildly broken and to add insult to injury, Tilden High was defeated as usual.

53

Leo's oldest sister May was now married to Al, very much in love, and very much subjected to his dominant will and personality.

He ruled their little nest, but her gentle appearing exterior belied her inner iron core. She would "Yes" him to death, but the dishes and pots and pans in the sink might reach the ceiling before she would yield to his meticulous needs and bullying. She, privately, was immaculately clean and well groomed. The drawers in her bedroom furniture were organized like a work of art, but to her the kitchen was just a place for minor culinary activity and for reading at the kitchen table. Al would often direct strong derogatory remarks to his wife as to the state of the greasy dishes residing in the kitchen sink no matter who was present, and May would smile indulgently and say something pleasant to soften the blow.

She frequently invited me to accompany her baby brother, as she often referred to him, to her house to visit and I was much surprised to learn that Leo's entire family called him Leon. The extension of his name seemed to give it more importance and I resolved that I would call him Leon from that moment on. May always treated me as though I was a person of importance and not twelve years her junior. I became extremely fond of her and grew accustomed to Al's way with words, somewhat empathizing and understanding his frustrations.

Al had graduated as a civil engineer during the latter 1930's. Times were hard and hiring was very tight for newcomers and especially for Jews. He could not get a job in his hard-earned profession, and he had to make a difficult decision. In order to earn a living, he took Civil

Service exams and scored high. He became a fireman for the city of New York and opted for the small salary, the danger, and the supposed ephemeral security of the job. That must have been a bitter pill for him to swallow, but I had the strong impression that he did not complain about it.

May gave birth to a little girl whom they named Joan Patricia. May laughingly told me the reason for their selection of the middle name Patricia. "In order to say Patricia," May said, " Joan will be compelled to pucker her lips, and that will make her kissable and irresistible to future swains."

The condition of May's kitchen did not improve. As a matter of fact, it was all downhill with the arrival of the new baby. Al's complaints were louder, more powerful and grew more insulting in relation to the amount of detritus lying about the kitchen and the height of the piles of dishes in the sink.

"Why don't you clean up this cesspool?" he barked, as he rolled up his sleeves to do the dishes. May smiled sweetly and answered, "In just a few minutes, Dear."

As a matter of fact the rest of the house was well kept and good-looking. I always enjoyed visiting since May was charming, and affectionate and the desserts were great. Our strongest bond was that we both loved the same young man.

54

The welcome summer warmth arrived and seeped into our receptive minds and bodies. School was out. I was sixteen and ready for life to reward me with vacation fun. Leon, as I now knew him, was accepted as my boyfriend in spite of the fact that I would occasionally "date" other boys when he, by choice, would spend some weekend time hanging out with his friends.

Barney, Leon's close friend, had moved with his family to a nearby neighborhood that was close to Lincoln Terrace Park. This was a small step up from our neighborhood. The larger cleaner looking candy store on their corner became a meeting place for many young men of eighteen and nineteen who lived in the area or slightly beyond. Leon and his other good buddy Lefty became part of that congregation. There was a sense of camaraderie and friendship that pervaded their get-togethers and their conversation. Many of them had girlfriends whom they saw on a fairly regular basis and after a while, I got to meet them.

We found out that wonderful concerts were being held regularly in Prospect Park in a special place during the summer. The Goldman Band had a respected tradition and performed to the delight of all that attended. Leon and I decided that we would take advantage of this free musical treat.

Izzy Paul was a handsome neighbor and friend of Leon's. He was perhaps a year older and looked more self-assured and mature. His girlfriend was extremely pretty, slender and considerably taller than I. I was always aware of my lack of height but my sense of security was bolstered by the fact that many tall fellows seemed to like small girls. I did not suffer from a lack of attention.

Leon arranged to double date with Izzy Paul and his girl on Saturday night. We would all go rowing in the lovely Prospect Park lake at twilight. Our escorts would rent two rowboats and the girls would have the pleasure of gliding along the silky smooth water observing the pale sky, the blue-green lake, the surrounding foliage and the beautiful muscles of our young men who would remove their jackets for this strenuous activity. They would be dedicated to satisfying our every whim, and I for one would be filled with contentment and young love. Afterward, we would all meet in the special area where the Goldman Band would be giving their concert. The stage was set for the musicians and the Parks Department would place hundreds of chairs on the grass for the occasion. We would enjoy the music and each other's company.

The sun was still shining when Leon called for me very early that particular evening. He seemed more self-assured when he entered my apartment than he had in the past. He was dressed in a new looking green tweed suit and he looked great. His white shirt, open at the collar, emitted a strong sense of young, healthy masculinity. I felt proud of his appearance and happy to be going out with him.

"How are you, Leon?" Papa asked.

"Good. Thanks, Mr. Dlugash. It's a beautiful day and Beulah and I are going to hear the Goldman Band concert tonight at Prospect Park. I guess she told you. We're going with some friends."

"That's very nice," Papa countered. "Have a good time."

He was not aware that we were planning to go rowing before the concert. I had not informed him of those plans. I felt that perhaps my parents might worry unnecessarily since I could not swim, and I was inclined to spare them any anxiety. I believed that it was not essential for them to know about all of my rather innocent activities. They seemed to like and trust Leon, and I preferred not testing their judgment.

When we came down, we saw Izzy Paul and his very pretty girlfriend waiting for us in front of Leon's building. Leon's family lived one flight up and their windows were wide open. We walked across the street and greeted our friends. Daylight's glow was still upon us. Leon's mother appeared at the window and softly called out, "Have a wonderful time." We smiled up and waved. She had a good face. I liked her a lot, particularly since she seemed so fond and accepting of me.

The bus trip was uneventful. All the windows had been opened wide and when the bus moved swiftly along, the soft summer breezes embraced us and contributed to our feelings of anticipation and contentment.

"Here I am in my prime," I thought, "sitting next to this strong brawny male." I felt satisfied and happy. I knew that he cared about me. He was not an easy talker and I always found myself filling up the spaces of conversation, but I knew that he enjoyed and desired my presence. I knew that I needed his. Leon obviously recognized the true value of the spoken word. He seemed to save it for important dialogue and not waste it too easily on the mundane.

Izzy Paul looked so handsome and he seemed to be a perfect match for his lovely looking companion Rosalie. He had a clever way with words and his company was stimulating and enjoyable. Every once in a while, however, Rosalie's response to Izzy Paul would be a little sharp. I wondered why she seemed to be delicately undermining their relationship that to my inexperienced eyes appeared to be "serious". Her smart piercing little retorts to his general comments seemed aimed to inflict subtle hurt.

"Why was she doing this?" I wondered. "Did he provoke this kind of behavior by acting a little bit puffed up? Did he think that he was G-d's gift to women because of his good looks?" I basically thought that he was charming and clever and deserved to be treated with more respect. She obviously did not completely agree.

When we reached the lush greenery of Prospect Park, we all stepped off the bus quickly and headed for the lake area where the boathouse was located. Our young escorts were ready to take us rowing in the blue-green waters of the Prospect Park Lake that reflected the profound mysterious loveliness of the darkening sky and emerging stars. Leon and Izzy Paul each rented a rowboat for which they were charged fifty cents an hour. Twilight was deepening and the fiery colors of the clouds in the sky had turned into an artist's dream. The delicate coolness of the lake and the oncoming evening drifted towards our overheated bodies. It was a lovely gift.

Izzy Paul and his girlfriend took their places in a rowboat and Leon took my hand and guided me into ours. I perched on the wooden slat opposite where he would be sitting and rowing our boat. He was sweetly attentive and considerate of my comfort. He took his seat, removed his jacket and handed it to me to hold. He placed the oars in their proper slots and proceeded to carefully row the boat away from the dock. He seemed to be in total control. I loved that. I waved to our friends who were already removed from us, and we were on our way.

Izzy Paul called out, "Don't forget. We'll meet you behind the last row of chairs at the concert."

"Fine," Leon replied. "We'll see you later."

We looked at each other and felt pleased to be alone in the stillness of the evening. His eyes seemed incredibly blue and I felt as though I could look through them into his mind. He was, indeed, a very complex personality. No doubt that was what made him so interesting and exciting to me. There was very little small talk but rather little surges of electricity that traveled between us. Knowing him, it almost seemed as though he needed to hide his sensitivity and vulnerability by setting up a cool barrier that would be difficult to penetrate. I never attempted it. I always waited for him to reach out to me. I intuitively knew that this was the better way and I inwardly thanked my parents' subtle and unspoken influence.

He rowed easily and smoothly. The moon showed its face and the beauty of its reflection in the water added to our feelings of serenity and contentment. Leon's arms looked strong and supple as the oars dug deeply into the resistant water and slowly propelled us along. I felt warmed holding his green tweed suit jacket in one hand, and placing the other in the cool moving water of the lake. The soft impact of the miniature waves gently rocked us with its continuing rhythm.

When we reached a little cove in a quiet private area, Leon stopped rowing. He secured the oars in the locks and carefully stepped across to my side sitting down beside me. We held hands and talked quietly and easily. He surprised and delighted me by talking openly about his friends and telling me how much he enjoyed their fun-filled company. He confided that he had a great desire to go to college but it appeared to be a closed door. That was a great disappointment to him. He believed, however, that he might change his supposed destiny and eventually make the effort to achieve that goal.

I felt tremendously moved when he told me how poor his family had been. They had moved frequently from apartment to apartment during the depression. Landlords were giving the first three months of rental free of charge to new tenants as an incentive for them to move into their buildings. Leon's family took advantage of this offer frequently.

"When I was five years old," he said, "a moving truck pulled up to our house one morning, and the drivers piled our shabby and much used furniture into it. The family walked the short distance to our new apartment and neglected to take me along. They were so distracted. I had been playing with my little friends and didn't notice that they had left. After a while everyone went in for dinner and I found myself alone."

"What did you do?" I asked.

"Well, I sat down on the curb and waited and waited for someone from my family to show up. I really did not know whether anyone would come to get me. I didn't seem to be missed. I remember feeling very much alone and frightened. I just continued to wait. I didn't know what else to do. Eventually someone did appear. It was getting dark and I saw my mother in the distance rushing towards me. She had a frantic look on her face. She hugged me, kissed me, and repeated very softly over and over, 'I'm sorry. I'm so sorry,' and practically carried me to our new apartment."

"How sad," I thought. "Did these devastating experiences contribute to Leon's somewhat closed facade? Could it be wedged open and childhood wounds healed?"

Leon had a terrific dry sense of humor, which he indulged freely. It came to the rescue and we laughed a lot when the course of conversation shifted after that sad intense confession. We kissed lightly and headed back to the boathouse. It was time to return the rowboat, get back his deposit, and take a long slow walk to the area where the concert was being held.

The fact that Leon had opened up and confided a sharp painful memory brought him closer to me. I knew that the confidence was not easy for him. We took the meandering quiet trail back through the park to meet our friends. We walked along solitary, earthy, tree-lined paths and did not hurry. "Let Izzy Paul and his girlfriend create their own experiences!" I thought. We were creating ours. Leon and I were in perfect harmony that evening and did not long for any one else's company. The time passed in a full flush of pleasure, and we finally met with our friends. Their company was engaging and it was enjoyable to be with them. Leon and I sat comfortably in the set-up chairs holding hands, waiting to listen and enjoy the wonderful spirited musicianship of the "Goldman Band." It was a great concert and a great evening.

When we got home, Leon escorted me into the small entrance foyer in the hall. It was quite dark with only a dimly lit bulb barely lighting up the stairway. He gently embraced me and soft kisses gave way to more passionate and meaningful ones. My response was positive, but a sense of responsibility decreed that it was time to part. That little downstairs foyer was like a home away from home. We were lucky. Eddie Krebs did not show up!

55

Leon enjoyed spending a lot more summer time with his friend Barney, whose family had moved a short distance away to a neighborhood near Lincoln Place and Eastern Parkway. The corner candy store was a hangout for their friends and more and more acquaintances arrived daily and joined their expanding group. These acquaintances turned into friends after a relatively short period of time. They had so much in common. However, Leon could only see them on weekends since he was now working every week day night from five thirty P.M. to one A.M. One of his new friends, Marty, had gotten this job for him and Lefty Glazer as a special favor at a mattress manufacturing plant where Marty worked the day shift.

Leon was in his last semester of high school when he started working on this job and it took its toll on his school marks. The lack of sleep drained his stamina and energy. The job involved feeding strips of metal into a machine that stamped the strips together. It was repetitious to the point of exhaustion, both physical and mental.

All of his earnings, with the exception of five dollars that he kept for his personal expenses, went to his mother to use for the family. His father was not able to work at this time because he was suffering from severe chronic bronchitis. Nevertheless, he continued to smoke. He admitted that for him it was impossible to put an end to this deadly habit. Both May and Rose were married and out of the house, contentedly established in their own little nests. Leon's job was debilitating and discouraging, but the need was compelling. His only reprieve were the weekends when he was free from school and his job.

The group of young men that congregated around the Lincoln Place candy store in the afternoons grew larger and larger. Eventually, there were eighteen compatible guys who came and went, and who generally liked each other most of the time. They were seventeen and eighteen years of age, all sharing the same religious ties and approximate family backgrounds. They enjoyed the mundane familiar conversations that consisted mostly of sports and girls, not necessarily in that order. Their knowledge of sports was profound and impressive. It dominated a special part of their lives. Some of the fellows were "Giant" fans, some "Dodger" and others were "Yankee" fans. They incessantly and good-naturedly argued the virtues of their favorite teams and happily denigrated the opinions of others. Of course no one ever changed his own convictions or beliefs. Their provocative conversations were inspired and ongoing.

Their other major topic of conversation, perhaps of much more importance to them was girls, of which they had very little knowledge. Most of it, no doubt, was intuitive. However, that never stopped them from expressing expert opinions on all the various aspects and facets of female psychology and female attributes. Leon told me that those who had ties and perhaps light commitments to particular girls were least likely to participate in that conversation. A sample of their dialogue would probably sound something like this:

"That Judy is really well stacked. I'd like to take her to the movies and sit in the balcony."

"Yeah, she'd really go with you. She's seventeen and taller than you are. She needs an older and taller man, like me." Jay was past eighteen, and feeling his slightly superior status.

"I really like girls with blue eyes," said Barney. "Those twin sisters who live around the corner fit the bill. Either one would do. The trouble is, I can't tell one from the other, and when I see them, I'm not sure who I'm talking to and I don't always know what to say."

"You don't have to say anything." Tony interjected. "Just give them one of your sexy, heavy lidded looks. As for me, I like the third sister. She's different. Not as good looking, maybe, but she's got more personality. The only problem that I can see is that they're all skinny."

"They'll fatten up after a while," said Lefty laughing aloud. "Look at their mother."

A lot of chuckling and ridiculing accompanied their gatherings. It was a relief for Leon to be part of this fun group of guys who considered him to be a welcome and intellectually motivated addition.

His deadly night job faded into the background when he was with his friends. School, on the other hand was a place where he could catch up on sleep a little bit. He spent weekend evenings with me, having his libido restrained.

The eighteen guys had a brilliant idea. Of course it was not original. Lots of other groups had thought of the same thing. They would rent a basement in a private house and fix it up as a cellar club. It would be used to bring girls and girl friends to hang out, listen to music on a record player, dance, and hopefully neck a little or a lot. The rental would be minimal, perhaps five dollars per month. Fifty cents weekly from each member would take care of all expenses. Since money was scarce, this would present an alternative to regular dating. The search for an ideal place was top priority. Fortunately, they were lucky and soon located just what they wanted and needed.

The basement was a huge dirty room that had an old couch and two shabby-looking chairs in it. The boys got to work and painted all the walls white. The floor was swept, cleaned, painted and waxed. It immediately took on a comforting and welcoming look. The "pies de resistance," however, occurred when talented Gladys, Monk's beautiful girlfriend, painted a huge mural on one blank white wall. She pictured men in a swing band wearing tuxedos, playing to an attentive audience. She painted musical black notes floating about the mural and young couples dancing to the silent music. What "class" this classy girl brought to Club 18.

The lindy-hop was the great dance rage of the time, and several of the boys were extremely talented dancers. The record player blasted, and the boys could shimmy and shake while dancing together putting on a performance worthy of professionals. Smoky and Barney would do their ever-changing lindy routine to the music of the masters of the "Big Band." Benny Goodman, Artie Shaw, Tommy and Jimmy Dorsey were at their peak and Benny Goodman was called "The King of Swing". The wooden floor of the cellar club resounded to the rhythmic, pulsating beat of the lindy. To all of us, who watched from the sidelines, it was exciting and exhilarating.

After the demonstration, which bordered on the gymnastic, the records were changed and several couples would get up to dance to the beautiful slow romantic melodies that issued forth from Artie Shaw's clarinet. Young bodies were locked in fanciful thoughts of love that emanated from the music that captured our emotions and imaginations. The enthusiastic members of Club 18 had contributed their favorite records for a good cause.

Club 18 was a huge success from the start. Barney and Smoky started dating the skinny twins, and Tony worked up the courage to ask the third sister to spend the evening with him at Club 18. They all seemed well suited to one another, and their relationships flourished.

Lefty Glazer had a no-nonsense, earthy, very likable girlfriend whose name was also Beulah. I liked her best of all the girls, not because she shared my name, but because of her complete lack of pretense and pretentiousness that some of the girls seemed to suffer from. Her common sense approach to daily dilemmas was sensible and liberating. However, even though I spent a good deal of time with Leon's friends and their dates I never felt completely comfortable with them, except for Beulah. The others seemed to be a little too sophisticated for my taste, and though I probably matched them in appearance, inwardly I felt a little timid when I thought that I was not really a part of their world. They seemed more grown-up and secure in their environment than I. Perhaps they actually felt the same way I did. However, my mind secretly informed me that I was on the outside, looking in.

When I look back, nostalgically, at those times from my early youth to my present elevated and advanced age, I sometimes laugh aloud at the frequency and the propensity of the nick-names that so many of the boys carried with no obvious ill effects at that time. There were three Leftys, a Smokie, a Monk, Mutty and a Tony, whose name was actually Irving.

56

Summertime immutably rolled around once again, and it was welcomed. No one was offering me a summer job, and that contributed to my sense of happiness and well being. I was free to enjoy the pleasures of friendships and the company of Leon. My responsibilities at home were minimal. I was expected to help out a little with the housework and keep an eye on my small brother from time to time. It was no hardship.

Pearl and I continued to be good friends, but she had met two boys whom she and her cousin dated regularly, which meant that I did not get to see her too often. Pearl's boyfriend Bob, was a very bright, very interesting, and very homely looking young man. However, when he spoke, he invariably became impressive and nice looking. His ordinary conversation had that effect on his listeners. His wonderful voice and his eloquence were delightful, and therefore he was always welcomed and well liked. He and Pearl seemed to be very much in love, and Pearl's family warmly invited him into their home. They recognized quality, which Bob possessed in abundance. Bob felt comfortable in their midst, but his political views were the antithesis to theirs. They were all careful when they expressed their scarlet tinted ideas when Bob was present. They were determined not to antagonize him.

Frances, Esther and I became a threesome and did summer things together whenever the opportunity arose. We came from somewhat different backgrounds. Esther lived within an orthodox Jewish environment, and would not or could not travel or hold money on the Sabbath. Frances and her family held together and conducted their lives in a respectable fashion without the benefit of parents. The lovely looking older sister, living at home, held a tight rein on all the siblings. She was engaged to a charming, gentle young dentist and they planned to many soon. His practice was newly established and growing slowly. When they married, the sister next in line would continue to hold the family together in spite of the usual minor disputes, and lovingly maintain order and discipline. The married siblings would always be supportive. They were an unusual and caring group.

My family, I believed, was pretty ordinary. I neglected to take into account the perhaps-unique total support system extended to each member of the family. There was the ever present bonding, the surprising lack of sibling rivalry and the pervasive quality of love that subtly but powerfully floated through the rooms of our apartment and into our lives and very existence. It was a good family.

Very often on a Saturday or Sunday morning, Mama would pack up a huge lunch of those special succulent thick fried hamburgers with its accompanying onions stashed into those large fresh crisp Kaiser rolls. I loved the soft doughy insides and the crisp topping of a generous sprinkling of poppy seeds. What a treat we looked forward to when my family all headed out to Coney Island for the day. It had been arranged that Papa's brothers, sister, their spouses and a number of cousins would meet us at 23rd Street on the beach.

When we arrived, old blankets were spread out carefully on the hot sand, and shoes and top coverings of clothing were removed to reveal hidden bathing suits. Jack and I and a few impatient cousins would immediately run into the spuming salt water of the ocean. I was a very poor swimmer and did what I was capable of doing. I would mostly jump with the waves when I saw them approaching, and occasionally was knocked over by their height and strength, which would mightily push me towards the shore. Coughing and sputtering, my eyes burning from the salt water, I would pick myself up and venture forth once again. Jack and my cousins swam about easily and gracefully, laughing, racing and teasing each other good-naturedly. I felt left out of their fun, yet lacked the skill to join them, but the drying out was wonderful. Our chilled bodies loved and responded to the welcome warmth of the sun's rays. How dear and vivid those memories are, even today.

Mama, Papa and our aunts and uncles would sit under large umbrellas catching up on family conversation, breaking apart once in a while to test the delights of the Atlantic Ocean. Then it was back to the blankets to dole out the delicious food that had been prepared so lovingly for their children.

My cousin Sidney was five years older than I and had unexpectedly come to the beach that day. He had a smiling face and personality to match. Everyone enjoyed his low-keyed fun-filled antics. I ended up that warm, wonderful day at the beach having my picture taken perched on Sidney's shoulders. That little photo always transported me to those easy, sun-filled days. Somewhere along the winding indirect paths of life, that picture has disappeared, but in my mind and memory I can always see sweet Sidney's face supplying bits of delight and pleasure to all. The strange thing is that I can also picture Mom and Pop sitting nearby, even though they were not included in the photograph. For me, they were always in it.

When the sun began to set in the sky and the intense heat was subdued, it was time to leave the beach. We all stayed out of the water long enough for our bathing suits to become relatively dry. We attempted to brush off as much sand as we could and donned our shirts and shorts over our still damp swimsuits. All supplies were gathered up, blankets and towels were carefully shaken out to dislodge the sand, and folded neatly. We slowly walked along the many streets back to the elevated trains. We were all very tired from sun and surf. It was a long uncomfortable ride back home but the day had been worth it. Our parents had done most of the hard work of organizing, packing up and getting everything together. We were content to contribute our minimum efforts.

57

Fair summer time was waning, drawing to its closing days. "A sad destiny," I thought, "back to school!" The cooler days quietly and determinedly announced the arrival of stimulating fall weather. The leaves abandoned their summer home high above the ground and ceaselessly floated down to cemented walks reminding us of wintry weather that would arrive too soon, bringing with it a need for warmer clothing. The falling leaves also heralded the beginning of my last semester in Tilden High School, and what I believed would be the end of my formal education. I was returning to school as a senior, and I would be graduating in January. High school had made very little impact on my life. I had acquired acquaintances there, not friends. Generally, the classes and teachers, I was sad to acknowledge, were not memorable for me, and the process of forgetting them had already prematurely begun.

What I do remember with feelings of deep nostalgia and loss, are the recollections of coming home one afternoon after taking the last of the "Regents," shortly before graduation. This was the statewide culminating test given when a particular course, such as Spanish, English or math had been completed. It supposedly determined one's status in that specific area of learning. I stepped down from the warmth of the bus that day, and into the purity of the fresh snow that had fallen all that morning. The continuing snowflakes landed on my cheeks and merged with my intense feeling of well being. The tests were over! For all intent and purpose, I was finished with high school.

"Home is where the heart is." I walked quickly from the bus stop down the long expanse of the white-sheeted street to my snow-covered stoop. The air was fresh and invigorating. My little world was filled with the soft cold cleansing descent of snowdrops.

I ran up the two flights of stairs to our apartment and opened the old wooden door with its "Siegel" lock guarding our premises. There was Mama sitting at our kitchen table reading the Daily News. Her welcoming smile brightened my entrance and filled my heart with love and contentment. Her coffee cup was empty, but she quickly volunteered to make a fresh brew to celebrate this special occasion. Her delicious "Mandelbread" had just come out of the oven and would provide a great accompanying dessert. The bonding was total.

58

Sylvia and Charlie were getting married! The family was in a high state of excitement. My parents were perfectly willing to go into deep debt to do the right thing for their beloved daughter. They shopped around at various catering halls comparing size, beauty, price and reputation and finally found one nearby that met with their complete satisfaction. Everything projected was up to their standards. Sylvia and Charlie were included in all aspects of their research and they learned that this beautiful catering hall, conveniently located several blocks from where we lived, could be completely depended upon to satisfy the needs of the most demanding couple for a wedding blessed with grace and beauty. Additionally, they had a fine reputation for serving elegant and delicious meals.

The marriage ceremony would be conducted in a lovely sanctuary laced with fresh flowers by a rabbi of their choice. All of our guests would be seated in their elegant finery sharing the religious, spiritual and loving experience.

I can still clearly visualize my big sister, my dear friend, my mentor, dressed in her gorgeous heavy creamy satin wedding gown with its flowing train. She was magnificent and her smiling image remains deeply imprinted in my memory.

My parents were inordinately proud and happy. They knew Charlie well. They loved and trusted him. He would be a fine husband for their daughter. It was a true love match.

Mama and Papa reflected the general happy mood of their family and guests. Tante Laikie, Uncle Panush and their two wonderful sons were among the honored guests. Simon and Hymie had been like brothers to Mama when she arrived from Poland and had lived with them. She had become part of their family, and had been nurtured and protected by them until she married my father.

Simon, the elder, was married now, had a fine family and was practicing law. He sported a large dark mustache and was an interesting looking and attractive man. Hymie, the younger, was Sylvia's age and full of fun and loving personality. He was studying to be a cantor. It suited his religiosity, the development of his especially beautiful voice, and his musical needs. Years later, he was present at one of the most important events of my life. He performed my marriage ceremony.

Tante Laikie looked frail and delicate. Her sweet voice still had an uncertain quivery timbre as she questioned my general health and well being. Uncle Panush stood beside her like a miniature ramrod protecting her frailty.

Mama looked particularly beautiful in her sea-green gown, which matched her eyes. Papa could hardly keep from glancing in her direction every few moments. His personality was reserved, but his eyes expressed his constant unchanging love for his Sarah.

Charlie, the slightly nervous groom carried himself as always with an admirable combination of relaxed demeanor and great dignity. He was a young man who commanded respect and was loved by all who knew him well. He had a large family and a deeply religious father. His mother had died many years before and was still mourned. Every one else was present for this momentous, joyous occasion.

The bridesmaids in their beautiful gowns, carrying small bouquets of flowers, were accompanied down the aisle to their appointed places by their ushers, elegantly clothed in tuxedos. Good friends and cousins were part of this ceremony.

Jack was the best man. He walked down the aisle accompanied by the soft ceremonial music of the band, which was ensconced in the far corner of the sanctuary. He reached the "Chupah" where the ceremony would be performed and he waited patiently, standing to one side. He tightly grasped the gold wedding ring that was to be handed to the groom in his closed, clenched hand.

I followed Jack and carried my lovely bouquet and a set smile on my face. I walked slowly and proudly down the aisle feeling the great importance of the occasion and my contribution. I was the "Maid of Honor." I reached my destination and stood next to Jack.

The groom appeared from behind the curtained door at the rear of the sanctuary and walked down the aisle to the sedate music escorted by his father and oldest sister. When they reached the "Chupah" Charlie separated from them and waited patiently for his bride. There was a little hush, and the band began to softly but animatedly play Mendelsohn's Wedding March.

Sylvia emerged with her satin train trailing behind gracefully. She was escorted by Mama and Papa. They slowly glided past the bridesmaids and ushers towards her husband-to-be. She looked radiant and expectant. When she reached Charlie, he claimed her and took her from her loving parents. I was filled with overflowing emotion that I barely managed to restrain. I remember thinking that I had better not cry. My mascara, so carefully applied, would run down my cheeks. My mind wondered, "What had I done to done to deserve such a great family?" Jack looked so handsome and tall in his dark rented tuxedo and little Murray was adorable and manly in his.

The ceremony was brief and emotionally moving. Charlie stamped his foot on the champagne glass, which had been placed in a napkin on the floor, and everyone shouted "Mazeltov!" which meant good luck. Sylvia lifted her lacy delicate facial veil and her new husband kissed his bride. My beautiful sister was now Mrs. Pravda.

The bride and groom were ushered into the main ballroom after many stops for words of congratulation from relatives and other wedding guests. The immediate family followed at a short distance. The band now ready and waiting in a corner on the dance floor struck up a "freilach," a joyful rhythmic Jewish melody to welcome the newlyweds into their new status of marriage. They were led to the head table that was decorated with lovely large bouquets of colorful flowers. My parents had arranged with a florist for this lovely, lush display, knowing that the multitude of blossoms would enrich the appearance of the large dining room and would spread its welcoming aroma to everyone. Every table had its own individual arrangement of exquisite color and loveliness. It was well worth the sacrifice to their finances. My mother, father, Charlie's father, and a few of the older members of the family would be seated at the head table along with the bride and groom.

The band now started playing a spirited "Hora". It was a call to everyone who cared to join the dancing circle to celebrate the momentous event, the sacred joining of two souls. The commitments of the times were of extreme seriousness and generally lasting, perhaps even when love was not.

My Uncle Joe was one of the first to rise from his table, and he firmly grabbed Mama along the way to join him in the dancing. It was the responsibility of the family and guests to help make the wedding a huge success and the music and dancers were an important part of the process.

"Come on, Sarah. You're the mother of the bride. You're needed in this circle."

Mama's green eyes gleamed with joy. She smiled broadly at her non-dancing husband and when he smiled back at her, she rose and joined his brother, Uncle Joe. My mother loved to dance.

Uncle Joe's idea of expressing fealty to his brother's family was by pounding and stamping his feet on the dance floor as he did the "Hora", the symbolic dance of the Hebrews. The sounds of music and moving feet reverberated throughout the hall. My cousin, Jakie Joe's, who had initially introduced me into that Israeli dancing organization that I had loved and enjoyed so much before we moved to Brownsville, emulated his father and stamped and banged even harder as he danced. Mama kept up with the participants in the large circle moving gracefully to the beat of the music. Uncle Joe and Jakie were working up a fine sweat and enjoyment and pride were evident on their faces. A successful wedding needed enthusiasm, and they were good providers.

The non-dancers stood on the outside of the circle watching and clapping in unison to the rhythm of the music. Papa was one of the observers and after much spirited dancing, he reached into the circle as Mama passed and pulled her out. He felt that she was over-exerting herself. Her complexion was too pink. He was there to protect her.

The band followed the spirited "Hora" with a slow romantic waltz and the bride and groom were invited to dance alone on the polished dance floor. As they gently glided and circled the area, they looked like a painting in motion with Sylvia's satin train resting on her arm. Charlie gently leaned over, softly planted a kiss on her cheek and whispered something in her ear. I silently whispered a prayer. "Please G-d, bless them!"

59

Long after the wedding had been forgotten by others, my whole family retained an inner glow of satisfaction. The fragrance of the flowers and the music persisted in my mind. Sylvia and Charlie moved temporarily into the very small front bedroom, next to our French Provincial living room. Charlie labeled their accommodations, "The Executive Suite". They would live with us until they were able to find a suitable apartment in their price range. Jack and Murray would share the bedroom next to Mama and Papa, and a folding bed would be set up for me in the dining room.

The arrangements worked out fine because very shortly thereafter, the new couple found a nice three-room apartment on Ocean Avenue in a lovely, old, tree lined area of Flatbush. It was located in a tall, still good looking building that boasted a large slightly shabby lobby, but sadly, it could not boast of an elevator. Unfortunately, their apartment was three flights up. However, they were young and healthy and they were thrilled to have a place of their own, besides which, their neighborhood was definitely a large step up from where we lived in Brownsville. Everyone was satisfied.

Papa supplied a huge quantity of elegant bed linens, blankets, face towels, dishtowels, tablecloths and anything else that could be classified in this category. He was able to purchase everything at wholesale prices through the dry-goods business where he continued to be an inside salesman. Sylvia's linen closet was packed to capacity. Papa strongly felt that this generous supply of linens for the newlyweds was a prerequisite for starting a new life in a proper way.

Sylvia continued with her responsible job as a full charge bookkeeper and Charlie worked as a grocery man in a large food store. He was soon recognized to be a hard working, extremely likeable asset to the business and was given the special job of cutting and dispensing the hand sliced lox and the various kinds of smoked fish and cheeses. He always accompanied his tasks with his usual good humor and engaging personality. His pleasant dealings with the sometimes difficult and troublesome customers, and his sound judgment and acumen was greatly respected by his bosses. The customers loved him. It became apparent that he was managerial material.

They filled their little third-floor nest with stylish furniture. Beautiful wall to wall carpeting and draperies decorated their living room. Their coffee table had a heavy beveled marble top that boasted a lavender and gray coloration that was unique and particularly beautiful. I had never seen marble that resembled this piece. Its subtle shades and blending of color drew my eyes to its smooth polished loveliness whenever I was in the room. Since Sylvia was the bookkeeper in an upholstery and drapery fabric business, she possessed a great deal of accumulated knowledge as to the quality of the material to be used for her furniture and also in her selection of the fabric for the draperies. She utilized her awareness and expertise to good advantage.

I loved visiting her on weekends. It was necessary to take two buses to reach their apartment, but somehow it seemed to be an adventure. Charlie had to work on Saturdays and Sylvia would welcome me with a special huge breakfast of steaming hot, crispy on the outside "French Toast" which we would delicately cover with jam and devour with two cups of freshly brewed coffee. In addition, there was invariably a platter of marvelously appetizing lox, whitefish and various cheeses from Charlie's grocery. The choices were wide and my appetite was happily fulfilled.

One of the kitchen drawers was always stuffed with assorted delicious candies. Charlie brought home only the best. My favorites were the chocolates. I tried to restrain my lust for these creamy delights, but Sylvia's kind encouragement to try a few was of little help to my somewhat uncontrollable urges.

"Have a little. It won't hurt you. You don't have to worry about your weight."

"I know that I don't have to at this time," I answered, "but if I keep on eating it I will. The trouble is that I'd like to eat that stuff non-stop."

"Just take a few pieces," Sylvia said jokingly, "and I'll lock up the drawer after that. Tell me, how do you like all that extra space you have now that Charlie and I are out of the house?'

"The extra space is great but I admit that I'm feeling a little lonely for you. I find that I'm doing the dishes more often." We both laughed.

"Are you still seeing a lot of that kid from across the street?"

"His name happens to be Leon, and as a matter of fact we're going to a football game tomorrow. Tilden is playing another high school. They'll probably lose as usual, but they always show plenty of spirit. A few of our friends are going too, and I hope that it's not too cold during the game. Tonight we're going to Club 18 and lots of Leon's friends will be there. They dance a lot, and I watch a lot. Leon says that he doesn't know how to dance, but when he occasionally gets up to do me a big favor, he does very nicely. I know he feels self-conscious. For a guy with a strong male image, he's a little shy about certain things."

"You have to encourage him a lot," Sylvia said. "Tell him how much you enjoy dancing with him."

"I try," I answered, "but it doesn't seem to do any good. However, he tells me that he's a great walker."

Together, in the warmth of her little kitchen, Sylvia and I laughed a lot, talked a lot, ate a lot and we had a sweet sisterly time. Once again, I openly admired her new home and her very good taste in furnishing it. I told her that I loved the unique coloring of the elegant marble that topped the coffee table in her living room. That thick beautifully shaped beveled piece of marble with its subtle streaks of lavender, white and gray rested heavily and securely on a strong wooden table shaped to perfectly fit its magnificent top. I continued to be impressed with that particular piece of furniture. The unusual cool colors of the smooth satiny marble drew my mind into a special place.

It was time to leave. I dashed down the three flights of stairs, through the large lobby, and smiled at the few neighbors who greeted me politely. I quickly walked the two long blocks to the bus stop and patiently waited along with several others for the bus to arrive. It was very cold, but thoughts of all that great food and my easy delightful visit with Sylvia warmed my soul, if not my feet. The trip home was uneventful and unpleasant. I had to wait for a second bus for a chillingly long time.

That evening at home, a delicious dinner meal of yesterday's soup with noodles, boiled chicken that had been recooked lightly and recreated with onions, carrots, bay leaves and allspice awaited me and the rest of the family. The side dish of creamy mashed potatoes was always welcome and would be further embellished with the gravy from the chicken stew. There was Mama's home baked filled mandelbread and tea for dessert. We all sat down together to enjoy the good food and the good company of family. Papa had a little shot of rye whiskey, "Three Feathers", before the meal. He thought that it gave him a better appetite. Perhaps it did, but he always remained a small thin man, probably due to all the energy that he expended. He was such a hard worker.

Papa and Murray cleared the table and I did the dishes. I felt so virtuous allowing Mama to rest a little after cooking a large meal and serving everyone. Jack and Papa sat down at the cleaned kitchen table for their nightly game of chess. It had been a good day.

60

My graduation in January of 1941 from Tilden High was fast approaching. It signaled the arrival of adulthood and an entrance into real life.

I did not feel quite ready for this momentous change. Was I really mature enough to accept the idea of getting a regular daily job? I would have to travel by bus and quiet nausea to the subway station where I would be propelled into the land of the grown-ups. I thought not, but I had no alternative. I was being pushed by time and circumstance. I was sixteen years old and college was unavailable to me at this particular time in my life. "Perhaps the opportunity will arrive in the future," I thought hopefully. My stubborn streak and academic leanings might make it happen. Jack was my encouraging mentor, and kept recommending reading material from his literature classes at Brooklyn College.

He was now completely fluent in Spanish and dating a rather robust, nice looking girl with thick ankles. He seemed pretty serious about her, and my parents liked her. She came from a nice Jewish family and that was important to them. They were very happy for Jack. I had some immature reservations about her, which I thankfully kept to myself at the time.

She and Jack did not seem to be on the same wavelength. Sometimes it appeared that their conversations were coming from different planets. She was primarily interested in material aspects of the world, which I could easily relate to, whereas his world was the more ephemeral of literature, art and music. They were basically incompatible and it ended up unfortunately as a failed relationship.

Leon's graduation from Hamilton High, which was an all-boy's school, preceded mine and he invited me to attend. I was flattered that he arranged for three of his friends from Club 18 to pick me up and drive me to his graduation exercises. The only problem that I could foresee was that they were all six-footers, and I barely managed to reach five feet. I would just have to cope. Leon's height was five feet nine inches and when I was in his company, I foolishly hesitated wearing flat-heeled shoes even when I knew that we would be doing a lot of walking. However, after some serious soul searching and a little more self-acceptance, I finally overcame that trivial problem. After all, he obviously liked me short.

Three tall handsome young men escorted me one evening to Hamilton High for the graduation ceremony. I tried to even up the score a little by wearing my highest heels, but it did not accomplish very much. They were charming and attentive and I thought that their interest and thoughtfulness for Leon's girl showed consideration and respect for their friend, as well as for me. I noticed Leon's parents sitting in another row in the auditorium. They smiled and waved to me, and I happily waved back.

My graduation was uneventful, and I thought that it would be eminently forgettable. I felt uncomfortable and uneasy dressed in my cap and gown. However, as the graduates marched down the aisle to our seats from the rear of the auditorium, and the school orchestra played the moving "Pomp and Circumstance," our emotions became highly charged and we were pervaded by a powerful feeling of temporary pride and satisfaction. Such little milestones encompass the passing moments of life.

I was surprised and delighted to receive an invitation from Leon's mother to have Friday night dinner with his family, excluding his two sisters who were married and living in their own apartments. Moe, who was seventeen months older than Leon and whom I secretly thought was a handsome sophisticate, would be there. From where I lived across the street I could see him often through our living-room windows, emerging from his building dressed meticulously and on his way to work or perhaps meet with friends.

My girlfriends were very impressed by this new turn of events. Frances, who probably still had a crush on Leon, was happy to find fault with the invitation.

"You still go out with other boys occasionally. How come his mother is inviting you up for a Friday night meal?"

"I guess she likes my looks and realizes that I'm a special girl. She knows that I'm good for her son," I replied, hoping to upset her a little. I still had not completely forgiven her, and probably never would, for not having invited Leon to my "Sweet Sixteen" party.

"Ha! That's a laugh. Mothers aren't interested in their sons having a girlfriend."

"Well, Frances, I guess you're wrong in this case," I said.

Esther good-naturedly chimed in, "Enjoy yourself. I think it's wonderful, but there might be one little problem. His brother is so good looking that you might concentrate on him and forget to eat the food. But I must tell you, Leon looks more interesting to me."

"I agree," I said, "and I know that my appetite will be fine. Mrs. Brown is probably a great cook. She's from the old school."

My parents liked Leon, trusted my judgment, and did not object to my going. My mother baked something special for me to bring. It was not polite to go empty-handed. "One has to be a "mensch," a person, a proper human being, and act accordingly," said my mother.

Leon called for me early Friday evening. He was dressed up in his green tweed suit and looked particularly virile and strong. A little thrill of anticipation danced through my body. I felt proud of him as though it was to my credit and influence that he looked so well dressed and presentable. I was already aware of the fact that clothes were generally of no great importance to Leon. The more his brother dressed up, the less interest Leon seemed to show in his attire.

I wore a relatively new dress in the hope of making a good impression on his mother. Leon and I sat with my family at the kitchen table for a little while before we had to leave for dinner at his house across the street. My mother had invited Sylvia and Charlie for that Friday night meal and conversation was light and pleasant. Papa and Jack were engaged in a pre-meal chess game. Papa was being soundly beaten by Jack's talent and expertise, and my father was delighted and extremely proud of his son. He always gave Jack a good game, but Jack's finesse had him coming and going. My father loved it.

Before Leon arrived, there had been a little conversational family fun. Charlie loved to tease me good-naturedly and I always enjoyed our exchange. Perhaps I even encouraged it a little.

"I guess we'll all have to start thinking about a June wedding," Charlie volunteered with a big smile on his face. "You'll be seventeen at that time. If you wait any longer, you'll be a candidate for old maid."

"Listen, Charlie, first I have to get a job so that I can support Leon in the style in which he'd like to become accustomed," I answered.

Mama laughed, but her mind followed a more serious route. "He's lucky to have such a smart girl like you, and his mother knows it, and I'm sure that she agrees with me."

"How about such a pretty girl like me, Mom?" I continued half jokingly. "Smart is good, but pretty is probably better. I always work towards that goal, you know."

"You are. You are pretty. You don't have to work at it," Sylvia contributed, "but you and Leon have a long way to go. I'm sure that there will be lots of other guys in your young life."

"Like there were in yours?" I queried.

She and Charlie laughed. It seemed to me that she and her new husband had been well bonded from way back during their early high school days.

The knock on the door announced my escort. Leon seemed to be more at ease than he usually was with my parents, and I could tell that he enjoyed the continuing light-hearted conversation with Sylvia and Charlie. We were all comfortable with one another and I felt relaxed with happy anticipation. We said goodnight to all.

"Goodnight, goodnight," they all echoed.

"Have a wonderful time, and enjoy a wonderful meal," said Mama as she handed me the cake that she had baked for Mrs. Brown.

We walked down the two flights of stairs holding hands and there was Eddie once again, walking up to his apartment. We dropped hands as he passed us on the stairs and he gave us one of his quizzical crooked smiles. "Where are you guys going all dressed up?" he asked.

"Around," Leon coolly replied as he opened the outside door and we exited.

He carefully guided me across the street grasping my elbow firmly as we approached his building. From another direction, we noticed a tiny, elderly lady. She appeared to be a half-foot shorter than I. She waved to Leon and we stopped and waited.

"That's my old tante. She lives on the East Side, and makes that long trip to see us all occasionally. She'll sleep over tonight and visit my sisters tomorrow. They're not too keen to see her but they'll be polite. You won't like her. She has a caustic tongue."

"I'm not going to make any advance decisions," I said. "I expect her to be very sweet to me."

"What an optimist you are!" he quickly responded as we quietly chuckled.

As she reached us, she looked me over carefully and immediately started talking. "Hello Labele. This is your girlfriend?" She did not allow him to respond, but continued with her "piece de resistance." "A za kleine nemst du?" which meant, "Such a small one you're taking?"

Leon did not even take a moment to think up a reply. His immediate response was, "Tante, it's not the quantity, but the quality."

I still remember her expression as she turned her full, intelligent, badly wrinkled face to me, and studied mine diligently. She paused momentarily. "That's a wonderful answer, Labele. Let's go up and see the family." If Leon had ever committed any minor sins or infractions in the past, and I could not think of any at the moment, he was completely forgiven and immensely valued. What a fast thinking gentleman my boyfriend was!

We made our way up to the first floor and the door was open. Mrs. Brown had seen us coming though the bedroom window where she no doubt had kept a concealed vigil. Perhaps she felt as nervous as I did. She greeted us with a warm smile and leaned over and lightly planted a kiss on my surprised, but welcoming cheek.

"Come in. Come in. Hello Tante. I'm glad to see you," she said. Mr. Brown came in from the other room and greeted me with a huge smile.

"Hello. How are you?" he said to me, putting forth his hand to shake mine. He placed his other hand over mine and pressed a warm welcome.

I felt a little shy, "Fine, Mr. Brown. Thank you," I responded with an answering smile.

"Hello, Tante," he continued. "My wife cooked up a great meal for us. You'll enjoy it."

"My teeth don't let me enjoy food too much," she replied.

Leon gave me a knowing look. "She'll eat like a vulture," he quietly whispered in my ear. I restrained my evil giggles and maintained my demure demeanor. I was very anxious to make a very good impression. I handed the box of baked goodies that my mother had prepared to Mrs. Brown and she thanked me politely. I would have preferred a little more enthusiasm for Mama's home baked delicious works of art, but perhaps that would be forthcoming later when she tasted a sample. I wondered whether Leon's Tante would display a positive reaction to me and the dessert that I had brought.

Ah! Handsome Moe emerged from the back room. He had a patronizing smile on his face as Leon formally introduced us. I was his kid-brother's girlfriend. I could tell that he wanted me to think of him as being older, more sophisticated, more handsome and certainly more fashionably dressed than his younger brother. I was a little disappointed by his manner. We had seen each other occasionally in passing but did not openly recognize or acknowledge our connection. He had a deep masculine voice reminiscent of a radio announcer, and the small black mustache above his lips flattered his face.

We were all ushered into the dining area where the table was beautifully set and the mood of the arrival of the Sabbath prevailed. Mr. Brown sat at the head of the table and his genial and welcoming behavior was palpable. Leon sat beside me and temporarily held my hand below the observation level. This certainly was not enemy territory but I enjoyed the feeling of being protected and cared for.

There was lots of pleasant small talk interspersed with mildly negative comments from Tante. She commented when Leon and Moe put a little ketchup in their chicken soup. She thought it was sacrilegious.

"What are you doing?" she loudly proclaimed with her inimitable accent. "Why are you destroying this beautiful soup?"

Mrs. Brown came to her son's rescue and laughingly suggested that anyone who cared to be part of the "Brown" clan would have to learn to appreciate this gourmet touch that her sons possessed. She meaningfully glanced in my direction.

A delicious meal was served and great appreciation was given for my mother's cake. Moe's company had turned delightful, and I decided to like him. Sweet attention had been paid to a sixteen year old girl and I felt as though I could easily and contentedly be part of this family even though I would never put ketchup into my chicken soup.

Leon walked me home, and I felt satisfied and mellow. I hoped that Eddie would not be finding his way home at the same time. It was a cold starry night, and I looked forward to my increasingly warming goodnight kisses in the little entrance foyer near the brass mailboxes.

61

I had to start looking for a job as a bookkeeper. That seemed to be my current responsibility. Papa's words logged in my brain. "Bookkeepers are important people in any business. They make a decent salary and they're shown respect. Sylvia knows that to be true. Ask her, you'll see." I saw, and I knew that he was right. I certainly was not going to work in a factory. "I need all the respect that I can get," I thought to myself laughingly, "to compensate for my lack of height."

The initial difficulty was to get leads for job interviews. This was generally accomplished by visiting an employment agency. A clerk would fill out forms listing your qualifications and hopefully send you out to a place of business that needed the services that you could supply.

It was a very nervous little girl that showed up at one of the many employment agencies in "The City," as Manhattan was called. Getting there was a semi-traumatic experience for me. I could either take what seemed to be a long cold walk to the subway station or wait a long cold time for the bus. I chose to take the bus, hoping to avoid a wind-blown tired appearance when I would finally arrive at the agency.

The bus arrived and transported the impatient transients to the subway station. I walked down the steps where I was greeted with a rush of that underground enclosing subway smell that permeated the entire area. The platform, which had train tracks on both sides for people traveling in opposite directions, was filled with waiting, persevering commuters.

The older segment of the population looked gray and weary. The younger appeared slightly more spirited and alive. Did going to work every day in this crowded never changing perhaps claustrophobic environment turn these young people into sad replicas of their elders? Perhaps it was their jobs that did not open doors to change, interest and advancement.

I fought back the slight sense of nausea as I entered the train that had arrived after a few minutes of waiting. I found a seat next to a young woman and settled in for a bumpy thirty-minute ride. I closed my eyes and thought about the good happenings in life. I repeated my philosophy to myself like a mantra, "Emphasize the positive and minimize the negative." Was this attitude part of my genetic makeup, or was it mostly parceled out by my parents early on?

I thought about my current and only boyfriend, Leon. It helped pass the time. There was definitely an electric current that existed between us that I often attempted to sedate. When we occasionally had cool differences I was lucky enough to be able to date others.

Forty Second Street station! I was pushed forward by the exiting crowd towards the opening doors when I rose from my seat. Which way should I go? I inevitably found myself in the very cold outdoors trying to determine the correct direction to take in order to reach the job agency. Since I did not know my way around the city, I stopped a rushing, hurrying woman and inquired. She pointed her finger and spat out, "That way." I barely had time to say, "Thank you." She had left me far behind.

I walked several blocks, gripping my coat collar to my neck for a little extra warmth, to no avail. Wintry winds had me in its icy grip. I was shivering, but suddenly, there was the sign announcing the "East Coast Job Agency." I dashed into the warmth of the lobby with a profound sense of relief. However, the relief changed to a mild case of nervousness as I was taken up to the fourth floor in the shaking, quaking old elevator.

I gently opened the office door and politely waited at the desk of the sour-faced receptionist. I could tell by her disdainful look and complete inattention that she was quite unimpressed with me. She finally looked up and frowned.

"How old are you?" she eventually asked.

"I'm sixteen and a half." That half seemed very important to me at that moment.

Her face remained uninterested and cool. She could not care less about my extra half-year. "Here are several papers that you have to fill out for our records," she said, handing me the forms and a pen. "You know that if we get you a job, we're due one week's wages.

I nodded. "Yes, I know. That's fine." In my heart I felt that it was not so fine, but what could a poor girl do? My innate sense of humor prevailed, and I inwardly laughed at my self-pitying thoughts. I filled out the necessary papers attempting to show myself to best advantage. Perhaps I exaggerated my sterling qualities and talents. It was tough getting started in the real world. I attempted a half smile as I handed the forms and the pen back to the formidable and unconcerned lady at the desk.

She quickly glanced at them without interest and said, "We have one opening at the moment. It's downtown in a sausage factory. They need a bookkeeper and they expect a beginner for twelve dollars a week. You might do." Her parting words to me as I left were, "Hurry "

Twelve dollars a week seemed like a good salary for a completely ignorant and inexperienced bookkeeper. I could be very satisfied with that weekly sum, while I learned on the job. However, when I entered the domain of ground pig, I knew that I could never function in an office that was immersed in that particular odoriferous environment. I would be back on the trolley-car full time with no escape.

I stayed for the interview, but they did not like me any more than I liked them. "How old are you?" was the first and only question. "I'm sixteen and a half." "Sorry, you're too young for the job. You look fourteen."

I danced out happily and took the train home. The subway smelled better to me on the way back. Anything smelled better than the sausage factory. I walked home from my subway exit instead of waiting for the bus. The frigid air gave me the feeling of fresh renewal and hope. I would try again tomorrow.

Mama did not seem at all disappointed at my lack of success. "You really did a lot today. You found your way around in the city and didn't get lost, and you talked to people about a job. I think you did very good and learned a lot. Remember, it's a big world." In my mother's vernacular, "It's a big world," meant that tomorrow is another day, and the situation could completely change for the better.

Perhaps I got my optimism from her. She always seemed to send an encouraging and strengthening word or thought my way. When I seriously considered it, I could not figure out what she had to be particularly happy about. She and my father had gone through some extraordinarily difficult times together. They never were able to go on vacations. Their children provided heavy doses of illness from time to time. They rarely ate out, although once in a while they would go to the local kosher delicatessen and order a succulent hot pastrami sandwich on rye bread accompanied by a half sour pickle. My mother relished that tasty repast and my father enjoyed pleasing her. This was one of his fundamental pleasures in life. I believe, however, that her basic overpowering satisfaction was derived from her family and her constant attempt to fulfill its needs. She knew that she was deeply loved by her children and her husband, who always seemed to be the epitome of loyalty and quiet devotion. When he arrived home after a long days work, the melodies that he softly hummed as he climbed the stairs to our second floor apartment was a welcome sound to our ears. We had made the transition from Papa to Pa, and sometimes to Dad. Regardless of what we now called him, when we heard his gentle humming, we knew that our guardian was safely home, and we were safe.

62

Club 18 continued to be the hangout for all those young guys with their dates and their girls. A sweet evening could pass without any money being spent. A lot of special "Lindy-Hopping" was happening. The "Big Band" sound took us into its sweet embrace and never released us. We were caught up in its rhythms, tremendous musical talent and marvelous melodies. The lyrics accompanying the ballads were mellow, romantic and unforgettable. Our teen-age moods were very often dependent upon what our music masters Benny Goodman, Artie Shaw, Glen Miller and Tommy Dorsey would feed us. How we loved their distinctive sounds and style, and still do. The slow dancing to those ballads is still deeply impressed on my mind and body. They encouraged romanticism, and a kind of reserved sensuality. We believed these were the best of times.

Even those who did not know how to dance could move slowly and sway to the rhythm of the music, holding their girl closely in their arms. Lots of hugging and concealed kissing was permissible. Gladys's mural looked down on us from the wall and kept watch. From time to time a great Lindy-hop record would be played, and Smoky and Barney would get up and dance together, giving the group a wild treat of their dancing talent. Everyone loved watching two guys performing at a near professional level. They were our stars, and their girlfriends looked on with unabashed admiration.

Leon and I saw each other quite regularly, but during one of our times of "cool differences," Marty, from Club 18, asked me to go with him to see "Gone with the Wind." That was a very attractive offer at the time and my immediate response was "Yes." Leon and I were still not absolutely completely committed to each other although the bonds were growing stronger and stronger. I continued to feel free to occasionally date other young men. He did not discourage this arrangement and that attitude encouraged me further. However, I did entertain the notion that he might not have extra money to spend on real dates too often, thereby suffering minor pangs of guilt.

Marty was one of the members of the club who was not too popular with the other guys, but he was tolerated in spite of possessing a weak personality. He was the only one in the club who had a steady job, and perhaps some of the boys were a little jealous of this. He was nice looking, pleasant and predictable. He lost points as a non-dancer and a less than stimulating conversationalist. I did not feel guilty about dating him. He wanted a companion for this occasion and he knew that it was not a love match. In his heart he was aware, as was I, that I was Leon's girl. I knew that we would both enjoy ourselves and have a good time. I would certainly make a determined effort to be my most charming self.

We went with another couple and fortunately the other young man had a car, which was much more convenient than taking the subway. My parents were a little distressed that we were going by automobile, and I noticed my father surreptitiously looking through the living room window with pencil and paper in hand. He was copying down the license plate number before we left. Perhaps this little action supplied a modicum of security for him. How hard it is for most parents to contain their worry. My parents were no exception. Obviously nothing in the world was more important to them than their children. Papa's unsaid words were indeed powerful.

The trip to the movie house seemed long and bumpy. The jalopy that we were riding in had long since given up its shock absorbers and springs. However, we were young, and happy to be going on this excursion that promised a wonderful reward when we arrived, if we arrived. Finding a place to park the car presented another little problem, but finally our young driver swung into a nearby spot and we happily emerged, glad to take deep breaths of the fresh cleansing air.

The Brooklyn Paramount had been built to resemble a palace. Many movie theatres of the time were huge and elegant and gave the viewer a feeling of complete luxury upon entering. "Gone with the Wind" was magnificent and we were overwhelmed by its gripping power and beauty. It was epic in scope and the actor's performances were thrilling.

The entire experience was unforgettable. Clark Gable and Vivian Leigh were at the peak of their extraordinary talent and the movie was indeed a classic. Our date had been a huge success but deep down in my immature heart, I missed that reticent, cool reserved boy from across the street.

63

Monday arrived, and as usual, everyone scrambled to get out on time to meet his or her obligations. Papa shaved at the kitchen sink glancing into the clear mirror that hung on the wall above it so that other members of the hurrying scurrying family could use the bathroom. There had to be lots of cooperation for this morning operation to succeed, and there was. Mama had already rushed to the family grocery store earlier that morning for fresh rolls, butter and perhaps a thick slice of cream-cheese and she was now preparing breakfast for all. The coffeepot sang its rhythmic inviting song. In retrospect, the morning scene did not appear to be too difficult.

Since it was not necessary for me to show up at the job agency at a specific time, I lingered a little while longer at the kitchen table after the others had left. Mama poured a cup of that freshly brewed coffee for each of us and we quietly sat together joined by love, camaraderie and respect. We sipped our flavorful coffee pensively, and Mama opened the conversation with, "So, what do you think of this new boy, Marty?"

"I really don't think about him too much, Mom. He's just another nice boy floating by. He probably doesn't take me too seriously, and I surely feel the same way about him. We had a good time seeing "Gone with the Wind" and it was nice for both of us. He basically knows that I'm Leon's girl."

"So, if you're Leon's girl, how come you can go out with other boys?"

"There's a kind of understanding between us," I explained. "I'm not ready at my age to make a commitment, and I think that he may feel the same way, even though I really don't think that he's interested in seeing other girls. As a matter of fact, I'm not particularly interested in other boys. We'll just see what the future brings."

"That's the best idea," Mama said. "Now I think a better idea for you would be for you to get to the agency early. Maybe they have some jobs."

"You're right, Mom. I'm on my way."

The routine had been established, but this time I waited at the bus stop along with several other travelers anxious to get to work on time. We saw the old yellow bus approaching, and we all piled on politely when it stopped. It kept releasing its toxic fumes that did not waste any time having its usual effect on me. We arrived at the subway station in a short while and I took a few clean deep breaths before scampering down the steps that led to lower level purgatory. The train to the "City" awaited us and screeched and howled its way on the tracks in the dark tunnels with its lights turning off and on intermittently. When it finally arrived at my station, I gratefully disentangled myself from the crowd of harried, hurrying people. I felt secure in the knowledge that today I knew the right direction to take to get to the agency, and suddenly my mind spoke to me. "Hey, you really know your way around. There's the job agency sign. Ignore that old biddy's frowning face and you'll get a job today." I laughed to myself and thought of the power of positive thinking.

That chug-a-lugging elevator carried me, rather unwillingly, up to the fourth floor. There she was, old pie face, looking me over and over. "Ah," she said. "Here's the fourteen year old back again. I do admit that you have stamina or perhaps you're just a glutton for punishment." She studied her open notebook and looked up at me with her piercing eyes. "O.K., try this. I don't think it will do you any good, but you never can tell. The owners are Germans, perhaps refugees, and their business is called The French Powder Puff Company. A Mr. Hersch runs it for them and he's a tough cookie. See if you can charm him."

"Thanks for the great encouragement," I thought.

She gave me a printed form from the agency to present to Mr. Hersch. It also contained another slip with hand-written directions as to how to get there. I felt more nervous about finding the place than I did about facing the inevitable interview. "If I expect the worst," I reflected, "I will not be disappointed with the results."

My destination was within walking distance from the agency, and I was grateful for small favors. I entered the building and there was the relic that was called the elevator. I momentarily hesitated and then bravely walked into it. I pressed the proper button and it groaned and jerked its way up to the third floor. The metal door creaked open slowly. My relief was tangible and I gladly exited and knocked at the glass entrance door that signaled my fate. There was a large powder puff painted on the glass.

The French Powder Puff Company was actually a factory located in a loft where the powder puffs were manufactured. They were partially sewn and then turned by hand on a stationary piece of metal. Some of the girls working at the tables in the factory would lightly stuff the powder puffs with soft filling whereby other workers would carefully sew the small remaining gap by hand.

The office that I entered was large and airy and boasted two oversized desks. Huge windows allowed much light to enter the room and brighten the scene. There were two well-rounded overweight persons present whom I assumed were the boss and his wife. They were sitting in strong chairs on the side of the office. Behind the centered desk facing me as I walked in was a middle-aged man who was stocky, short and dressed in a dark suit. He looked very serious and not particularly friendly. I guessed he was Mr. Hersch.

I handed him the requisite form and said, "Good morning. I'm here to apply for the bookkeeping job."

"How old are you?" he questioned in a deep rather mellow voice, which did not seem to belong to him. "You look fourteen. Are you a high school graduate?"

"Absolutely, sir, and I'm sixteen and a half."

"I'm sure the half will help a lot," he responded. "Do you know anything about keeping a set of books?"

"Oh yes," I lied. "I majored in Bookkeeping," which was true, but I patently realized that my school experiences were practically worthless. I did not even know how to insert a new sheet of paper in the ledger. "I don't have any practical experience yet, but I'm a fast learner and a hard worker," I bragged, hoping that my face, if not my words, displayed some modesty.

He sighed heavily as though he had been attacked. He studied my face for a long moment and decided to take a chance on me. The two owners did not utter a word. Mr. Hersch did not seem too terrifying in spite of his slightly scowling demeanor. It was those large Germanic faces sitting on the side watching me perform my little act, taking it all in and certainly knowing me for what I really was that further undermined my meager self-confidence. They deferred, however, to their business manager and mentor and allowed his decision to hold.

"You can start right now if you want to," Mr. Hersch declared. "You know the salary is twelve dollars a week and we're responsible for mailing a check for this amount to the agency from your salary. If you prefer, however, we can send them four dollars a week until it's fully paid up."

"Thank you. That would be much better. I can start now, but I would like to make one phone call, if that's alright."

He gave me an unexpected smile. It seemed to light up his face. "That's fine. Here's the phone."

I felt a little embarrassed calling my mother to let her know that I was now a working girl, with Mr. Hersch standing nearby. I had gotten the job and was elated, but it seemed rather unsophisticated to display my enthusiasm especially when those very attentive ears were so close.

When Mama answered the phone, I spoke in a subdued tone and what I hoped was a rather mature manner . She was delighted with the news, and clearly got the message that there were other people present. She knew that I could not express any ideas on the subject of my new job at that particular time. We said our good-byes without delay and looked forward to the evening when I would return home.

Mr. Hersch suggested that I follow him and have a look at the adjoining space. We walked into the next area of the loft and there were several young women sitting on high stools facing a long wooden table at which they did their work on the powder puffs. They looked up as we approached and Mr. Hersch stopped and introduced me. Their smiling faces welcomed me, and I knew that I would be very comfortable working and learning in this environment, if I could keep the job.

Mr. and Mrs. Braun were the owners of the French Powder Co. They appeared to be completely distant, cool and uninterested in me. As a matter of fact, Mrs. Braun was cold, but uninterfering. I was just too unimportant. I was shown to my desk and given a simple bookkeeping job to do by Mr. Hersch. He kept me busy for the rest of the day, and I told myself, "So far, so good." Occasionally I would glance out of the huge window next to my desk and notice people working in the loft opposite mine on the other side of the street.

Those old buildings seemed to be a mirror image of ours. These buildings lined both sides of the street.

At lunchtime the girls in the back trudged out past the office talking and laughing quietly. They were on their way to a little coffee shop for lunch. Mr. Hersch openly suggested that I join them, and they immediately stopped and offered loud, insistent and kind invitations. I was happy to agree and thanked them profusely. It would feel good to have some pleasant female companionship during my lunch hour. The sandwich, good coffee into which I generously deposited several packets of sugar and the sweet talk of my luncheon companions revived my tired spirit. My unknown future seemed more encouraging with the smiling support of these factory "girls". I squelched a little hidden desire to be one of them. They enjoyed a camaraderie while doing their repetitive chores, while I no doubt would struggle to learn the inner workings and complexities of bookkeeping, alone.

Five o' clock finally arrived and I was satisfied that I had been able to follow Mr. Hersch's directions without any difficulty. His instructions had been explicit and I felt reassured and encouraged particularly since he appeared to be pleased with my work. I decided that beyond that scowling face was a rather nice but harried person. It would take a lot longer to judge the Brauns.

When I finally got home, it was close to six o' clock. Papa was not due home for at least another hour, but Jack and my mother made much of me. Even little Murray joined in and gave me a big kiss of approval. What a sweet little guy he was. I knew from that reception that I had climbed one more rung on the ladder of life. I was really growing up whether I wanted to or not. Sylvia called that night when she got home from work. She sounded delighted to learn that her little sister was a bona fide working girl earning a real salary, no matter how minimal. "Some day," she said, "you'll be taking over my job when Charlie and I decide to start a family." Her intuitive words, casually expressed, seemed to foretell the future.

When we heard Papa's sweet humming floating up the stairs leading to our door, Mama opened it quickly and welcomed him with the words, "She got a job. Beulah got a job."

He entered the kitchen and looked at me proudly. An affectionate and warm smile spread over his sweet tired face and into his loving eyes as he quietly said, "Congratulations. I'm never surprised at your success."

64

The next morning I struggled out of bed very early so that I would be sure to get to work on time. I wanted to try to elicit a smile from Mr. Hersch's scowling, troubled looking face. My self-confidence which last night had soared and reached the stratosphere had gradually lost its strength and impetus during the restless night with its lack of sound sleep.

Mama had prepared some medium boiled eggs for breakfast, which were placed in a little egg-cup. The next step to culinary enjoyment was to slice off the top very carefully with a spoon and delicately sprinkle a smidgen of course kosher salt on the open, waiting, welcoming egg. Each spoonful was eaten with a concomitant bite from one of the delicious warm Kaiser rolls that had been picked up earlier at our local grocery store by my mother. At this point, another few grains of salt were added to the remaining egg. Mama strongly felt that a good breakfast was important to successful living. This favorite breakfast was replete with hot coffee that was made every morning in the shining, scrubbed aluminum coffeepot. The satisfying singing sound of the coffee percolating on the stove always contributed to my feeling of pleasure and well being. I still love that special kind of breakfast.

I walked briskly to the bus stop, running the last few feet when I noticed the yellow bus approaching. I recognized some of the people waiting on line and they smiled their recognition. This was good. It was like a club one belonged to. I thought of my friends who were still struggling to get good grades in high school. I did not miss that routine. It seemed that my new life was much more exciting and hopefully more rewarding. Frances and Esther would have more than one year in high school before they had to start hunting for a job.

The subway train propelled me noisily towards the French Powder Puff Co. I closed my eyes and my mind gradually filled with thoughts of Leon who was now attending a radio school sponsored and funded by the government and administered by the state in order to train young people for jobs and careers in various fields. It was a program that was akin to the W.P.A. of the depression. These new trainees were taught by experienced teachers who explained and repeated their lessons until they were well absorbed by the students and they were able to be put their expertise into practice. Leon was interested in the complex components and study of radio and therefore selected that particular area of learning. He believed that if one could not attend college, it was absolutely necessary to have a trade. At that time, he did not foresee how very helpful his selection would be in the future. There was no charge involved in taking the course. As a matter of fact, the government wanted to encourage young men to participate in this program by paying them one dollar a day. It barely covered their meager expenses and carfare, but knowledge and interest in the subject matter was accumulating and giving them a feeling of pride and accomplishment.

The people who were in charge of the program generally were retired army officers. Leon's teacher had been a colonel in the Signal Corps. The inside knowledge was that the United States would probably be involved eventually in the great ongoing international conflict and the army would be in great need, if this occurred, of experienced and trained radio operators and signal corps men.

Europe was being overrun by Hitler's "Blitzkrieg" and England was bleeding. It was the recipient of sustained bombings by Germany's "Luftwaffe." Most nights Londoners and their families had to leave their homes and dash to underground shelters to spend the cold nights. Their cities were being bombed and burned, but Churchill their Prime Minister, dispensed copious quantities of courage and hope.

Mama had not heard from her family in Poland since Hitler had invaded and quickly conquered it in September of 1939. Russia had joined the Axis forces at that time and formed a partnership with fascist Germany and Italy. Russia immediately occupied eastern Poland and the western half had gone to Hitler's forces. Most of Europe was under the domination of Germany, including France, which had fallen quickly in spite of their supposed impregnable Maginot Line. Hitler had made it very clear that he was in favor of the demise of all Jews and other minority groups, such as the gypsies. Worry, and a vague feeling of helplessness and sadness seeped into our not normally contented environment.

Leon was very much interested in his classes and the material that he was learning. He had great respect for his teachers and the job that they were doing. Perhaps this would lead him to a satisfying career.

65

French Powder Puff Company," I sang out when I answered the telephone. Several weeks had passed since I had arrived on the scene and I now felt comfortable and secure with all my debits, credits, and a rather simplified system of bookkeeping. I could easily handle this one girl office. Mr. Braun had loosened up considerably and was almost friendly. Mrs. Braun, who accompanied her husband to the office frequently, remained cool and distant. I thought that this was to my benefit. I did not require her friendship or her company. Mr. Hersch was the man who ran this operation. He was the "brains," and he was a surprisingly pleasant boss.

There was not always enough work to keep me busy, and I would occasionally glance out the huge window on the left of my desk to the huge window facing my office from across the street. It seemed to me that every time I looked in that direction, a pair of eyes planted in a good-looking young man's face was looking back at me. It became a subtle game between us but I knew that it was a mistake to persist. He was an outside presence, and I could tell that he was from a completely different background. He was an unknown who seemed to possess and project an aura of danger. I felt the loss and it was difficult, but I stopped looking.

My full salary of twelve dollars per week was now coming my way regularly. The job agency had been paid off. My friendly co-workers in the area next to the office continued to manufacture the powder puffs that were then neatly packed into cardboard boxes and shipped out to various wholesale buyers. I could hear the girls talking and laughing softly during the day as they did their work. I enjoyed their company at lunchtime, and missed them a little when I did not have enough work to keep me busy. On rare occasions I would join them and help them out for a short while. It was completely relaxing, but I experienced pangs of guilt about participating in factory work. That no doubt, was my father's influence.

Little green leaves were emerging from Mrs. Gensburg's dry bushes in front of our three family house and the trees on our street and Eastern Parkway began taking on a changed look. A fresh soft green covering began to appear on their colorless winter branches. How our spirits welcomed the reminder that spring was on its way. Life was renewing and reawakening, and our buoyant steps reflected the change.

At the time that we were celebrating the coming of spring, involuntarily thoughts of the suffering in Europe invaded our minds. Was my mother's family being starved, beaten and perhaps burned in the ovens set up by Hitler's master plan to rid the world of my people? The hazy, obscure information leaking out that hinted of horrendous occurrences in Europe, we assured ourselves, was merely evil hearsay, vague and ephemeral. The rumors, we hopefully repeated to ourselves, were certainly no more than rumors.

Passover was approaching and it was the occasion for our family to sit down together at our beautiful dark mahogany dining room table to celebrate this unique holiday. There would be a huge specially prepared dinner to be served later on that evening that would do justice to the long tiring hours which my mother had spent cooking, roasting, boiling, and baking a vast variety of delicious foods that were laced with love, great care and elaborate effort. This exceptional meal was called a "Seder." For this particular holiday which lasted eight days, all dishes, pots, pans and cutlery had to be exchanged for others that were only to be used during this specific time. Many ordinary foods could not or should not be eaten. They had to be kosher for this special holiday. During Passover, bread would be replaced by "matzos," large flat pieces of unleavened bread.

Prior to the serving of food at the Seder, there was the reading from the "Hagadah," which told the story of the Hebrews' escape from slavery in Egypt. The reading was lengthy and beautifully ceremonial. At one point, the youngest male would have to ask the "Four Questions," which were listed in the Hagadah. It was little Murray's responsibility. He had just turned seven, and he felt slightly nervous and insecure even though he knew his part perfectly. However, regardless of his feelings and his vulnerable age, he would fulfill his obligation. He knew that his role was important and that he would experience a strong sense of pride and satisfaction when he had completed his task. He would be praised by all. To ease the way, there had been much rehearsal prior to the event. After Murray would ask the "Four Questions," the reading from the Hagadah would continue with the answers.

The table was set with Mama's beautiful old white lace tablecloth and lovely Passover dishes that had been removed from the top shelves of the kitchen closets for its temporary service. They would be returned once again to their yearly resting-place after the holidays. Delicate crystal stemware for the pouring of the ceremonial wine graced our table, and lighted our lives with its brilliance.

We were all seated and waiting in quiet anticipation. Papa's face assumed a pleased gentle demeanor as he surveyed his beloved family sitting around the table in their best clothes waiting expectantly for him to begin. He did not acknowledge to himself that he was the patriarch of the family, but we knew that he was. A slight familiar smile played about his lips. Perhaps it was a little nervous display while he contemplated the importance of the rite. It enriched his sweet face. He lifted his wineglass and sang the "brocha," the prayer for the wine, and we were content. The Seder had begun. Charlie sat next to his wife, our Sylvia, and recited the prayer after my father, followed by Jack's resonant beautiful voice. After a while, when the readings in Hebrew by those who really knew how and who were proficient at it became slightly tedious and seemed never-ending and ongoing, a little whispered conversation could be heard. The women, the three of us, were guilty of this minor indiscretion that was mildly acceptable, but there were songs to be sung, interspersed with the readings, and we raised our voices enthusiastically at the proper times and enjoyed the melodic interludes.

Finally, finally, it was time to eat! Very carefully my little mother carried in a twenty-two pound turkey on a huge platter from the kitchen. That was the "piece de resistance" that would be eaten after the wonderful tasty beginnings. Mama paused for a moment, leaned against the wall as she entered the dining room with her luscious and ponderous burden and smilingly commented, using one of her favorite expressions. "Please, kinderlach, eat very slowly. It took me a long time to prepare." We had difficulty following her amusing instructions. What a feast we experienced and enjoyed! What a feeling of family bonding and friendship! No doubt Mama was exhausted after so much preparation preceding the holiday, so much cooking and baking for the Passover Seders, so much serving and catering to the family's needs and desires.

The evening's festivities came to a quiet and satisfying conclusion. Sylvia and I slowly rose and started clearing the table. Everyone else remained seated and pleased with subdued conversation. We insisted that Mama join them, in spite of her protests, while we washed and dried the never-ending supply of dishes, pots, pans and delicate glasses. A dishwashing machine had never seen the inside of that apartment. I noticed that Jack leaned over and whispered a welcome compliment in Murray's ear for a job well done. It had been a great evening. However, for me, the evening was not over. When Sylvia and Charlie were ready to leave, I felt free to go outside to meet with Leon. There was still enough time left for us to enjoy each other's company for a while. My parents said, "Go. Have a good time." I bounded down the steps, paused, and then walked slowly across the street in what I thought was my most casual and sophisticated manner. Frances, who lived in the building next to Leon, was on her stoop with Mutty from "Club 18." Leon was there too, waiting for me as we had prearranged.

Frances had continued to be a somewhat close friend. I had partially forgiven her for her treachery during the time of my sweet sixteen fiasco when she had purposely neglected to invite my boyfriend Leon to my big and important celebration. However, I never forgot. My friend Pearl would never have been capable of such duplicity. The April air was mild and fresh, stroking and lightly caressing our cheeks with its gentle breezes. We were in high spirits. We were all supported by the underpinnings of positive and happy high-voltage teen-age emotions and we tried not to think about the serious nature of life and the difficulties that occurred when they were least expected. We depended upon our inner resources and any available outside support to successfully handle and cope with these moments, these exigencies that regularly cropped up. We had a good time together talking and laughing and we decided to take a little walk along budding, tree-lined Eastern Parkway. After a while, we sat down on an inviting bench that was dimly lit by a street lamp and chatted and joked. Fun and laughter continued until the hour dictated that it was time to go home. Leon walked me to my door and entered the little entrance foyer for his goodnight kiss, or two, or three. It was good.

66

Club "18" became a hangout, a retreat. It was also a cheap date which was fine with all the girls who understood and empathized with the fact that their boyfriends finances were indeed limited.

Once in a while, some of the guys would get together and decide to take their girls on a special date, a real date. Leon surprised me by arranging for us to go out with Mutty who had an old vehicle that resembled an automobile, along with Mutty's current girlfriend. Another two couples would follow us in their car to the Rustic Cabin, which was a little nightclub located in the wilds of New Jersey. This unusual, almost thrilling event, was set up to celebrate my seventeenth birthday.

I did not want my parents to be too concerned about our little pilgrimage, and therefore did not fill in all the details. They were aware of the fact that Mutty was parked downstairs waiting for Leon and me to come down and join him. I once again noticed Papa walking casually into our living room from the kitchen, looking through the window, and writing down Mutty's license plate number. I restrained a little laugh that was mixed with love. He was so caring, and he hoped, protective. What could he really accomplish if I ran into trouble? Not much, I assumed.

We drove and drove and the other two Club 18 couples followed us in their car. Finally we arrived at a little out-of-the-way nightspot that sported flashing lights that surrounded the sign, "Rustic Cabin." Four very young men and their younger companions gratefully emerged from their uncomfortable, unchanging sitting positions and happily followed the leader, Smoky, who had been there once before and had made the reservations for this evening. He and Barney had told us that we would dance to a great little band, and that we would love the music. "The lead singer is wonderful," Barney exclaimed.

We entered the hazy, smoke-filled scene and I immediately absorbed the surrounding excitement. The music was soft and its beat was insistent. I succumbed and enjoyed its entry into my psyche and inner being.

I had never experienced this particular kind of environment. It seemed so sophisticated and grown up. I was extraordinarily impressed, and felt a little out of place.

We were lead to a table nearby and seated. Very soon, a pretty young waitress wearing a very short black skirt enhanced by a small white apron approached our table. We all ordered non-alcoholic drinks and snacks and settled in for a good time. The music was inviting and the other guys all got up to dance with their girls. Leon who never felt too comfortable on the dance floor was nevertheless anxious to please me. He rose and led me to the crowded postage-stamp dance floor where our friends were already expressing their enthusiasm and natural ability. The music turned mellow and the female singer, ensconced and enclosed in a red sequined gown, approached the raised podium, joined the band, and softly and melodiously began singing a romantic ballad. Her appreciative audience started swaying to the warm, slow rhythm of her song. Leon and I were doing very little dancing, but much hugging and swaying. This was such a perfect birthday celebration, and Leon was so special. I silently wondered, "Why did I also enjoy going out with others? No doubt I was still an immature person."

Leon edged me over to a darkened corner of the Rustic Cabin and said, "I have something to show you. It's for your birthday." My look of pleasure and open delight must have spurred him on. "You know, you look so pretty tonight." That was a great deal for him to express romantically. He always seemed to be afraid to reveal too much of himself, but that latent trait that some might consider a flaw, always made him more exciting and interesting to me.

I could barely contain myself. "What do you want to show me?" He reached into his pocket and took out a little jewelry box. He handed it to me and I felt my heart fill with what must be taken for love. I stood on my toes and reached up as far as my five feet allowed and planted a light kiss on his welcoming cheek. A mere "Thank you" can never be sufficient, but perhaps a look of love is. I opened the box and there on a golden chain rested a very beautifully etched heart-shaped gold locket. How elegant and lovely it was. I was truly surprised and delighted. I turned it over, and on the back the following words were engraved, "To Beulah, with love, from Leo, 6-20-41." I'm wearing that locket today, fifty-seven years later. Its beauty has never diminished. Its importance has never diminished. When I touch its smooth cool surface, it transports me back to nostalgic innocent love.

We had a great time that night. Smoky, who looked skinnier than ever, and handsome heavy lidded Barney, could not restrain their high spirits and talent. When the band struck up the Lindy Hop, they rose as one and took over the miniature dance floor as others willingly gave way to their exciting jitterbug performance. Their talent was overt, and its pleasure and power extended to all. Everyone present watched and smiled their approval and enthusiasm. There was a good deal of applause when the dance ended and Barney and Smoky made their way back to our table with the satisfied smiles of conquerors on their faces. Their girlfriends looked on in justifiable pride and admiration. "You were wonderful!" they loudly exclaimed.

The band continued playing, pleasing all with its great sound and selections. To us, this was the real thing. We loved the pseudo sophistication, the crowded room, the smoky atmosphere, the music, loud and rhythmic, alternating its pace with mellow romantic ballads.

Suddenly the band stopped playing. There was a darkening in the Cabin and two waiters approached our table, one carrying a small birthday cake lighted with candles. Both waiters started singing and harmonizing "Happy Birthday to You." My mixed emotions made me want to laugh and cry simultaneously. I sensibly did neither. Our friends joined in, and I had to make a wish and blow out the candles. It was embarrassing and wonderful to be the center of attraction. The lovely gold locket hung around my neck and was noticed, complimented and commented upon by all.

The drive home was long and tedious. We were contentedly tired but very much wide-awake. The excitement of the evening still had us in its grip and the music continued to resound in the silence. Mutty was a good careful driver and brought us safely home. It had been a special celebration and Leon's goodnight kisses were a little deeper, and more meaningful.

It was quite late when I tread ever so lightly upon the stairs and quietly opened the wooden door with my key. I felt breathless and exquisitely happy, particularly in anticipation for the moment when I would share the pleasure of having received my beautiful locket with my parents. I knew that anything that made me happy would have that effect on them.

There was a soft light in the kitchen to welcome me home, and sure enough my parents were still awake in their bed. Now that I was safely home, they could sleep.

"Beulah, did you have a good time?" whispered Mama. "Wonderful. It was wonderful!"

"That's good," said Papa. "Now, let's get some sleep." "Goodnight," I answered. I'll extend my pleasure, and show them the locket at breakfast, I thought. "Goodnight."

67

Pearl had one more year of high school' before graduation and she and her boyfriend Bob, were an inseparable twosome.

Much to my amazement, she and Bob were talking about getting married. It was hard to accept the fact that sensible Bob was willing to think about such a serious step at this vulnerable time of their lives. She was seventeen and he was two years older. He was an extremely verbal and clever fellow and appeared to be quite mature for his years. Nevertheless, his powerful libido got in the way of his common sense. The times in which we were growing up dictated to most of us the unspoken rule that girls should remain virgins, or as close as possible to that pure state, until marriage vows were exchanged. Pearl decided to drop out of her last year in high school to become a bride. Bob was ecstatic that she had succumbed to his pleas. "How foolish they are," I thought, but once again I kept my opinions to myself.

Pearl's family was supportive, and her sisters gathered round her with exuberance and encouragement. A little wedding party for some relatives and friends was arranged. Bob's homely face smiled through the ceremony and the blessings given by the local rabbi. Pearl looked queenly and radiant. She carried herself with dignity and grace.

"I must be wrong," I thought, "to have such negative feelings in the midst of their joy." My heart opened and allowed their love to gently infiltrate. Leon stood beside me during the ceremony and held my hand. He seemed so dear and I was exquisitely aware of how closely bonded we were. However, my mind declared privately, "We would never be so foolish."

Bob stepped hard on the champagne glass that had been carefully wrapped in a cloth napkin and placed near his foot after the rabbi had ceremoniously intoned, "I now pronounce you husband and wife." Upon hearing the breaking of the delicate glass, everyone shouted, "Mazeltov! Good Luck," while Bob passionately kissed my best friend.

A lovely celebration followed the heart melting bonding of two very young souls. Bob's family, politically right of center, educated and elegant, responded in a quiet respectful manner to some of the casual leftist and radical conversation issuing from Pearl's earthy side of the family. Tense moments were not permitted to develop, and we all happily partook of the wonderful food and refreshments presented as a buffet luncheon. We enjoyed watching the loving looks that the bride and groom exchanged. The sun shone in a cloudless sky, and "All was right with the world."

The French Powder Puff Co. continued to occupy the major part of my world. The daily routine became pleasant and productive. I was able to fulfill my responsibilities while learning some of the heretofore hidden aspects of running a business. Mr. Hersch was a good teacher and I was an avid learner and grateful to him for his patience. Mr. Braun turned out to be the kind of person who possessed a kind, blustery personality. I felt comfortable in his presence and I began to like him a lot. His wife remained a cold bystander who had very little interest in me and did not hesitate to display it. I was happy with this development. I subsequently learned that they were refugees from Hitler's Germany. That knowledge brought uneasy thoughts to mind regarding my mother's family.

Poland had been invaded and quickly conquered in 1939. It continued to be a closed slave state of Germany and knowledge of its internal affairs was unknown and unavailable to the outside world. The German propaganda machine issued the political news that it wanted the world to hear, believe and absorb. However, little alarming rivulets of rumors had begun to flow into the news channels.

France had been successfully overrun by Germany, and England continued to suffer heavily through the consistent air attacks and bombings of their cities. London was burning and bleeding but its dreadfully harried populace continued to display an inordinate supply of courage, and it continued to cope and fight back as best as it could.

Russia and Germany had signed a peace alliance but Hitler's "Mein Kampf" had made it perfectly clear and steadfastly maintained that the U.S.S.R. had to be destroyed. The Ukraine, part of Russia, was the breadbasket of Europe, and oil, which was not available in Germany, was partially supplied by Russia at this time. Germany secretly and diligently planned to obtain these essential items for its own use.

For the first time since 1918 the United States had instituted a draft for military service, and young men were being inducted into the armed forces. This occurred in spite of the fact that the country was settled in the midst of an intensive, powerful isolationist attitude that was pervasive and prevalent. Huge conventions were being held all over the country that was paid for by Germany, German agents and sympathizers. The evolving premise was that the draft had been initiated and instituted because of President Roosevelt's tremendous influence and desire to prepare the country for the possibility of war that to him appeared imminent. He was an adamant Anglophile, and made it plain that he hoped to be of aid to England during its fight for survival. England was on the brink of total disaster, and to the Allies, Hitler represented the "Devil."

Russia, still in the midst of a pact with Nazi Germany, fed its loyal American communists their orders that they object loudly and fiercely to the United States joining the British in their fight against fascism and totalitarianism.

Pearl's family joined their communist comrades by loudly proclaiming their isolationist slogans in support of Russia. A song emerged.

"The Yanks are not coming,
One hundred thousand strong,
We're staying in our own back yard,
`cause that's where we belong."

This song went on for several stanzas, loud and clear. Pearl was disassociated from her family's politics in spite of the fact that she and her new husband shared their apartment. She appeared to be oblivious as to the precarious status of the world. She was a married lady and happy in her role. She remained uninvolved in the views and interests of her parents especially now that she was fully aware that her husband silently and strongly disapproved of their political opinions.

68

The summer's arrival with its concomitant heat had its advantages. The longer days were filled with eagerly awaited opportunities. The parks welcomed our presence when the heat of the sun's rays subsided. They invited us to partake of its soft evening breezes, its tree-lined quiet pathways and its cool lakes where our youthful muscled companions rowed us about. It was a gift that was given us occasionally at the end of a long day spent at a desk.

The welcome break in the workday always came at noon when I combed my hair quickly, refreshed my lipstick and joined my factory friends for lunch. I ordered what I considered to be a delicious and inexpensive afternoon meal of scrambled egg on a fresh, crisp Kaiser roll. It was topped with poppy seeds that provided a special taste that I loved. It was always accompanied by a cup of coffee to which I generously added several spoonsful of sugar. The caffeine jolt was reinforced with a second cup. I felt raring to go! The girls from the back remained fun companions during our lunch hour. The longer I knew them, the more I liked these real earthy, no nonsense, basic women. I always look forward to their company and this pleasing break in the day.

I told them about Pearl's marriage, and they laughed when they responded, "Your friend is nuts. She should have stayed in high school and married a year later, after getting her diploma. Maybe she's already pregnant." The ironic fact was that not one of them had graduated from high school. Perhaps that was why they understood the importance of education and the implications of what they considered to be a serious mistake of sound judgment.

"When are you getting married?" tongue in cheek, from Tessie, who was built like a small fortress.

"I'm in no hurry," I laughingly responded. "Leon and I don't even talk about it. I feel much too young to even think about it," I added adamantly. Actually, I privately thought about it a good deal, and was mildly jealous of my best friend and her subtly approved and accepted sex life.

Leon was studying and continuing to work hard at the government radio school that he was attending. He was becoming proficient at learning the Morse code, and was also gaining a great deal of knowledge about radio and electricity from his talented and dedicated teachers. The radio industry was always searching for competent technicians, and the school had contacts with Emerson Radio, Columbia Broadcasting Company and the International Telephone and Telegraph Company.

The students hoped to eventually gain employment with one of these prestigious companies or any others like them. Meanwhile, the moments, the minutes, the weeks and our lives raced by.

69

Saturday morning, I waited at the bus stop on Saratoga Avenue for the ride that would take me part of the way to Sylvia's apartment house. I had to transfer for the "Avenue J" bus, which would bring me into the lovely residential tree lined area of Flatbush. My family was happy that she had moved to what was considered to be a better neighborhood. The fact that her little apartment was on the third floor with no elevator to ease the way was of little consequence. Sylvia was young and strong. The neighborhood that she and Charlie had moved to was the important factor. The large, old, once elegant lobby was also a positive feature. It lent a vague reminiscence of having seen better days. It was a long walk from Sylvia's apartment to the shopping district but that was almost accepted as an asset. No crass commercial enterprises nearby!

Charlie could and did bring home lots of groceries and culinary bonuses from the large grocery establishment where he was employed. He worked a long day on Saturday, which meant that I could spend several hours in Sylvia's company, not sharing her with anyone. What a sweet treat it was to knock at her door and wait expectantly until she appeared and greeted me with her smiling, welcoming words. Breakfast was almost ready and hunger pangs would be satisfied in a little while, when it was time once again to bite into her freshly prepared "French Toast" and relish its soft buttery egg flavor. This had to be a preview of heaven. Sylvia had quickly become a great little cook. She was such a married lady!

Unfortunately, it is not a perfect world and Sylvia had a well-meaning, loud-mouthed neighbor living in the apartment next to hers. There was an abrupt knock at the door and Mrs. Branlow presented herself. "How about offering me a cup of coffee, Sylvia?" I held my breath. Our time together was so precious to me and it was about to be destroyed. My sister did not wish to encourage Mrs. Loud-Mouth, but she was too polite and kind to turn her neighbor away. Perhaps, too, Mrs. Branlow filled a need for a little companionship on occasion.

Sylvia invited her in and served her. We were compelled to listen as she endlessly discussed her neighbors and their failings in a very loud, headache inducing voice. I felt my eyes glaze over with helplessness and boredom, but at last, after downing two cups of coffee, she rose and thankfully left.

"Now that she's gone," Sylvia said, "I want to give you some very exciting news. I was going to hold out until Charlie and I came to dinner next Friday night, but I can't wait. I'm pregnant!"

"Wow," I exploded! "That's wonderful! That's great! I can hardly believe it. I'll be a 'tante.' Imagine being called Aunt Beulah."

Sylvia calmly continued. "Mom and Pop will be here a little later to visit. They're bringing some cake that she baked, something that Charlie particularly likes, and I'll tell them then. Beulah, I'm so happy about this and so is Charlie. I feel very much at home here. Our little place is wonderfully comfortable, and I think kind of pretty. There are some very nice women in the building with little children and they're quite friendly. One of the big things that I think about is my job. It's an important one, and it pays well. I make as much as some of the salesmen. I hate the idea of giving it up, but I'd feel much better about leaving if I knew that you could take over my job when it's time for me to go. My boss doesn't have any idea of what's been going on in my mind and body, but he's a good person and I really like him. More importantly, he likes me and he likes the job I do. I'll try to talk him into taking you on, and naturally I'll give you a fantastic reference." We both laughed a lot at that predictable statement. "I'm hoping that he'll request you at our union, and that they will allow you to replace me when the time comes. I could break you in for two weeks which wouldn't be enough time for you to learn the ropes, but it would have to do."

"I'm having a lot of difficulty absorbing all this stuff," I said, "but to me the most incredible thing, Sylvia, is the amazing fact that you're having a baby. You're so matter of fact about it. I still think about it in terms of miracles. The most important thing to think about, I guess, is your health and taking care of yourself. How do you feel?"

"Great," she answered, "except for a lot of morning nausea. After a little while it disappears, and I'm fine."

"Wow!" I repeated stupidly. "Wait until Mama and Pop hear the news. Mom will faint!"

"Don't kid yourself She's stronger than she looks. She's been through so much in her life that this good news will be like a marvelous present to both of them. Maybe they would have preferred for us to have waited a while, but I can't wait to see their faces when I tell them. Beulah, I know I'm repeating myself, but I'm so excited and happy about this. You know one of Mama's many favorite sayings is that a baby brings its own luck."

We got through with breakfast at noon, and then we raided the candy drawer that Charlie kept filled with luscious chocolates and a variety of other sweet delicacies. We were anxiously anticipating the arrival of Mama and Papa, and I was filled with excitement at the thought of my parent's reaction when they would learn the overwhelming, completely unexpected news. The anticipation and arrival of new life was the most profound experience that I could envision. That emotional and visceral response has never changed.

The time had passed quickly and we had enjoyed good food and good conversation, but now we were caught up in a spirit of impatience. Where were my parents? They should have been here a little while ago. Finally, there was that welcome awaited knock at the door and there they were at last, smiling and laden with packages containing food stuff and some baked goods that Mama had prepared in advance. Murray was with them, holding a little shopping bag. He looked so sweet and happy to be helpful. "We brought you some good things to eat. Mama baked them yesterday," he breathlessly said. As a matter of fact, they all seemed a little breathless after hiking up three flights of stairs.

"Come in. Come in," Sylvia called out as she ushered them into her bright little kitchen. "I've fresh coffee and we'll have some of Mom's goodies with it." I could not believe that she had room for any more food. Perhaps it was true that one ate for two when pregnant. Sylvia kissed our parents lightly, but gave Murray a hug and a resounding kiss on the cheek.

"You're growing up so fast," she said to him. "I can't believe that you're such a big fellow." My small pipsqueak brother smiled shyly and could not hide the pleasure he felt at hearing her words. He was one of the shorter boys in his second grade class and needed all the encouragement he could get. I could relate to that. Jack was a wonderful big brother to him, and he seemed to have taken Murray under his wing now that I was quite grown up. Jack had always been a strong influence in my life, and I was delighted that Murray could share that benefit.

The apartment filled up with excitement and joy at Sylvia's announcement of her pregnancy. Mama could hardly contain herself. "How wonderful! Mazeltov! How wonderful!" she repeated and repeated and repeated. Papa's face lit up and the reserved quiet little smile that always indicated extreme pleasure appeared on his lovable face. I laughed aloud with delight. Their expressions were so readable, so typical and so endearing. They gave themselves away so easily and did not even know it.

As my family was experiencing total acceptance and tremendous joy in learning of Sylvia's pregnancy, another family was also being informed about a forthcoming blessed event. On the other end of the continuum, my friend Pearl's family was experiencing an overwhelming sense of doom when she and Bob announced, two months after her seventeenth birthday, that she was going to have a baby. Her parents had hoped that several years would elapse before they would receive this kind of news. They naturally felt that their daughter was too young, and economically and psychologically unprepared to deal with motherhood. I don't believe that abortion was ever considered. Babies were much too valuable. My mother's favorite aphorism came to mind once again. "Babies bring their own luck."

Pearl was married to a fine young man and the only option was total acceptance and loving support that her family was very capable and desirous of giving. When Pearl told me of her condition she appeared to be happy and content, but perhaps reconciled would be a better description of her true feelings. Her young husband Bob loved her dearly and was very positive and encouraging. They would continue to live with Pearl's parents until they could hopefully make it on their own. Bob was always bringing Pearl a token gift of a single rose or a very small bouquet of flowers to help express his complete love.

Pearl's mother presented another picture. Whenever I visited my friends, she would manage to get me alone in the kitchen and her eyes would fill with bitter tears. "Wouldn't you think that they would know enough to be more careful, Beulah? If they were old enough to get married, they should have known how to be more responsible. Bob's a fine boy, but he still can't make a living for a family. My poor husband, his blood pressure is way up."

"Mrs. Becker," I responded, "don't underestimate Pearl or Bob. They'll make it on their own after a little while. Your son-in-law is a special person, and he will make a good living for his little family. He just needs some time. Remember that they're both very young. Pearl's lucky that she has parents like you. You know, Bob's a good husband and she'll have a fine baby."

Her mood lifted and she gave me a limited smile and a total hug. "Tell my pregnant daughter and Bob to come into the kitchen. We'll have some coffee and cake. Maybe Pearl should have milk." I did as I was told and we enjoyed being together.

70

The isolationists and their strange bedfellows the Communists, were still pushing their agenda in spite of the fact that Japan had signed a ten-year military pact with Germany and Italy. This evil triumvirate joined together with the expectation of taking over the world. Hitler was perpetrating and perpetuating unbelievable acts of horror, cruelty and death to Jews in the hope and desire of wiping them out. Many of the countries that he had conquered were happy to give up their Jews to Hitler's deranged tortuous plans. Later knowledge confirmed the establishment of death camps and gas chambers for quick disposal of Hitler's innocent victims whom he hated with fierce insanity.

The months flowed by and I continued to grow up and hopefully mature with the passage of time. Sylvia felt fine and in spite of her progressing pregnancy and daily nausea, she remained conscientious and continued to work hard. As I sat at my desk at the French Powder Puff Company and attempted to pass some empty time, my eyes were drawn occasionally to that loft across the street where that strange peasant Slavic face often stared back at me. His eyes were like black marbles that reflected the light that drew me to them. They were mesmerizing and elusively frightening. Why did I look? I prayed that I would never encounter him during my lunch hour, and I fortunately never did.

Americans could barely believe the blasting and often hysterical and frenzied announcements issuing from their radios on December 7, 1941. Japanese planes had attacked Pearl Harbor even while their representatives were in the United States talking peace. Sixteen hundred sailors aboard the Arizona were drowned when their ship was bombed and sunk. Six hundred others of the armed forces lost their lives during the unprecedented and unexpected bombing. The United States was in a state of devastating shock. However, the entire country for the first time in years, was totally united because of Japan's complete and deadly treachery. They had talked peace, but had attacked and dropped bombs before declaring war.

President Roosevelt went on the radio and spoke of December 7th, 1941 as a day that would live in infamy, and announced that he would ask that Congress declare a state of war against the Empire of Japan. Congress responded with but one negative vote from Janet Rankin of Montana. We were at war with Japan! Now the country was anxiously waiting to see what Germany and Italy would do. We held our breath. Four days later Hitler made up the mind of Germany and his ally Italy, which was more like a satellite at this time. They both declared war on the United States. It was not assured, but it was expected.

Hundreds of thousands of Americans rushed to enlist in all branches of the armed forces. Leon went down the following day and the lines that had formed at the selective service office seemed to extend for miles. A uniformed sergeant emerged from the building and informed groups of twenty to return on subsequent days since their office was only set up to deal with draftees. They would begin to induct small groups of volunteers each day along with the draftees. Leon's group was told to return in February.

Meanwhile, Leon continued to attend radio school and the benefits were accumulating. He was learning more and more as time passed. The instructor informed the class that now that the country was at war, those who wished to enlist would do well to join the "Reserves." In this way, their education in this particular field would continue and they would not be in uniform until their training was complete. Moreover, the top ten percent in the class would be moved along for more advanced training. The instructor told those men that wished to join up, to see a particular individual at the "Reserves Center" where they would be sworn into the Reserves. When they finished their courses they would enter the Army Signal Corp.

Leon appeared once again at the induction center on his twentieth birthday in February. He went through the entire physical, including a short session with an army psychiatrist who asked him, "Leon, do you like girls?"

Leon passed the test with flying colors, but was refused induction into the Reserves when they noticed that he was under age for enlistees. He needed his parent's permission. They handed him a form to be signed and he was back the next day with the necessary signatures. Much to his dismay, he had to repeat the entire physical. The same psychiatrist asked him the same question. Obviously, he thought that perhaps Leon had changed his mind. Leon was now a bona fide member of the army reserves.

Things did not change for a while except that he continued studying radio in an army-training center. That was the way the people in the Reserves wanted it. They needed knowledgeable and experienced men for the Signal Corps and they moved the top ten percent in the class along to more advanced classes from time to time. Leon was one of them.

71

Sylvia continued her work as a full-charge bookkeeper in the upholstery, drapery and fabric corner store on the East Side of Manhattan. The owners were jobbers and sold fabric to upholstery shops all over the city. They also did a large retail business, particularly on Sundays. Wives, who were ready to buy beautiful fabric for new drapes, or to reupholster old furniture, were accompanied by their husbands who had the day off from work. Lots of cash and checks exchanged hands and the three salesmen, the boss Mr. H., and his very bright, energetic son, were out there on the floor dressed in their most attractive personalities. They were ready and highly motivated to do business. They were all skilled at promoting sales and measuring out all kinds of exotic and ordinary fabric by the yard. They accomplished this with precision and artfulness. No doubt it helped build customer confidence. The salesmen would also suggest and recommend particular upholsterers, who just happened to be our wholesale customers and were in the retail business of upholstering and creating custom-made draperies. Several of the salesmen had become proficient and experienced in hanging the draperies for those who requested this service. They earned extra money in this moonlighting venture.

Sylvia was nearly at the end of her pregnancy, and was anxious to have me replace her in what she considered to be a good job and a very satisfying, friendly business environment. Of course, working on Sundays was a distinct disadvantage, but no job was ideal, was it? She was treated with respect, and she loved the sense of camaraderie that existed. The pay was relatively good, and it was true that she was earning as much as some of the salesmen. The head honcho salesman, Sylvan, was the union representative in our store, and he thought that if Mr. H. vigorously requested me, the union would acquiesce even though I was not a union member at the time. I immediately applied for membership and was accepted because the owner of the business, Mr. H., strongly insisted that he wanted and needed my services as a replacement bookkeeper. I paid my union dues, and was in.

I happily gave two weeks notice to the "French Powder Puff Company" and much to my surprise and satisfaction they gave me one extra week's salary as a bonus when I left. My loyal factory friends treated me to my sandwich lunch and insisted on ordering a large portion of chocolate cake for dessert on my last day. I was already beginning to miss them. I knew that my new job would lack the easy calm that I enjoyed and had become accustomed to.

My new job opportunity filled me with mild terror. I knew that Sylvia's phone kept ringing too often. Cash, checks, invoices and bills of lading were constantly being handed up to her tiny office that was located on a little balcony above the main floor of the store where all the selling took place. Six wooden steps led up to this compact refuge from customers and salesmen below. Sylvia assured me that I would rapidly become accustomed to the busy routine and grow to love it. She promised that it would be an interesting and gratifying job. I had confessed to my sister that I was often bored with my first job since there was not always enough work for me to do. That was why I probably spent time looking out the window. "That will never be the case here," she promised. Sylvia and I went to work together for the next two weeks. She, accompanied by her big belly and lots of minor and occasional major discomfort, sought to encourage and instruct me in the job. She was my heroine and I trusted her judgment implicitly. The bookkeeping system had been set up many years before by a certified public accountant and was professionally sound. The accountant and an auditor made monthly visits to her office to check on all entries and calculations. I would have to learn and relearn the correct methods of coping with all aspects of this new challenge.

The entire staff of salesmen, two bosses, Mr. H. and his son Julie, plus the sweeper reached out to welcome me on my first day. They were a fun-loving group, and Mr. H. thought that it was entirely appropriate to lightly pat my seventeen year old rump as I attempted to walk up those six wooden steps leading up to my new home away from home. I smiled politely at this old reprobate who warmly smiled back.

A cigar, which I later learned was ever present, was rooted in his mouth at a rakish angle giving him a charming, impudent look. I surely did not want to antagonize him so early in our relationship. Besides, I surmised and hoped that he was being fatherly, albeit completely unlike my own father. I also overwhelmingly loved the thought that my starting salary was twenty-three dollars a week, just about twice what I had earned at my previous job. Sylvia had preceded me up the stairs and was already seated at her desk with an open ledger to start my intensive learning period.

The two weeks of the so-called "breaking in" period was over much too quickly, and it was time for my sister to leave. Mr. H. gave her a generous bonus and took her out for an elegant lunch with the staff. I realized how difficult it would be for me to attempt to replace her. Everyone marveled at her efficiency and enjoyed her loving personality. It was terrifying to contemplate being responsible for any errors I might make now that she would not be around to correct them. There was sure to be an outbreak and result in many embarrassing moments. I sadly realized that I was a novice and that I was on my own!

Part of the job involved handling a good deal of cash and numerous checks that were received from wholesale and retail customers. It was my responsibility to make sure that all the figures balanced and the money that was received from those who had accounts with us was properly credited to their particular page in the Accounts Receivable ledger. Each day I made up the daily deposit that I carried to the Bowery Bank, which was located several blocks from where I worked. There was absolutely no thought of fear in my mind. I, and apparently all the bookkeepers in the neighborhood, felt secure and safe. We walked calmly and serenely to the bank and made our deposit. We never considered the possibility of being robbed even though our deposits to the bank very often consisted of many hundreds of dollars in cash in addition to the checks that buyers submitted for their purchases. We were not really naïve. The times were different.

The ringing phone was a welcome interruption to my intense concentrations, and I enjoyed the little break to socialize and perhaps mildly flirt with the older upholsterers who were sweet and safe, and who needed information about obtaining a few more yards of a particular piece of cloth. Very often the upholsterers would try to economize and buy a little less yardage than was necessary for the job. Therefore their shortages. Retail customers also called regularly to find out if their draperies were ready, and when Sol or Murray would be ready to hang them.

Sylvan, our big bluff union representative who was always fighting for his people in our store, was our main man and the main salesman. Certainly Julie, the boss's son, was his equal in selling with his strong motivation and equally strong likeable personality. Each man had a particular talent. The boss Mr. H., with his persuasive soft manner inspired trust. He was subtle, but powerful. His cigar was always in place in his mouth and his fingers encircled it lovingly as he gently puffed away. Very often his middle finger would lightly embrace his nose. He appeared a picture of contentment with this favorite pose.

I was still "breaking in" and learning on the job. The boss was patient with me, but there was so much to learn. Mr. H. would dictate a letter in his slightly foreign accent and slightly broken English. I would take it down in broken shorthand, and have to type it in proper English. We were a good working team. I was turning into his editor. The responsibilities were growing greater and greater and becoming easier and easier. The days flew by and when I made out the payroll on Fridays, which proved to be a formidable job for a beginner, I was delighted to collect my salary. However, I was not delighted to have to work on Sundays. That was one of the days that Leon and I used to spend together. Another day during the week was offered as a replacement, and it was an offer that I couldn't refuse.

Sundays, surprisingly, turned out to be the best and most interesting day of the week. The store filled up with retail shoppers all hoping to get a great buy on their purchases. The East Side of Manhattan was well known for its bargain prices. Some of the clientele came in with their upholsterers or decorators who almost always managed to get a commission on the sale. The customers would have received a lower price very often, if they came in by themselves. Relatives were the easiest mark.

The rush started relatively early and usually lasted all day. The noise, the conversations, the indecisions, the exchange of money, and the ringing of the telephone all added to the interest, excitement and the quick passage of time.

The union allowed an hour for lunch, and everyone in the store took turns rushing to a coffee shop located a block away. It seemed to be the main meeting eating-place for the bosses and their staff. When Sylvia was still with me initially, she introduced me to a number of bookkeepers from various stores who ate at this restaurant daily. They were a congenial welcoming group, several of whom were middle-aged and unmarried. Every day, with unvarying taste, I would order poached eggs, a baked potato and toast. I would place the eggs on my delicious buttered mashed baked potato and happily devour my favorite midday meal. Dessert was always the same. I had no desire to deviate. The chocolate covered éclair, stuffed with custard and downed with two cups of coffee graced with cream filled me great joy.

Sundays were the exceptions. There was always a feeling of holiday spirit when several bookkeepers would meet at one P.M. at Ratner's Dairy Restaurant on Delancey Street. This meal was above and beyond special for me. Their baked halibut and vegetables in a savory tomato sauce was a gustatory delight that I could not and would not resist. The accompanying little onion rolls were superb. Dessert was not required and kept the price in line. I thoroughly enjoyed the company of those lovely hard-working women, and they began to treat me like a little sister. The job was getting better all the time.

72

It was hard to bear the pleasure. It was overwhelming, excessive! After a long and arduous labor Sylvia presented the family with the greatest gift, a healthy little baby boy. Charlie was thrilled and expressed his emotions openly and happily. Mama cried with joy and happiness. Sylvia's ordeal was over, and everyone was filled with delight and a strong sense of thanksgiving.

Papa unwittingly expressed his satisfaction and suppressed preference at the arrival of a grandson by repeating, "It's a boy. It's a boy!" We all thanked G-d for the well being of mother and child. Baby Leonard was a sweet-tempered and beautiful new member of our family and he was adored.

Leon's mother continued to invite me for occasional Friday night meals, and I found the friendly family atmosphere very pleasant and compelling. His father was an interesting gentleman who was a Norman Thomas socialist. He was an ardent anti-Communist in spite of the horrible depression that seemed to have bred many Communists among the depressed and unemployed working class. He teased me often about my union affiliation with "Local 65" which definitely had leftist leanings. I was not in the least interested in politics at that time, but did feel that our union strongly protected and helped its members in many ways.

Moe was always present at these meals and I could not help but admire his handsome demeanor and meticulous dress. The more conversational he was, the quieter Leon became. It was evident to me that there was a mild spirit of dissention between them. Moe did not hesitate to utter a lightly disguised demeaning remark regarding Leon's mode of dress, which he cloaked in what he considered to be humor. He was the big brother and felt free to dispense his brand of kindly criticism for Leon's benefit. I knew that Leon couldn't care less and was ostensibly uninterested in clothes, but I found Moe's smiling and loving disapproval of his brother, in front of his brother's girl, slightly offensive. However, no doubt aware that he was good-looking and charming, he obviously believed that I appreciated his supposedly humorous, brotherly jabs. I never did. His attention to me remained polite and slightly flirtatious.

The Friday night meal, as usual, was carefully prepared and delicious. Leon's mother always treated me warmly and made me feel very welcome. She seemed happy that I was her son's choice, and so was I. Mr. Brown treated me with sweet affection. Nevertheless, I still preferred my chicken soup without Ketchup.

73

My best friend Pearl delivered a healthy baby boy when she was not quite eighteen. She and Bob continued to live with her parents who never ceased to spout and repeat the slogans of the party line. This was fed to the baby along with mother's milk. The baby preferred mother's milk. It seemed to me that her parents had swallowed what had been fed them, and regurgitated the information with regularity. They did very little thinking for themselves. The Communist party told them what to believe, what to do, and what to repeat, and they never deviated from these instructions. Bob continued to maintain a mild mannered negative response to their vehement Communist propaganda. He realized that peace in the household was of utmost importance and that it contributed to the good health of his wife and cherished son. He was a young man with much wisdom.

Pearl proudly paraded her new baby in his shiny new carriage up and down our street. He looked like a miniature old man. When Pearl happily showed his wrinkled little face to neighbors and disinterested observers, their non-committal comments ranged from, "Oh. Ah, what a baby." Pearl looked radiant and gleamed with pleasure and good health. The exigencies and emergencies of motherhood came easily and naturally to her and she relished her new role in life. I had some deep-seated, suppressed feelings of muted pity for her. The war was coming closer and closer. More and more young men were being drafted, many with a child at home. She did not have a home of her own and she carried the heavy responsibility of motherhood. Her family continued to remain as always, supportive and loving. Her situation had very little to do with politics. They adored their baby grandson and he was practically the focal point of their existence. Pearl could hardly cease looking deeply into the jet black eyes of her new treasure. In him, she saw the renewal and true meaning of life.

She brought her little son up to our apartment for my mother's viewing on one of my days off from work. She expected and received positive comments and loving approval. "He looks a lot like you," my mother lied. Pearl's eyes shone with satisfaction and happiness. "My mother is so sweet," I thought, as my heart embraced her. I looked at Pearl and perceived her brilliant aura of contentment. "There is no doubt," my silence echoed. "Love is blind."

"I hope that he's as smart as his father," Pearl responded to Mama.

"Amen," I uttered to myself. Inwardly, however, I realized that I did have glowing faith that this sweet little monkey would grow into a nice little boy. He slept soundly, covered by the feathery soft, light blue blanket that I had bought for him as a gift. Mama set the kitchen table with her prettiest dishes and served some of her rich, tasty, home-baked filled "Mandelbread" along with her heavenly freshly brewed coffee. She was delightfully kind and generous. She was so easy to love. Pearl reached out, hugged her warmly, and said, "Mrs. Dlugash, you're just like another mother to me."

After a while Pearl left with her little bundle and I helped Mama clear the table and do the few dishes. When our cleanup was completed and everything was back in place, we sat down together for another cup of coffee and were welcomed by the serene quiet.

My mother softly said, "I keep thinking about Sylvia, and how she manages to carry a baby and bundles up to the third floor."

"She's very efficient, Mom," I answered, "and she has a good routine. She handles her new life like an old pro. She's made friends with some of the women in the building who also have small children, and she told me that she's very happy and loves her life and her little family. Lenny's a good little baby and brings lots of fun and pleasure, besides work, into their home."

"I guess you're right. We'll be seeing all of them this weekend," Mama said with a big smile on her face, "and they'll be here all day on Sunday. Papa can hardly wait to see the baby." She took off on another subject. "Pearl seems to be doing fine." There was a short silence as she waited patiently for my opinion.

"I don't think she has much of a choice, Mom, and she has to make the best of it. She told me that the baby is up a lot during the night and that she and Bob try to keep him quiet. It doesn't always work too well. She doesn't want to wake her parents and that builds up a lot of tension for her and her new husband. She also worries that Bob could be drafted. He told her that if it looked as though that would ever happen, he would enlist in the "Medics." Of course it all depends upon how many young men are available from his particular district. If there's a surplus at the time that they call him, he won't be drafted. If the supply of young men dwindles, he could be called. I wonder how Pearl would handle her life then." Mom and I sat quietly for a while immersed in our own private thoughts

74

Leon and I spent a lot of our free time, which was not too plentiful, with his friends at Club 18. For some reason, which I could never fully understand or was able to arrive at any meaningful conclusion I did not feel completely comfortable with the very nice, friendly young women who frequented the downstairs cellar club. They necked and danced with their boyfriends to the beat of the inimitable and insistent music of our big band sound which blared forth from the old "78" record player. I could not figure out, and was not quite sure why I always felt slightly ill at ease with them. I always felt a little removed as though I were on the outside looking in. They remained friendly, but strangers. It didn't matter. I had Leon.

The war was moving relentlessly into our lives. The weather turned cold and blustery and mimicked our wintry emotions. Leon was to leave the Reserves and enter the actual uniformed army life in November of 1942. He had to report for uniform and assignment at Fort Dix. His father, Robert, was an outwardly strong man with soft emotions that were generally well hidden and not allowed to emerge for public viewing. He insisted on accompanying Leon to the train, which would transport him into a separate and alien mode of existence. Leon much preferred to go alone. The muted good-byes would be difficult, but he did not wish to counter his father's love and need to be with him at this precarious moment of separation. Leon gently embraced his father and received a strong reciprocal hug.

"Take good care of yourself, Sonny," his father said, with an unexpected tear making its slow descent down his tired and anxious face.

"I'll be fine, Pop. Don't worry about me. You know I can take good care of myself," he said. He paused for a moment. "I love you," he whispered. The train pulled out and Leon's eyes turned red with restrained tears, more in empathy for his father's feelings than his own.

He stayed at Fort Dix, located in New Jersey, for one week of orientation and outfitting. The days passed with early confusion and loneliness amidst the crushing crowd of new recruits. Everyone seemed to be heading in different directions, depending upon the varying sections of service where they would be assigned. Leon was sent to Camp Edison, New Jersey, from Fort Dix for basic training. Because they were technicians, the Signal Corps men would train for four weeks. Everyone else had sixteen weeks of basic training. The new recruits in Leon's group appreciated the distinction and special privilege. They understood that they would be pushed hard in another direction.

Two weeks after Leon arrived at Camp Edison, he notified his family and me that he would be allowed visitors for the day. His mother and father invited me to accompany them on that Sunday. It involved a two-hour train ride to get to Camp Edison. I was delighted with the invitation. I had been experiencing a heavy sense of loss and loneliness for this very important person in my life. My parents thought it was absolutely acceptable for me to go, as long as I was being escorted and chaperoned by Leon's parents. There was no doubt they felt that I would be well taken care of.

They were good company on the train and made me feel very comfortable. Conversation never lagged. Mr. Brown was articulate and funny. They displayed their approval and fondness for me offering me little cakes and delicious chocolates, with frequency. They were good people, and I felt welcomed and easy with them.

We arrived at our destination along with the billowing dark gray clouds that had accompanied us from Brooklyn. They lent a sad, oppressive covering to the almost colorless gray barracks in the background.

There he was, still not quite at home in his soldier's uniform, waiting for us on the station platform along with many other young soldiers who kept looking for their loved ones as they stepped from the train. Leon spotted us from a distance and dashed forward. He hugged his mother, kissing her warmly on the cheek, shook hands enthusiastically and happily with his father, then deciding to hug him. He finally turned to me. My quiet, reserved Leon took me in his arms and kissed me warmly while his parents looked on approvingly.

Our new soldier led us to the camp, ostensibly to show us around, but there was a minimal amount of sightseeing in store for us. The basic training camp bordered the Atlantic Ocean at Sea Girt, and visitors were not permitted to pass particular boundaries. We walked to the PX where the soldiers could buy a wide variety of supplies and food items, more than they needed or wanted, but it helped fill the void and emptiness of separation. Our need was to spend quiet time together, but we were outwardly animated and for the moment pretending complete satisfaction. There was a great need to bolster each other's spirits. The loneliness or little signals of suppressed fear were not allowed to surface. It did not matter that the "piece de resistance" of the camp was the cafeteria. We were together. Leon's father was in fine form and continued to display his kindness and keen sense of humor. His mother showed her strong friendly personality. It was easy and comforting to like her.

The hours passed and the heavy clouds filled up with tears which turned into huge snowflakes. It was time to go. Leon's parents kindly suggested that they would walk to the train station and meet me there after their son and I exchanged our farewells. The snow fell gently and heavily from the skies. It all seemed unreal. I was in a movie scene saying goodbye to my beloved. I still remember it that way. Leon's piercing blue eyes evidenced the disbelief that we were separating. Our parting kisses were a little hungrier and prefaced our loneliness for each other's young love. I walked away slowly, turned back, and my misted eyes saw him standing against the fence alone. The brim of his cap was covered with snow. The scene ended.

75

The country was geared up for total war. Young men were being drafted at a quickening pace. Many married men with a young child went to work in defense factories or shipyards in the hope that they would be temporarily deferred. They sought to protect their little families, but being called upon to serve in the armed forces still depended upon how many young men were available in their particular district. Several of Leon's friends from Club 18 enlisted, and most of the others were drafted. None of them were married at this time.

My brother Jack was drafted shortly thereafter and he became a Spanish translator for the Army when our country had dealings with Spanish speaking countries. He had found his niche. My parents were proud of him and missed him greatly. Leon's brother, Moey, as he was called most of the time, was pulled into a branch of the Air Force and he looked the part. The uniform he wore fit nonchalantly, but meticulously, and he carried himself like a general. No doubt he would attract the girls.

However, much to his family's surprise and concern, he disclosed the fact that he was deeply in love with a woman who was several years older than he and had previously been married and divorced. He announced that he intended to marry this slender, attractive, heavily made up woman without delay.

He strongly suggested to his parents that they allow Hedda to move in with them since she was out of funds and could not afford to maintain her own apartment. Moey would send a small monthly army allotment home each month to cover the cost to his parents. It appeared that Hedda did not anticipate working although jobs were plentiful at that time since so many young men were necessarily removed from the work force. Leon's parents could not find the courage to refuse, in spite of their strong and fearful doubts regarding their son's decision. They suffered their fate discreetly, and suffered even more worrying about their son's hasty judgment.

"What's the hurry? We don't even really know her. Does she have a family? Is she Jewish?" questioned Mrs. Brown.

"Look, Mom. If I'm old enough to be in the army, I'm surely old enough to get married if I want to. Sure she's Jewish and when you get to know her, you'll love her."

"Listen, Sonny," Mr. Brown addressed his handsome son. "We would like to back you up in whatever you want, but we just want you to think about it a little more. Let's face it. You may have to go overseas and leaving a wife behind is no small thing."

"Pop, we both thought it over and that's what we decided."

An intimate wedding for the immediate family was arranged. It would take place in May's house in her living room under a folding, transportable "Chupah" that boasted a red velvet top with four attached wooden poles that opened and held it in place. The marriage ceremony would be performed and completed under the "Chupah" by a rabbi with proper decorum and perhaps a little sage advice would be directed to the newlyweds. After the rabbi would declare them to be man and wife, a family celebration would ensue with lots of lovingly prepared food and dessert. Big sister May and her husband Al were generous and enthusiastic hosts.

Unfortunately, Leon was not able to get a weekend pass, but I was delighted when Mrs. Brown called me and asked me to attend the wedding. It would be a strange, sad ceremony. Moey would be shipping out to another state very soon and Hedda would remain with her in-laws. She had previously made it known that her parents were dead, and the subject was never mentioned again. She made it clear that no one would be attending from her side of the family and that she did not care for any discussion.

On the day of the wedding, Moey appeared to be slightly ill. A private dialogue between him and his bride to-be took place shortly before the wedding in a small side room in May's house. The rest of the family and the rabbi waited patiently in the next room for them to come out. Everyone pretended that they weren't trying to listen to what was going on behind that closed door. Their conversation that could barely be heard was cool but obviously upsetting to Moey. Finally Hedda opened the door and displayed a huge reassuring smile directed at Mrs. Brown. She seemed to be in total control of the entire situation.

Moey emerged from the room a few minutes later looking as though he was suffering great uncertainty regarding their future together. He was very pale, and unlike his usual careful, scrupulous demeanor he appeared slightly disheveled. There was a distinct impression, from the little that had been heard by those in the living room, that he now possessed heretofore unknown information that he was not likely or willing to share with anyone. He had been captured and was completely enmeshed in Hedda's potent, womanly wiles. All of us experienced a suppressed desire that he courageously back out of this somewhat distasteful and precarious union, but the die was cast. It was too late. He and Hedda were pronounced man and wife.

"Mazeltov, mazeltov," resounded under the "Chupah" as Moey put his foot on the delicate glass wrapped in a cloth napkin and successfully broke it. The ceremony was concluded and Moey kissed the bride.

76

The following week Hedda moved into the Brown's clean but threadbare apartment. She established herself in the small bedroom that had been Moey's and made herself at home. She was lively company for Mrs. Brown who somehow did not completely trust her motives. The thought that Hedda had married Moey for his army life insurance should he be killed in service, floated endlessly in her mind.

"I don't like to think about things like that," she confided to me one day. "She's a lot of fun to have in the house and she acts very nice, but she is very strange. She goes out and stays out for the whole day. Where does she go? She's not working."

"Try not to think about it," I answered. "She certainly is very friendly and likeable. Just try to enjoy her company. I know that you like her and feel sorry for her knowing that she doesn't have parents. She told me the other day that she loves you and Mr. Brown."

"Well, that's nice to hear. I hope she loves my son."

"Of course she does. She never would have married him."

"Listen, Beulah, she's not you. I'm going to see Dr. Alex later. He gives me a shot for my nerves."

Hedda had a deep husky voice, probably aided by a heavy smoking habit that resonated and gave forth a sensual aura that was not fully appreciated by the family. The smoke from her constantly lighted cigarettes permeated the air. Mr. Brown hid the fact that it negatively affected his asthma. In spite of the inconveniences of having a virtual stranger in the house and concomitant underlying worries, Mr. and Mrs. Brown treated their daughter-in-law with generosity and affection.

After all, she was their son's wife, and they hoped that this marriage would turn out well for his sake.

I saw Hedda one morning without her makeup. It was as though a mask had been removed. Under that heavy covering of illusion was a rather plain ordinary older face, but the flash of her eyes appeared to emit electricity, great strength, self-absorption and perhaps deceit. I had been invited to come up for Sunday breakfast. I think that Mrs. Brown hoped that I might be a stabilizing influence, little goody-two-shoes, and she believed that Hedda could use a lot of stabilizing.

Hedda was not at all embarrassed to show up and seat herself at the kitchen table in her nightgown and empty face. She seemed delighted to see me and I, like Moey, found it easy to be captured by her charm. I was flattered by the thought that this sophisticated and older woman liked me. Her strong overt personality and her take-charge attitude tended to disguise her potential failings, but never lessened her self-esteem. Her smile was wide and constant. She loved being served a special breakfast by her mother-in-law. She realized that she had indeed arranged a good place for herself, and she generously dispensed a double dose of her charm. She was almost irresistible.

Unfortunately, there were some minor strange occurrences that proved to be unsettling and perplexing after Hedda moved in. Little unimportant items, like a pretty scarf or an inexpensive piece of costume jewelry started disappearing from the apartment. Mrs. Brown became concerned and confided to me that she thought Hedda might be responsible. There really was very little of value that could be considered worthwhile with one exception. Leon had been interested in studying coins and their value since he was a young boy. It started when a neighbor offered him two cents for his Indian penny. He decided not to give it up.

Very slowly by dint of carefully collecting Indian Head pennies that came his way and which were fairly common at that time, and keeping selective nickels and dimes, he accumulated coins that he believed to be worth several hundred dollars. This mother lode of wealth that had been collected so assiduously and painstakingly through the years from boyhood on was dearly valued by him, and was left in a secret compartment of his dresser drawer when he left for the army. Much to his chagrin and deep disappointment he discovered on a weekend leave from camp that it was gone. How did she discover his secret hiding place?

He was aware of the consensus of opinion from his parents that Hedda was stealing. Leon was furious but the situation was hopeless. It truly appeared that Hedda was a kleptomaniac or a plain run of the mill thief. She could not resist the challenge, the small financial benefit, and the call to own other people's property even when she had no use for a particular item.

When Hedda left the house, Mrs. Brown told me that she would enter her room and examine the contents of her dresser drawers. There she found the offending missing stolen loot resting comfortably under her delicate silk underwear. The coins, however, were nowhere to be found.

Hedda had originally told Moey and the Browns that her parents were dead, but she was suddenly overcome with an attack of conscience and decided to divulge the truth when Moey came in on leave. It looked as though he might be shipping out to another camp very soon. Her sleeping conscience awoke. Although it was now very difficult for her to belatedly confess, she hesitatingly announced to her new husband and his family that she had a child, and that her four year old little boy was living with her mother who was very much alive.

She further acknowledged, "My mother doesn't have a very good opinion of me. She thinks that I'm not qualified to raise my own child. As a matter of fact, I'm happy that she's taking care of him. I do get to see him once or twice a week. That set-up suits me fine."

We were all horrified by this new turn of events. Poor Moey! How could he be capable of coping with his strange troubled wife? He had to spend many more weeks in basic training and would only be able to see his wife infrequently to hopefully work out their problems. The urgency was great, but the opportunity was lacking.

May and Rose, Moey's two sisters maintained a minimum contact with Hedda. They knew trouble when they saw it and vehemently empathized with their parents' ordeal. They blamed their handsome brother for his poor judgment and self-serving ways, and were more angry than sad for the situation that he had gotten himself and his parents into.

Even though we could see right through her, Hedda continued to hide under a covering of positive pretense, applying heavier coats of attractive face paint, and exuding abundant charm along with interesting conversation. Mrs. Brown and I could barely resist her powerful personality, and found that we surprisingly enjoyed being in her company. We realized when we discussed our feelings, that we felt very sorry for this fascinating and corrupted lost soul.

I still regarded my friend Frances as a friend in spite of a lingering, latent modicum of distrust on my part that stemmed from her actions during that long ago sweet-sixteen party when she had purposely neglected to invite my boyfriend Leon. Obviously, I had no difficulty carrying a grudge ad infinitum. However, our personalities meshed and we continued to have a strong affinity for one another. We were always comfortable with each other's company in spite of my deeply buried mistrust.

77

Frances started going out with George, the iceman's son who lived with his parents on my side of the street. In spite of her little somewhat squashed in face, and her sweaty palms, which caused her a great deal of consternation, embarrassment and suffering, she was a classy girl. Her manner was cool and almost sophisticated, and her intelligence was evident.

George worked for his father and helped him with his deliveries of ice to those people who still had iceboxes. He carried big blocks of ice on his shoulder that were gripped by large metal pincers up to the apartments that very often were located on the upper floors of apartment houses. He would carefully slip his icy burden into the section of the icebox especially constructed for that special purpose. Meanwhile, a rapid transition was being made to refrigeration, and the ice business was slowly going out of style.

George was very plain looking and sloppy in appearance when working, but he had developed an attractive well-muscled body that Frances noticed. He in turn realized and understood her supposed casual interest and began to pay great attention to her. Girls had never seemed to be attracted to him in the past. Frances appreciated and enjoyed his overt consideration. She could see the potential in encouraging that relationship. When George was drafted, he evolved into a neatly dressed army man. His body looked wonderful in uniform, and his face took on a leaner, stronger more forgiving look.

Frances's home life was not an easy one without parents. Her older sister, who had kept their family together with disciplined love, had married. Her new husband was a young handsome practicing dentist with a friendly sensitive personality. Frances's sister was lovely and dedicated to her family. She deserved a good man.

Meanwhile, Frances's twin brother Joseph, at age eighteen, decided that he was going to marry his cute little girlfriend who was seventeen years old. The world was going crazy! Ellen had a sharp personality and a pert little nose sprinkled with freckles. As the intensity of the war quickened, more and more very young people were opting to plunge into the excitement of a war marriage. They became part of a large youthful population that decided that they did not want to defer instant pleasure when the strong possibility existed that they might not have a future.

Leon and I were invited to this hastily catered small wedding, as was our friend Esther and her soldier boyfriend Aaron. They sat at our table and we anticipated having a good time at this celebration. All of Frances's sisters were present for this important family occasion, and what an impressive number of females they were! They were dressed simply and beautifully, and were responsibly and enthusiastically participating in young Joseph's wedding. The actions and behavior of this large supportive family, growing up without benefit of parents, always produced a strong impact. Everyone respected and admired them. Frances told me that before the wedding date had been set, they had all tried to influence Joseph to wait a few years before entering the state of holy matrimony. However, he had one main interest in mind, and one only. He was feeling his manhood. The date was set.

The young bride's family was not enthusiastic about their daughter's relationship with Joseph and her new status in life. After all, he had hardly crossed over into manhood. However, Ellen's stubbornness persisted and prevailed. Her parents did not want to take a chance on a possible elopement. Their daughter had that kind of determination and "chutzpah."

They arranged for this wedding with a minimum amount of fuss, a minimum serving of food, a meager display of flowers on scattered tables, and a minimal wedding ceremony. However, the bride looked breathtakingly adorable bedecked in her youthful innocence and a magnificently beaded and sequined cream-colored satin wedding gown. This was where her parents had heavily invested their money.

Joseph looked exceedingly young and handsome as he stepped strongly on the wrapped ceremonial champagne glass that had been placed on the floor near his foot, and the shouted "Mazel Tov" echoed from all the guests. The rabbi pronounced them husband and wife!

Frances and George joined us and sat at our table, and the mood was joyful. Our escorts, although not really friends with one another, were compatible and conversation was spirited. Complimentary packs of cigarettes had been placed on each table. George opened one and offered cigarettes to all. Esther, Frances and I were non-smokers but we all felt a surge of pretentious affectation and daring. My friends lighted up for the first time with a minimal amount of coughing.

When I picked up the proffered cigarette, Leon quietly said, "I really prefer that you don't smoke." I must have shown my surprise, because he laughingly added, "Lips that touch cigarettes, will never touch mine." Everyone chuckled, and I had to make a quick decision. I intuitively knew that it was important to him that I yield. I decided to be generous and not challenge his masculinity before our friends.

I put the cigarette down, laughed softly, and said, "The music is great. I'll trade the smoking for a dance." Leon had never felt completely comfortable on the dance floor, but he gave me a loving smile and rose immediately. His body was strong and persuasive against mine. I never smoked. He had saved me from that addiction.

78

From Camp Edison, the basic training camp, Leon was transferred to Camp Wood, New Jersey, where he would learn the technical aspects of radio according to the army ways and methods. Most weekends he was able to get leave to come home. I could hardly wait to see him and we spent as much time as possible together. His parents shared my feelings, but they seemed pleased to take their turn after me. I relished the idea of their approval. Leon looked strong and virile and he resembled my vision of a hero in his soldier's uniform that now seemed to be a part of him. His quiet reserved demeanor lent a mature grace to his features.

It was terrible to have to go to work on Sundays when he was home for such a limited period of time. The weekend went by too quickly. If only we could slow down the passing hours. Leon would meet me for lunch and we would spend most of the hour communicating in silence. He would soon be leaving for camp. Our meal was mostly ignored and we felt the pangs of loneliness in advance. We were lovesick.

We impatiently looked forward to Saturdays. They were the best. The entire day belonged to us, but Friday nights presaged the emotional highlights of Leon's arrival from camp for the weekend. I was flooded by powerful feelings, which I carefully kept hidden.

A wonderful meal of Jewish soul food awaited us on Friday nights. It was lovingly prepared by his mother. Comfort food like chicken soup and matzoh balls was served, followed by roast chicken, mashed potatoes and vegetables. Desert was always delicious and welcome. I was happy to be part of this family scenario. The white tablecloth and lighted candles celebrating the Sabbath delighted the eye.

On occasion Moe's wife, Hedda, would be present. She would flutter her fake eyelashes, smile widely and make interesting conversation as always, but it was becoming evident that she was separating herself from the family more and more as time went by. There was generally a sigh of relief from Mrs. Brown when she was absent. It appeared that her marriage vows had been a farce and had only been self-serving. We all sadly believed that her relationship with Moey would not stand the test of time.

Mrs. Brown suspected that she was stealing from Woolworth's and other department stores as well. Pretty little things appeared to be hidden in Hedda's dresser and were found when Mrs. Brown looked for evidence of her deviant behavior. She was worried sick and did not know whether to confide this information to Moey who was due in on furlough pretty soon. She told me in confidence that very often Hedda stayed out till all hours of the night often returning slightly drunk with raised voice. Mr. Brown had no doubts about giving his opinions and relating all known information to Moey when the opportunity would arise. He was not going to sacrifice his son to this sick soul. He felt sorry for Hedda, but he knew that she would never be an honest or faithful wife and he had the responsibility of being a faithful and protective father wherever and whenever possible. He would attempt to correct his son's mistake.

After dinner and much pleasant conversation, Leon and I left to take a walk to Club 18. By this time, most of the fellows had either been drafted or had enlisted and this signaled the end of an era for these young men and their sweethearts. They had loved to congregate, dance to the great music blasting from the record player and perhaps make minor but devoted love during quiet moments. This meeting place that had created a sense of close camaraderie for eighteen young men was just about coming to a close.

Leon turned his key in the lock and opened the door. We were greeted by a musty, unwelcoming breath of stale air. Leon pressed the light switch and "Club 18" reappeared. The huge mural on the wall that depicted happy dancing couples, looked down upon us and invited us in. Leon turned on the record player and the sweet notes of "I'll Be Seeing You" flowed into the room and into our young hearts. I felt the need to dance to the music, and my love willingly succumbed.

We embraced into a dance position and moved and swayed to the lovely rhythm and poignant lyrics of this war song. The rough cloth of his uniform scorched my arms. It was getting more and more difficult to separate and say goodnight.

79

Big changes were taking place in the business. The large bolts of incoming drapery and upholstery material were becoming more and more expensive and the supply was diminishing. The shelves were emptying and becoming devoid of their previous abundance of beautiful fabrics. The tremendous needs of war were a priority, and this priority did not dwell on furnishings for the home. Most of the younger generation of men were being filtered out of society and were headed for the armed forces, but the remaining population shifted all efforts towards supporting their soldiers. Thousands and thousands of women who had never held outside jobs before left their homes to work in factories on assembly lines to help build weapons of all kinds. There was a huge influx of workers into the shipbuilding yards. The country was totally bonded in their war efforts. The home front was dedicated to preserving and protecting its country against the evils and barbarism of Adolph Hitler and fascism. Patriotism was a good word.

The bolts of fabric started disappearing more and more rapidly from the large shelves that lined all the walls of our corner store. Instead of delivery to our place of business, the materials were shipped directly from the manufacturer to our customers who were the upholsterers and drapery producing companies. There was lots and lots of money to be made, and less and less work for the employees.

Julie, Mr. H's son, who was a great salesman and so well liked by all, was drafted into the army. Mr. H. made a difficult and surprising decision. He took Sylvan, his top salesman and our stalwart union representative who had always fought for the welfare of the staff, into the business as a partner to help share the difficulties and responsibilities of running a successful business now that Julie was away. Sylvan would naturally share in the profits. It was an unbelievable opportunity for him and he grabbed the brass ring.

Sylvan was married and had one child, a little boy who was lame due to some trauma in childbirth. He was a very loving husband and father. Sadly, after he became a partner in the business, his views about the union and his co-workers underwent a drastic transformation. Greed entered the equation. Although the war was creating greater and very sizable profits, and Sylvan was reaping the financial benefits, he, unlike his former self, did not think the workers deserved any part of it. He did not believe that they merited even a small raise in salary when the union contract came up because their workload had actually decreased. Of course he chose to think that his tremendous increase in income was well deserved. He had become a boss. Fortunately, Mr. H. was more realistic and empathetic and chose to satisfy his staff with modest raises when the contract came due. He always reinforced the good feelings that everyone had about him. He had always treated my sister and me with generosity and affection and we automatically responded in kind. We were faithful and devoted employees. Love begets love.

When Julie came home on furlough after basic training wearing his neat, sharply pressed soldier's uniform, his overt friendly personality and good looks made him welcome everywhere. The uniform set him apart and we showered him with attention and affection. He had always inspired our trust and he was our star. His father's smile of happiness was non-stop at having his son at home, even though it was temporary.

Julie told us about his basic training and the hardships of army life. He presented his views in an honest non-complimentary manner. He hated the routine, he hated the food and most of all, he hated the separation from his very pretty little wife. He spent part of his furlough at the store and seemed to enjoy taking care of the retail customers on Sunday. He engaged them in lively conversation and his enveloping personality captured them completely. Customers utterly trusted his judgment and taste. Very often he would find himself selecting the drapery and upholstery fabric that they were buying.

He showed us his dogtags that listed his name, serial number and religion. The salesmen in the store had never before seen dogtags and they were very much interested, particularly in the letters that were embedded in the metal. They commented on the capital letter H, which signified Hebrew. Julie commented, "That always puts me in a special category."

He asked me about Leon and I told him that he had been transferred to Fort Monmouth, which was a Signal Corps camp. "He's very lucky to be stationed in New Jersey, so close to home."

"I agree," I answered. "He comes home practically every weekend and his family and I fully appreciate it. We all say small `thank you' prayers. But when he can't get a weekend pass," I added, "his mother and I take the train to Fort Monmouth armed with our little weekend suitcases.

We quickly make our reservations in advance, confirm them, and stay at the "Guest House" on the campgrounds." A customer caught his attention and Julie warmly smiled at me as our conversation was ended and he turned to serve her.

It was thrilling for Mrs. Brown and me to spend some time with the young soldier we both loved. She and I were a compatible team and we felt comfortable sharing a room. It worked our very well even though she did snore. We were supportive of each other, and she was a very cooperative chaperone giving us chunks of privacy. She would pretend that she was tired and needed a little nap. However, Leon was not always able to be with us. He had to be available to fulfill some minor responsibilities and duties when we were on the grounds, but there was always a good deal of time left for us.

There was a small restaurant attached to the PX where we all ate our minimal meals. That was about the only recreational activity available for the three of us, although we found it supremely recreational just being together. Mrs. Brown would not eat the meat served there because it was not kosher and for the weekend she existed mainly on cheese sandwiches. However, she looked forward to what she usually considered the best part of any meal. It was the dessert. She invariably ordered pie-a-la-mode. I always joined her in her choice. We were soul mates.

Our mood saddened as the hour of departure approached. During the train ride that had brought us, we had been filled with joyful anticipation. The trip home, however, always left us with a feeling of emptiness. We were incomplete. Our conversation slowly came to a halt as the train noisily rumbled along covering the miles that made our separation complete. We were quiet, enveloped in our own dark thoughts of loneliness and assailed by a pervasive feeling of sly anxiety.

"Don't complain," my mind insisted. "We can look forward to seeing Leon next week, in all probability." Meanwhile, I would receive the letters that he wrote daily.

Mrs. Brown and I acknowledged our greed. There were so many soldiers who were so far away from home, and so many who were already overseas and in battle. We fully realized how grateful we should be and we were, but would the situation continue to remain the same? Aye, there was the rub. Leon's serial number, 12147462, had become a part of his name and the daily letters that I wrote and received seared that number in my mind.

80

Pearl visited often with her little boy. He had evolved into a precocious and delightful baby and my family enjoyed having him around. Babies were the real stuff of life. Sylvia's Lenny was my parent's delight and they could not get enough of his company. His sweet little face and his actions, no matter how foolish or insignificant, brought loving smiles to their faces. He was pure enjoyment! They were glad that Charlie had left the grocery business and was now working in the shipyards doing important defense work. More importantly, Charlie was glad that he had made this significant change. The work was more physical, but he did not mind that. There were compensations. He worked out of doors, which he considered to be a great advantage and he felt that he was making a definite and concrete contribution to the war effort.

Jack was stationed on the East Coast and although we did not get to see him very often, we were happy that he seemed content in his work. He continued to be a Spanish translator, and was well suited for the job. When he did get home on leave, we were all very impressed by how handsome he looked in his uniform. He played chess often with Papa when he was home, and the quiet pleasure that Jack gave him showed plainly on my father's face.

Pearl's eyes filled with tears as she gave me the shocking news that Bob had enlisted. Many men who had children tried to avoid going into service. They were very concerned about leaving their wives alone with the tremendous responsibility of taking care of a child. Psychologically and economically it was not an easy path. Bob had felt that he was going to be drafted shortly because of the paucity of young men in his district, and he wanted to pick the branch of service that he preferred. He no doubt knew that his wife and child would be surrounded and helped by a loving family. It is also possible that he wished to temporarily escape from the unpalatable communist propaganda of his in-laws.

In spite of the non-aggression pact that Russia had signed with Germany, Hitler's legions had invaded Russia in June of 1941. Hitler's "Mein Kampf" had predicted this development. The people who had followed the communist line formerly did not give up their pact with the devil and they continued to follow and preach the political dictates and philosophy that issued from Moscow.

At first the invasion by Germany into Russia was enormously successful, and effective and excellent progress was made. However, "General Winter" came to the aid of the Russians and slowly and inexorably the tide began to turn. The Russians sustained tremendous losses, but they did not allow death to deter their defensive measures. Their historic bravery was lauded by the Allies and feared by the Germans who were mired in the freezing grip of winter. Within six months the Germans were on the run. The defense of Stalingrad was a phenomenon and would go down in history.

Pearl was overcome with emotion and could barely continue to tell me about Bob's enlistment. Little sobs escaped from her lips as she explained. "He didn't want to kill anyone and so he enlisted as a medic in the Marines."

I could barely catch my breath when I contemplated the negative aspects and possibilities of such a dramatic move. What motivated him to enlist in the Marines? Why did he select the most dangerous branch of the service? What could I say to Pearl to comfort her?

81

The young people of that generation were carried high on a wave of patriotism and frustration. These forces were on opposite ends of the continuum, but they existed simultaneously. The frustration of separation and imminent incipient danger was a powerful sexual stimulant and many young people rushed to marry to help fill the oncoming void in their lives. Many feared to wait for fulfillment that might never arrive.

My friend Frances, who had always appeared cool and calculating, decided to marry George, the iceman's son, when he began to court her seriously in his well pressed and beautifully fitted uniform. The homely, pleasant former iceman's assistant became a glamorous figure in Frances's eyes. When he was transferred and then stationed in Lubbock, Texas, there was a copious exchange of long distance letter writing. I was a little surprised at Frances's interest in George. He had always impressed me as a plain, earthy kind of individual with no apparent intellectual leanings that she had always seemed to admire so much. Was she selling herself short? In spite of her little squashed in face and sweaty palms, she definitely had class, and boys were attracted to her. They liked her style and strong personality.

When George proposed marriage, long distance, Frances accepted happily. She excitedly discussed the details with me. "You know, the bottom line is that I feel so comfortable and relaxed when I'm with him. He constantly tells me that he loves me and will always take good care of me and I do believe him. Of course, with the war on, sometimes I wonder about that."

"Well," I answered, "If he's lucky, he won't be shipped overseas. He might spend the rest of his time in the states and you can be together. He's a caring person and I'm sure he'll be a good husband."

"I know you're right," she said. "Besides it's time to get out from under my family's thumb. I always feel the pressure of my sisters loving domination. You don't know how hard it is and how different it is when you don't have parents. Eugene's mother and father have been wonderful to me. His mother bought me a beautiful pendant and I've been to their apartment for dinner a few times. She's a great cook, maybe too great. I can't believe how fat she is! When we're together, I always think, 'Fat and skinny had a race.' She never comments on how very thin I am. She just urges me to eat more. George's father smiles a lot, but he never says a word."

She showed me the pendant that she was wearing. It had been covered by her sweater and it was truly beautiful, elegant and in good taste. Frances loved it, was impressed with it and I could easily see why. She was already being welcomed as a future daughter-in-law with this expensive gift and she was ready to assume the roll. As a married woman she would achieve an elevated level of respect and status in her family. Certainly her young friends would be impressed by her actions and her bravery. She would be travelling alone to Texas to meet and marry her future husband without the benefit and security of the presence of her family or George's parents. It seemed a little sad to me, particularly that her future husband's parents were to be excluded from this most important occasion. I believed that she was acting too hastily, perhaps considering only her own immediate desires and needs. However, I did give her high marks for courage and determination.

Frances did make that long trip alone to Texas and she married the iceman's son. She settled contentedly into the life of a soldier's wife. She wrote me often and told me what a wonderful husband she had and how happy he made her. I was glad that her dream had materialized. She and George had rented a tiny apartment in Lubbock close to campgrounds, and she had made friends with other young army wives who had relocated from various parts of the country in order to be near their husbands.

82

Moey was going to be shipped overseas shortly. He came home on furlough knowing this but he exhibited a strong covering of bravado. His smile was pasted on his handsome face and he did not allow anyone, including his parents, to uncover or penetrate the facade. He did not wish anyone to view the fear, the anxiety and the sadness that filled him. He was aware of the terrible mistake that he had made when he married Hedda. He realized that he had only known her obliquely and superficially, but he had never suspected her devious life style. He was aghast at the thought that she was a kleptomaniac, or perhaps merely a thief, and that she did not come home many nights. Hedda was an inveterate liar. She had never told him that she had a child, a little boy who lived with her mother. Moey was under the impression that her mother had died many years before. He now believed that she had married him for his small monthly allotment and a free place to live. If he were killed while he was in military service, she would be the beneficiary of his ten thousand dollar G.I. insurance policy.

Hedda had not been home for several days, but when she finally showed up one morning steeped in her glamorous makeup and vivacious smile, Mrs. Brown notified her that Moey was coming home for ten days on furlough. She greeted everyone lovingly, not yet aware of the turn of events.

Mrs. Brown told me later that when Moey finally arrived home, he faced his wife and wearily questioned her. "Where have you been staying nights? My father told me that you didn't come home often, and that you didn't even show them the courtesy of calling. What's been going on?"

"Whatever do you mean?" She countered, flashing her expressive eyes. "I've been busy taking care of a million details in preparation for your furlough. I've arranged for us to spend a few days at a hotel in the mountains."

Moey gathered his courage unto himself. His feelings of weariness and vulnerability subsided. He felt supported by his parents and circumstances, and answered, "I don't think that I'm interested in going to the mountains. We're at the end of the line, Hedda. I think that you had better get your stuff together and leave. We're finished." Her face became transformed and hardened into a mask of venom. "I'm happy to be rid of you. You're a worthless fop and I know you for what you are."

Moey's parents stood by unhappily, abysmally depressed watching their handsome elder son fade under Hedda's scathing attack.

She dashed into her room, slammed the door and packed her meager belongings. When she emerged, she approached her mother-in-law and embraced her. She whispered, "You were always good to me, and for that I thank you." She lifted her head, glided down the hallway past the kitchen and out the door. Hedda had walked out of their lives.

83

The neighborhood had emptied out. Most of the young men were in uniform and many had been sent to the European theatre of war. Others had gone to do battle with the Japanese on steamy islands that harbored strange tropical diseases and had names that were completely unknown and unfamiliar to Americans. Malaria ran rampant in the South Pacific, and the soldiers received their daily quota of Atabrine for protection against this malevolent and devastating disease. It turned their skin yellow, but was absolutely preferable to the alternative. In spite of this temporary stopgap, many men developed a mild case of malaria even though they faithfully took this medication. Others listened to a false rumor that had been circulated by "Tokyo Rose" that Atabrine caused impotency. A few men preferred malaria.

The Japanese culture inculcated the philosophy that death was eminently more acceptable than surrender. Young Americans suffered their fanaticism and our losses were heavy and frightening.

However, the country remained locked in the throes of patriotism and worked hard and steadfastly to defeat the enemy.

Leon was still stationed at Ft. Monmouth, New Jersey, and he continued to come home almost every weekend. I hopefully thought that he might be stationed there for a long period of time, perhaps for the duration of the war. The weeks went by slowly especially since there was less activity on the job, but on Friday my level of impatient excitement would escalate until I could barely get through the day. By evening, Leon would be home and we would be together. Romance was a top priority and manifested its presence during the most mundane pastimes. Taking a quiet walk together hand in hand, exchanging the warmth emanating from our bodies into our joined palms was thrilling, but it demanded more. The darkened tree-lined streets of Eastern Parkway beckoned and we hurried to exchange sweetly charged passionate kisses. The huge leafy trees with their overhanging branches tenuously embraced us and granted us a modicum of privacy, chaperoning us and keeping us company.

His mom and mine subsequently served succulent meals, each doing her best to please his palate and fatten him up a bit. He had lost some weight and did not miss the few pounds at all, but our parents thought that he was bordering on thin. To me, he appeared powerful and strong in his army uniform. He wore his parade cap with its brim low on his forehead and looked particularly handsome. Every once in a while I would inquire of him, "Doesn't it give you a headache to have the brim so low on your forehead?" His answer as he pushed the hat back was, "Now it does." We often laughed at that little bit of nonsense, which lightened the thought that he would soon be leaving once again.

Even though we were able to spend some time together most weekends, Leon wrote a letter every day that we were apart. He had a definite imaginative flair for writing, which I always found appealing. He was clever and funny and I invariably responded to his dry wit with much laughter. He wrote of his daily experiences and the minor frustrations of army routine and accompanying red tape. He wrote of his love for me and surrounded it with his keen sense of humor. He always maintained that actions were the fundamental expressions of love and that words were secondary and less important. However, he needed to learn that to a woman, words emphasized the actions and were a necessity. I responded to his letters with loving words of my own that were etched in my brain. Sunday evenings, when he had returned to camp, I would be seated at our kitchen table with a sheet of blank paper waiting to be filled. The envelope had already been addressed to Leon Brown, 12147462.

Little by little, we edged closer and closer to the idea of marriage. After all, our long-standing relationship had begun when I was a novice teen-ager of thirteen. Our emotions were heightened and inflamed by our constant separations and by the danger and uncertainty of the state of our country at war. Europe was in flames and our soldiers were fighting and dying in the South Pacific. We were being caught up along with so many others in the quiet pervasiveness of the need to experience life before it was forcefully removed. Many of Leon's friends had already been shipped to foreign soil, but it continued to appear that Leon's situation was relatively stable. He might stay in Ft. Monmouth for an extended period.

We discussed the matter of marriage with Leon's parents, and they thought that it would be better for us to wait until the war ended before we took such a serious step. They thought that we were much too young to be married and that perhaps we did not fully understand the responsibilities involved. They were certainly more practical than we cared to be. However, our relationship had lasted and persevered, and Leon decided that this important change in our lives could and should be taken now.

My mother and father gave us their response, thoughts and opinions concerning marriage. It was true, they said, that we were both very young, and the war foretold a risky future. However, when two responsible persons, which they considered us to be, loved each other deeply and knew each other for many years, outsiders, indicating themselves, did not have the ethical right to keep them apart. Risk was one of the payments of life, and they prayed that G-d would protect Leon.

We decided to go ahead with our precarious plans. Leon, my quiet "Rock of Gibraltar" husband to be, exhibited tiny flashes of private nervousness that only I could discern. However, he was determined to make me his wife, and I was completely and happily overwhelmed by his inner strength and resolution.

My parents consulted with our immediate family and my future in-laws, who lived directly across the street. They hesitantly put on a happy face and agreed that perhaps it would be a good thing for the children to be married after all. They would not stand in the way.

I went along with my mother, father, Sylvia and Charlie to look for a suitable place to celebrate a wedding. Leon remained at camp. The nearby "Twin Cantors" located on Eastern Parkway was decided upon and I was delighted. It was a truly beautiful place to be married. It had a wonderful reputation for elegant service and fine dining. Mom and Pop were going overboard once again to do their best for us.

We were unexpectedly shocked and dismayed when Leon unexpectedly got orders to ship out of Fort Monmouth. We hurriedly cancelled our reservations for our wedding. A state of insistent terror and disappointment sharply invaded my mind and threw my former happy spirits into a sinkhole of despair. We waited and waited and finally Leon received notice that the shipping orders were rescinded. He was going to continue serving at Fort Monmouth. Such were the vagaries of the army. We rushed back to the "Twin Cantors" to attempt to reserve another evening. However, "Twin Cantors" was a very popular place and was now solidly booked for the entire summer. New decisions would have to be made.

We finally decided on a small nightclub restaurant that was available and had a large private kosher dining room for guests. Tante Lakie and Uncle Panush's younger son Hymie was now a cantor, and he would marry us. How appropriate and fitting it seemed. Tante Lakie and Uncle Panush were old and frail, but we were all filled with quiet joy that they would be present and celebrating with us along with their older son Simon who had been practicing law for many years, and now had a beautiful family of his own.

My mother's aunt and uncle were the epitome of generosity and had welcomed Mama when she had arrived from Poland at age fourteen. They had treated her like one of their own. My mother never forgot this and appreciated and valued them during their lifetime. This remarkable display of unselfishness and sharing on their part, even when finances were inordinately limited, was not unique. Many other families were doing the same for their incoming relatives from Europe.

My job as a full charge bookkeeper had grown and developed into an environment that contributed to my modest self-esteem and growing self-confidence. Mr. H., my boss, had always treated me kindly and with a modicum of humorous respect. I even felt little subtle messages of love in his somewhat fatherly behavior. It was generally a happy place where I spent so much of my life and effort. All of the salesmen and Mr. H. expressed great joy when I told them the momentous news of my forthcoming marriage. They out-shouted one another with their loud congratulatory phrases followed by lots of warm hugs and kisses.

Sylvan declared, "Leon is one lucky guy. I don't know what he did to deserve a little winner like you."

"Thanks," I replied, "but I feel like the lucky one."

All the staff and their wives were invited to our wedding to share in our happiness. I looked forward to their presence and wanted them to take part in the festivities, enjoy a social evening and hopefully be served a wonderful meal. The dance floor was small, but a great band would encourage guests to get up and dance between the serving of various courses of the dinner. This most important, nerve-racking event of my life was scheduled for Saturday evening, June 3, 1944. My twentieth birthday was coming up on June 20th.

Prior to the wedding, there were many details that demanded my immediate attention. I had to make advance reservations at what was then called "Hotel Pennsylvania" in Manhattan. Leon and I were to have a one-day honeymoon since he was due back at camp on Sunday night. That meant that I would be coming home from my very abbreviated honeymoon all alone. That seemed sad to me, but I tried to push negative thoughts from my mind and dwell upon the positive aspects of wedded bliss. Using the telephone to make the reservation was not acceptable to the hotel. It appeared that the New York hotels were giving service men a ten percent discount and they would only give confirmations in face to face meetings.

I left my office one afternoon with my boss's approval, and headed uptown on the subway to arrive at the busy streets and ongoing frenetic activity of Manhattan. I emerged from the subway feeling a little insecure. I was out of my immediate and familiar environment, but I breathed deeply and attempted to remain calm. I proceeded to my destination, "The Hotel Pennsylvania" trying to maintain a knowing and dignified facade.

Apparently, my feeble attempt at pseudo sophistication was not apparent and did not produce any reaction from the truly sophisticated receptionist at the "Pennsylvania." She contentedly allowed me to wait for ten minutes before she deigned to speak to me.

"Can I help you?" she asked, in a cool unfriendly tone while a false smile made its way to her pretty face.

"Yes. I'd like to make reservations for my husband and myself for Saturday, June 3rd for one night. He's a serviceman."

She filled out the reservation form with all the necessary information and responded, "That's fine. Everything is all taken care of. You do know that servicemen receive a ten percent discount?"

"Yes. Thank you." I turned away and headed out of the beautiful lobby of the hotel. A crowd of images raced through my mind as my state of turbulence accelerated. "What a lovely place to spend our brief honeymoon," I thought, "but how little time we'll have to be together. We'll probably arrive in the early hours of the morning after the wedding and we'll have to be out of our room before noon on Sunday." I was suspended between exhilaration and an undercurrent flow of sadness. Were we doing the right thing? We loved each other deeply, but we were so young. Shouldn't we have waited for the war to end? Would that day ever arrive? Our uncertain future loomed ahead, but I forcibly pulled my optimistic nature out of its murky hiding place and returned to my office full of smiles and strained confidence.

Leon continued to come home most weekends and we hid our nervousness from each other. We encased it with private, determined, impenetrable shields and did not permit it to escape from our inner depths where it unhappily resided and grew stronger.

In the interim, while waiting for the big day to arrive, Leon's mother would sit on my sunny stoop and knit woolen scarves and warm protective woolen head coverings that had openings for the eyes and mouth. These were among the items for our men in the armed forces in preparation for the future cold winter that they would be experiencing in Europe. I went with a few of my friends and neighbors to the Red Cross center nearby where we rolled bandages several evenings each week. We were filled with patriotic fervor.

The streets were strangely empty. Most of the young men had been moved from relatively carefree life-styles into the disciplined, controlling mode of wartime living. They adapted because there was no alternative and more importantly, they believed in the cause. An undercurrent of quietness pervaded our lives. We were waiting for something to happen. The anticipation was palpable. Perhaps the whole free world was waiting for the allied invasion into Europe. No one could foresee where or when it would occur. There was only conjecture, but the sense of inevitability persisted and hung over our heads like the sword of Damocles. We trembled when we contemplated what the cost would be of young lives, and we could not help wondering how it was possible to be brave in the face of possible extinction.

Rumors were washing ashore that Jews had been rounded up and sent to concentration camps in Poland where they were being used for slave labor and medical experiments. The rumors persisted that those who were not useful to the German State were being exterminated. These were images that had to be pushed from our thoughts and released from our minds. They were too horrific and painful to retain and dwell upon. Hitler had announced over and over in his screaming speeches his intention to rid the world of Jews, but many Jews in Germany could not allow themselves to absorb or accept the reality of his abusive words and threats. Their families had lived in Germany for hundreds of years and very often, they felt more German than Jewish. How could this attack on Jews be a reality? Those citizens who were losing their rights rapidly, and who were more realistic and farsighted, made attempts to leave the country and a small percentage succeeded. Those people were obligated to leave their homes and all their belongings to the Third Reich, but they were happy to do so, leaving everything behind in order to get out of that completely painful, destructive and deadly environment. Their eyes had been pried open. They were wise enough to envision their ultimate fate and that of their families if they remained.

84

Everyone at our place of business decided that it would be a good thing for all of us to go together after the day's work and give blood for the war effort. The country was completely dedicated and mobilized in its support for our armed forces. Our young men were fighting in the steamy, malaria ridden South Pacific and on the European and African front, and much blood was needed. It was the least we civilians could do, and we enthusiastically signed up.

One day after work, when the store was closed for the night, all the salesmen and I walked together to the subway station and took the train to the "Red Cross" center where nurses, aids and laboratory technicians were waiting and working. They wore their white jackets and professional appearance with ease and confidence. They looked genuinely efficient and their routine and procedure for bloodletting was scientifically set up to move along quickly. They welcomed us, along with a crowd of others who were happy to release their blood for the great cause. Good humor surrounded us. We shared the thought that this relatively insignificant act on our part might help save a life that was so dear to us, any American service man. We were told where to place our jackets, packages and pocketbooks, and we anxiously cooperated.

A young lady patted the blue veins on the soft insides of my left elbow to see which vein would give up its precious fluid most easily. She then proceeded to swab the area with alcohol. She seemed a little unsure of herself, but I firmly placed my confidence in her supposed expertise. She indelicately jabbed a needle into the vein that she had selected. Nothing appeared to be happening, except for the pain that her needle had provoked.

She finally removed it and said, "I think we'll try a different vein. That was not a very good one and the needle pierced it." I had experienced some pain, but I nodded cooperatively, not wanting to upset her concentration. She started once again to pat the area with her fingers and decided that she would try an adjacent vein. She proceeded to butcher the left arm, and then explained, "I'll have to try your other arm. Your veins are very small and narrow." Mea culpa.

When she finally completed her work by bungling and mismanaging the job, also piercing the vein in my right arm, she hesitatingly told me, "You'll have to come back another time. You can't give blood today."

My eyes filled with tears. "You don't know your job," I said. "You have no right working here." She turned red, did not answer, and turned away. All of my co-workers who had been attended by other technicians had given blood and had received little drinks of orange juice.

They were gratified and fulfilled.

They had accomplished something worthwhile.

I had difficulty putting on my jacket and lifting my pocketbook. On the train ride home I cried very quietly, gently dabbing my eyes and hoping that no one noticed. I was completely disheartened and dejected. I had particularly wanted to accomplish this mission for Leon. All my former joy clouded, leaving me with heaviness of heart. I had failed.

85

Our wedding date was rushing towards us. I hated the thought of all the tension that the actual proceedings would evoke. I was disappointed that I would not have the opportunity to walk down the aisle wearing a magnificent white wedding gown in a beautiful flower filled chapel. The change from the "Twin Cantors" which provided this kind of environment, to the little nightclub, alias restaurant, where we were to be married, was not a satisfying comparison, but it was available and that was the first priority. Fortunately, it did have a large private room for the ceremony. Tables would be set up in advance for the catered dinner that would be served afterward.

These tables surrounded the small dance floor where the ceremony would take place and where Leon and I would be wed.

I went shopping with my mother and Sylvia for a special dress to be married in, and was happy with our joint selection. It was sky blue in color and beautifully crafted. The soft lovely quality of the fabric further enhanced its appearance and I felt it was a good choice. When I tried it on, it clung to my young shapely body as though it had been delicately created specifically for me. I could envision my future young husband's approval. I could visualize those penetrating blue eyes enveloping me with love and lust.

It lifted the slight undercurrent of dissatisfaction that I felt at being deprived of "Twin Cantors." I knew that I would be a very happy bride. My main source of joy and fulfillment, after all, would be my groom.

The fateful Saturday finally arrived. It was June 3,rd 1944 and Leon was scheduled to come home early that afternoon from camp. I prayed that nothing would go wrong, and I tried to control the feeling of nervousness that would not leave me. Mom and Pop put on a good show of relaxed behavior, although I knew what a tremendously difficult act it was for her to exhibit and maintain. The afternoon hours were rolling by and it was getting a little bit late for comfort. Still Leon had not arrived. I carefully brushed, combed and recombed my hair into its fashionable current upsweep until it shone as if I had buttered it. My coiffure looked as though a Hollywood expert had prepared me for this most important appointment in my life. I took great pains to carefully insert a small bunch of blossoms in an appropriate place in my hair, and I studied my face carefully in the mirror.

I was reasonably satisfied.

My eyes could hardly accommodate or contain the excitement that was striking my mind. They stared back at me with a degree of comprehension and intelligence, but they could not prognosticate the future.

He was here! Everything would be all right. I discerned a look of vulnerability, but Leon covered it with a mask of genial happiness. His soldier's uniform was beautifully pressed and his trousers had a knife-edged crease. He had taken his obligations very seriously, I could tell. The brim of his cap was low on his forehead and he looked very military. He greeted my family warmly and feverishly and hastily kissed me. After a minimal amount of inane conversation, he dashed down the stairs and ran across the street to greet his parents. Where was that super-cool demeanor that I had come to expect from him?

We all met downstairs at the appropriate time. Neighbors gathered round us extending good wishes, wide smiles and occasional handshakes. Mr. and Mrs. Gensburg, our landlady and landlord, would be attending the wedding, as would Eddie's parents who occupied the apartment directly below ours. They would all arrive later. Leon and I were scheduled to take photographs and we were to be dropped off initially at the photographers by one of the cabs that had arrived. Another cab would arrive shortly to transport Leon's parents and my family to the wedding.

We did not have much to say to one another in the cab. What were we doing here? Was this a giant mistake? A vague feeling of numbness was settling over my body. It was a protective device that acted on its own accord.

The professional photographer took our wedding pictures in his studio, where we were arranged to best advantage. When the session was completed, Leon called a cab that transported us to "Arele's Romanian Restaurant" where we were to be married.

When we arrived we were directed into a small side room where we had to sign some documents to assure that our marriage would be legal. There was my mother's cousin, hefty, corpulent Hyman Blankstein waiting patiently for us with a welcoming smile on his face. He would sign his name as a witness. Unfortunately, Hyman signed in the wrong place. He set his John Hancock on the line meant for the groom's signature. His name was quickly crossed out and replaced with Leon Brown above it. Hyman finally made it to the correct space for the witness and his second attempt was successful. I thought Hyman's mistake was hilariously funny. However, I muffled a few laughs after getting a disapproving look from the man in charge. Leon leaned over and whispered in my ear. "I think that you're marrying Hyman Blankstein." At this little quip, I laughed aloud. "Perhaps that would be an improvement," I answered. Hymie, who had been like a younger brother to Mama when she had first arrived from Poland and lived with his parents, Tante Laikie and Uncle Panush, contributed his smiling presence to our little group. He was now a cantor and was going to marry us, with his golden voice blessing our union. Hymie always seemed to find the implicit fun in any situation or any occasion and he laughed along with me at Hyman Blankstein's innocent mistake.

We all entered the main dining room together where the tables had been previously set up for our guests. The band was welcoming everyone with its inviting, lilting rhythmic musical sounds and a number of people were already dancing on the small highly waxed dance floor. Later it would be used for our wedding ceremony. It was no "Twin Cantors," but a rush of happiness and satisfaction rose within me when my mother and I exchanged deep looks of unequivocal love and friendship.

My future mother-in-law approached me, embraced me and told me how lovely I looked. In my eyes, she looked lovely too. She would always remain a supremely loyal friend.

I glanced around and saw many relatives and friends who had come to share our happiness. There was a powerful air of festivity. The band started playing a spirited "Hora," and Uncle Joe and his son, Jakie Joe's, immediately stood up to join the circle that had quickly been formed. They danced forcefully, and as usual, stamped harder than anyone else to the rhythm of the traditional music, thereby demonstrating and proving that they were more sincere than most.

Pearl was sitting at a table with some of my other friends. Her husband Bob, had joined the Marine Medics in spite of her protestations and was now somewhere in the South Pacific. She had not heard from him for quite some time and she and her family were in a quiet state of panic.

Leon and I greeted all of our friends and continued on, walking hand in hand, to pay our respects to Tante Lakie and Uncle Panush. They appeared frail and delicate, but responded to our greetings with beaming smiles and good wishes. I kissed Tante Lakie warmly and her skin smelled of ripe peaches. She gently hugged me and I lightly held her fragile body against mine for an extra moment. Simon, their older son, sat at their table with his family. He looked to be, as he actually was, a person of significance. His carriage was one of kindness and responsibility. This small family that had rescued my mother when she was only fourteen years of age, dispensing love and devotion, was destined to remain in my heart for a lifetime. At this juncture of my existence their younger son Hymie, he of the golden voice, would officiate at our marriage tonight. It was fitting.

The evening passed in a haze. Reality seemed set aside. I waited impatiently for this small portion of eternity to come to a close. We were pronounced man and wife.

86

We made our way to the Hotel Pennsylvania where I had confirmed reservations in advance. It was three thirty A.M. and our mood and impatient dispositions continued to expand as we approached the prominent desk in the beautiful lobby of the hotel. Leon requested our reserved room and much to our chagrin and astonishment, the self-important Machiavellian clerk responded, "Sorry. Someone called and cancelled your reservations."

My quiet generally restrained new husband loudly and forcefully said, "No one knew that we were going to spend the night here, and I'm sure that nobody called! No doubt you gave our room to a civilian in order to save the ten-percent discount for servicemen. My wife and I are very tired, and we insist that you find us another room. This is our wedding night and you are certainly not going to perpetuate my virginity."

The clerk sensibly realized that Leon did not mean to be humorous. He appeared unsettled and looked a little uncomfortable. He noticed that several people nearby had no doubt heard what this young soldier had so vehemently expressed. He knew that he had to cooperate. "Corporal Brown, please sit down and I'll see what I can do."

"Yes. See what you can do. I'm ready to start a small riot."

We waited patiently for about ten minutes and the clerk motioned us to the desk. "We were able to accommodate you, sir. I think that you'll be very pleased."

We followed the young man who carried our small piece of luggage to the elevator. When we reached the proper floor we walked down a long hall until we reached a door that the bellboy opened for us. We were both quite surprised. It was a three-room suite that boasted an elegant sitting room, a walk-in closet and huge bathroom. Leon tipped the boy generously and gratefully closed the door and locked it. He did not want any more surprises. We realized that we had to vacate this lovely honeymoon retreat by twelve noon, Sunday. It was already four A.M. We showered in record time and got into that huge wedding bed. My husband kissed me gently and held me close. I felt as though I had finally come home.

We reluctantly left our suite at twelve and decided that we would treat ourselves to a large delicious breakfast. We went to "Child's Restaurant" and innocently thought that we were in the lap of luxury. We ate with great appetite and greater satisfaction. When we left the restaurant and emerged into the busy city, the rays of the sun brightly reflected our happiness. The day was cool and I wore a soft, scarlet boy coat. I felt very beautiful. No doubt my new husband had contributed to that attitude and to my feeling of utter contentment. I was encompassed in a passage of love.

We walked along Broadway studying the various big movie houses and theatres with their blazing marquis. They flamboyantly advertised the films and plays that were currently being offered to the public, along with the names of the important stars involved. The stage productions with their accompanying billboards and photos of the stars were housed on the side streets. The theatre scene was exciting and tempting to passersby.

We only had a few hours left to spend together before Leon would have to head back to camp. I was sadly prepared to return home from my honeymoon all alone with only my small suitcase to keep me company. However, our present happy frame of mind carried us along and we decided that we would continue to celebrate our contentment and innate joy by going to the movies. Our choice was "Going My Way" starring Bing Crosby and Barry Fitzgerald. We made our way across the street to the theatre with Leon holding my elbow and guiding me protectively. I felt well loved.

There it was, that impressive movie house, "The New York Paramount," waiting for us and welcoming us. The timing was perfect. The show was due to start shortly. Leon purchased our tickets and we entered the beautiful lobby of the theatre. We were greeted by the plush richness of the carpeting, the lovely sculptures and the serene elegance of its surroundings and ambiance. We found our way in the soft darkness to our seats, and appreciated the lack of patrons attending the performance at this time of day. We moved as closely as we could to one another. As we waited for the movie to begin Leon leaned over, warmly kissed me, and whispered, "My sweet wife." The striking realization and reflection kept recurring and rejoicing in my mind. "We're married!"

The movie was perfect. Bing Crosby and Barry Fitzgerald were perfect. The day was perfect. We left the theatre and Leon noticed a U.S.O. center for servicemen. The wind had changed and had become colder although the sun continued to shine and bless our day. The U.S.O. would be an ideal place for us to spend a little more time out of the chill of the wind before Leon had to leave. However, he quickly learned that only servicemen, and no one else, would be permitted to enter these sacred grounds during these particular hours. Leon protested loudly. "This is my wife." The receptionist was unimpressed. "Sorry."

Leon was upset and disappointed but it did not bother me at all. All I experienced was fulfillment and contentment. We walked along Broadway and Leon spotted one of his buddies from camp. They happily greeted one another. I was delighted when Leon introduced me, and said, "This is my wife." The sun shone brightly on my happiness.

We stopped at a small restaurant and had something to eat. Our animated conversation started to wind down. Sadness was softly edging its way in. It was time for him to leave. Hopefully, I would see my new husband the following week. I knew that I did not have the right to complain. I had foolishly convinced myself that our honeymoon was sufficient to ease the pain of separation.

My high heels clattered their way along the street leading to the subway. Leon accompanied me and we both smiled our goodbyes encouraging one another to remember the sweetness, not the separation. I wearily descended the stairs and entered the subway alone and lonely. Leon had to follow another route back to camp. It seemed so strange to be coming home from my honeymoon without a husband. I found a seat and rested the small suitcase on the floor. I closed my eyes. The rattling of the cars and the resounding reverberations of the trains carrying me home lulled me into a quiescent state of acceptance.

The little entrance foyer, where I had experienced so many furtive purloined kisses from my love, was empty. I made my way up the two flights of stairs, opened the door, and there to welcome me was my affectionate, tenderhearted family. Tears welled up in my mother's beautiful green eyes as she rose to embrace me. My devoted mother-in-law was sitting with my family patiently waiting for me to return from my abbreviated honeymoon. She grabbed my little suitcase, opened it and laughingly examined my satin nightgown. She had a lusty sense of humor, which seemed to embarrass my mother, but we both happily put up with it. "All's well that ends well."

Everyone around the kitchen table discussed and analyzed every aspect of the wedding in minute detail.

"You looked absolutely lovely," Sylvia generously volunteered. "Doesn't she always?" Charlie laughingly added. "Look at her."

I joined in the laughter. I knew that I was certainly not at my best at this time. The excitement and tension of the wedding and the unwelcome wrenching separation from my husband had exhausted me emotionally. The noisy train trip home had also taken its toll. My hair was in mild disarray, my makeup had faded, lipstick was gone, and I was mentally tired, lonely, and very sad to have come home, half of a couple, from my honeymoon.

"The flowers were gorgeous," Leon's mom said. "I took home the center-piece that was on our table. I felt the happiness of Beulah and Leon, and I thought about them, that old couple."

This statement evoked more laughter from all. As tired as I felt, I started to enjoy being the center of attraction. Meanwhile, Papa stood up and started setting the table. He had given me a warm welcoming kiss and hug when I first came in, and I relished seeing that faint subtle smile on his face that indicated that he was so very pleased and happy to see me. I knew that he was most happy that I was once again at home. It seemed to me that his primary purpose in life was to create a contented, pleasant environment for his children and I believe that he generally succeeded, spreading his natural innate cheerfulness to those with whom he came in contact.

At this point, Mama opened the refrigerator and took out a huge sponge cake that she had baked that afternoon and surrounded with thick hand-whipped cream. Her freshly brewed coffee was then poured into her best china cups, which had been set out in my honor. A little party ensued and warmed my empty heart.

Long after Sylvia, Charlie and my mother-in-law had left and the rest of the family had fallen asleep, I lay awake in the dark reliving the scenes and the passion of my brief honeymoon.

87

I walked to the subway station the next morning, my mind and body filled with inner turmoil. I hoped that the modest amount of exercise on this sun filled day would release some of my pent up emotions and tensions and allow me to do my job. Everything important in my life now revolved around the coming weekend. I visualized Leon's smile, as he would greet me on Friday night when he would come home on his weekend pass. It would be a continuing celebration of our marriage and togetherness. Unfortunately, my job continued to require my services on Sundays. I was very anxious to retain my good position and embark on a project of seriously saving some money for our future.

Before we were married, when Leon was able to come home from camp for the weekend, he would take the subway on Sundays to the Eastside where I worked and pick me up in time to take me out for lunch. What an appetite I developed, but not necessarily for food. It was his company I craved. However, my appetite was partially satisfied when I looked into his blue eyes and saw the look of love prevail.

Everyone working in the store made it a point to greet him. They intermittently stopped what they were doing and treated him like a conquering hero.

"Hi, Leon. How's the army treating you?"

"Hey, it's nice to see you. You're keeping our little girl happy."

"Listen, have a good lunch."

In spite of his reserved manner, I could tell that Leon was delighted. He probably did not expect such a rousing welcome. Mr. H. gave him a resounding pat on the back and surprised me by saying, "You don't have to hurry back."

We would make our way towards Delancy Street, our hands enclosed, palm pressing tightly against palm and enter Ratner's Dairy Restaurant. My solid appetite returned when I smelled those delicious little onion rolls.

We were led to a table covered with a white tablecloth and settings for two. In the center was a small vase with a single flower resting in crystal clear water. The white tablecloth satisfied my occasional need for what I assumed was elegance. We would feast on my favorite baked halibut with its delicately and deliciously cooked vegetables, lots of little onion rolls, butter and mutual love. I thought my corporal looked like a general.

Many of the bookkeepers that I had lunch with regularly during the week showed up at Ratner's often on Sundays when I was proud to introduce my fiancée. They discreetly sat at other tables but often looked in our direction. They were a wonderful group of caring women. My joy reached out to them and they accepted and blessed us. After lunch, I had to go back to work and Leon went home until early Sunday evening when he had to return to Ft. Monmouth. He reluctantly took that long train ride back to that home away from home.

88

The post-wedding week passed interminably and I impatiently anticipated Leon's arrival for the weekend, but it was not to be. He could not get home. My boss, Mr. H. had been very kind to me in the past months and had allowed me to take Sunday off to visit Leon at camp when he could not get a weekend pass. The war had changed and softened his perspective. His son Julie was a G.I. I greatly appreciated his show of innate generosity and understanding and gladly made up for my absence on Sunday during the week.

That Saturday morning I found myself in this situation. The mountain could not come to Mohammed, therefore Mohammed would go to the mountain. I would travel to Red Bank, N. J. to spend the weekend with my new husband. Leon had experienced a difficult and anxious week and was relegated to remaining in camp. He and his group of Signal Corps. men had been transferred out of Fort Monmouth to a nearby camp named "Camp Misery." That name had been legitimately given because of its relative proximity to Mount Misery. It was an appropriate name for the camp since it had been organized specifically as a place to prepare soldiers who were to be shipped overseas shortly.

Here they would receive particular inoculations, depending upon which direction they would be heading, and appropriate gear and clothing for special climate conditions. They would also obtain much information regarding the area where they would be sent.

My mind could barely accept the fact that Leon would be going overseas within the next few months. It was a long slow train ride to

Camp Misery crowded with a profusion of teeming humanity. There were soldiers who looked as though they had barely begun to shave, parents anxiously travelling to see their beloved offspring, and young women like myself all rushing towards their yearnings. We all belonged to a special brotherhood of man.

A young marine sat down in the vacant seat next to mine. His face seemed to be devoid of color, and his hands which were set quietly in his lap, trembled almost imperceptibly. He flashed me a charming and unreserved smile and introduced himself. "I'm Jim Murphy, home from the South Pacific temporarily. What good luck to sit next to such a pretty girl."

"Thank you," I responded. "I'm happy you made it home." "I'm happy too. I wasn't sure I would," he said. "I made it back from Tarawa."

We made small talk all the way to Red Bank, which was my stop. We did not discuss the horrific consequences of that particular invasion of a small island that incurred 38% casualties. Young bodies were strewn along the beaches. It was to be remembered and go down in history as a "blood bath."

Leon's parents knew that he had been transferred to another camp but were not yet aware of its significance. I did not have the inclination or desire to contribute to the furtherance of their state of anxiety. Moey had recently been shipped to England and was writing relatively cheerful letters home. I thought that was courageous, particularly in view of his utter dejection over the total failure and outcome of his marriage to Hedda.

I could hardly absorb the idea of this complete change in our lives. Leon and I had anticipated that he would be at Fort Monmouth for an extended period of time. That had seemed to be a strong possibility when we considered marriage. We did not allow ourselves to reflect on the fearful possibilities of the future. Our dreams and yearnings resided in a post-war world where we would not have to suffer separation, and love from a distance. Our expectations up to now, had been hopeful and positive. However, looking out the window, barely noticing the miles rushing by, I felt encased in an immovable sheath of tightly packed padding that even the radiant spark of optimism could not penetrate. I attempted to control my dark emotions and lock them away before arriving at Red Bank.

I stepped off the train and there were those blue eyes seeking me out. They sent me their forceful message of love and hope. I dropped my weekend suitcase, ran towards him and hugged him as hard as I could. He laughed aloud with the spontaneity that comes from joy and gave me a resounding kiss of welcome. It promised more to come. My flagging spirits soared.

Leon had made reservations for us to spend Friday and Saturday night at Mrs. Darling. She rented rooms to soldiers from Camp Misery, which did not have any guest facilities. We took a bus to her house and I was delighted and charmed when I saw our old fashioned room with its lace curtains. The windows looked out upon a lilting rivulet. I could hear the hushed running watery murmurings that sounded like flowing music. Mrs. Darling resembled her name. After she had shown us to our room and handed us the key, she returned shortly with a small platter of cookies and cold lemonade.

The door closed and we quickly decided to have the cookies later. We hastily fortified ourselves with some lemonade and wasted no more time. We made love, inexperienced, natural and completely satisfying. The melodies of the flowing stream lulled us to sleep.

89

The weekend passed quickly and I was back in the usual daily routine. I had purposely neglected to tell Leon that Pearl had received official notice that Bob was missing in action on Tarawa. It seemed like a death sentence and she was devastated. Her eyes maintained a look of strained disbelief and were constantly awash with tears. Her little boy could not figure out what was wrong or what he might have done to cause her complete and utter despair. "Why are you crying, Mommy? Would you like me to bring you a cookie?" He was a precocious and sweet child and it seemed as though he could be her salvation. Pearl's supportive family continued to be just that, supportive.

My family did what little they could to ease the way. It was not much. Her terror and grief were palpable and contagious. Pearl and I would separate ourselves from others and sit in my living room in silent communion with one another. There seemed to be a measure of comfort in quietly allowing the stillness of the room to settle upon us. Pearl's little boy, Gary, sat on the couch, his small legs dangling many inches from the floor patiently waiting for us to break what he must have considered to be a smothering silence, and speak.

"Would you like to hear the Warsaw Concerto, Gary?" I asked. I knew that this was his favorite piece of music and he could be counted upon to say, "Yes." He had heard it played on my record player a number of times and always expressed his delight. His eyes gleamed as he gave me the expected answer. What a dear little four-year-old he was. It was intriguing to witness his reaction to the stirring music. His little old-man face reflected the various moods of the music and I could hear him humming the familiar melodies in tune. Pearl and I derived a deep sense of gladness watching and listening to his response. These feelings were mixed with aching pain when we observed this little boy. He was so much like his father whom he might never have the opportunity to know.

90

Most weekends Leon was still able to come home on leave, but time was running out. He had told his parents the distressing news that he would be shipping out soon, and they were trying their best to accept the inevitable. They put on a happy face for him even when their insides were churning with despair. Many of his friends from Club 18 were already overseas and writing letters home from various parts of the world. These letters were called V-Mail and were written on special stationery that was read and censored by officers in charge. They eventually became the basic substance and essence of our lives.

Leon could not get a pass to come home one weekend early in October of 1944. He called to tell me that his group would not be allowed off grounds, and that I would not be able to visit. He could not say more, but I could project the inference of his imminent departure. His love poured through the telephone lines and I was transformed. I was no longer a separate entity, but part of a being that needed Leon to complete me.

The week passed slowly and painfully. A letter finally arrived and Mama handed it to me hesitatingly. Her green eyes glistened with restrained tears. Leon's address had been changed. It now had an APO number with a California designation. He was on his way to the South Pacific.

Would prayers protect him? Should I attempt once again to give blood to the Red Cross? How little help was rolling bandages! I would buy "War Bonds" regularly. I would write every day.

"Come back safely to me, my dearest. Goodbye for a while, my husband. Goodbye for a while, my love.

"Goodbye 12147462."

Made in the USA
San Bernardino, CA
01 July 2013